India's Economic Reforms
1991–2001

India's Economic Reforms 1991–2001

VIJAY JOSHI

I. M. D. LITTLE

CLARENDON PRESS · OXFORD

1996

Oxford University Press, Walton Street, Oxford OX2 6DP
Oxford New York
Athens Auckland Bangkok Bogota Bombay
Buenos Aires Calcutta Cape Town Dar es Salaam
Delhi Florence Hong Kong Istanbul Karachi
Kuala Lumpur Madras Madrid Melbourne
Mexico City Nairobi Paris Singapore
Taipei Tokyo Toronto
and associated companies in
Berlin Ibadan

Oxford is a trade mark of Oxford University Press

Published in the United States
by Oxford University Press Inc., New York

British Library Cataloguing in Publication Data
Data available

Library of Congress Cataloging in Publication Data
Data available
ISBN 0–19–829078–0

1 3 5 7 9 10 8 6 4 2

Printed in Great Britain by
Bookcraft (Bath) Ltd.,
Midsomer Norton, Somerset

Contents

Preface

This book was mostly written between August and December 1995. Events of 1996 have been almost wholly ignored. The main exception is that figures given in the 1996/97 budget papers have been used in the sections concerned with stabilization and the fiscal deficits. The book went to press before the results of the national elections of 1996 were known.

Acknowledgements

The UK Overseas Development Administration (ODA) provided some funding for this book. However, the views and opinions expressed do not reflect the ODA's official policies or practices, but are those of the authors alone. We are indebted to Merton College and Nuffield College for facilities and other support.

The persons who helped us in India are too numerous to name individually. They include politicians, officials of the Government of India and the Reserve Bank of India, academics, journalists, businessmen, and members of the IMF and World Bank resident missions. But we wish particularly to thank Sudhir Mulji for his hospitality, Professor S. Guhan who organized our meetings with the Government of Tamil Nadu, and Professor P. V. Shenoi and Mr Dinesh Afzulpurkar who helped us similarly in Bangalore and Bombay.

A. B. Atkinson, Omkar Goswami, Michael Lipton, and M. Govinda Rao have read parts of the book. We are grateful for their comments.

We thank Elaine Herman and Judith Kirby for their secretarial help; and Hilary Hodgson and Alistair McMillan for skilfully editing and preparing the book for the printer.

Acronyms

ARF	Asset Reconstruction Fund
BFS	Board of Financial Supervision
BIFR	Board for Industrial and Financial Reconstruction
BJP	Bharatiya Janata Party
BOT	build operate transfer
cif	cost, insurance, and freight
CPI	consumer price index
CPSE	central public sector enterprise
CRR	cash reserve ratio
CST	central sales tax
DFI	Development Finance Institution
DOT	Department of Telecommunications
EAS	Employment Assurance Scheme
EPCGS	Export Promotion Capital Goods Schemes
FCI	Food Corporation of India
FERA	Foreign Exchange Regulation Act
FII	foreign institutional investor
GATT	General Agreement on Tariffs and Trade
GDP	gross domestic product
GDR	global depository receipt
GFCF	gross fixed capital formation
GIC	General Insurance Corporation of India
GNP	gross national product
GOI	Government of India
IBA	Indian Banks Association
IBRD	International Bank for Reconstruction and Development
ICICI	Industrial Credit and Investment Corporation of India
IDA	International Development Association

IDA	Industrial Disputes Act
IDBI	Industrial Development Bank of India
IFCI	Industrial Finance Corporation of India
IMF	International Monetary Fund
IRDP	Integrated Rural Development Programme
JRY	Jawahar Rozgar Yojana
LIC	Life Insurance Corporation of India
LPG	liquid petroleum gas
MANVAT	manufacturing value added tax
MEGS	Maharashtra Employment Guarantee Scheme
MMMF	Money Market Mutual Fund
MODVAT	modified value added tax
MOU	Memorandum of Understanding
MP	Member of Parliament
MRTP	Monopoly and Restrictive Trade Practices
NABARD	National Bank for Agriculture and Rural Development
NAS	National Accounts Statistics
NFPS	non-financial public sector
NIPFP	National Institute for Public Finance and Policy
NPA	non-performing asset
NSE	National Stock Exchange
NSS	National Sample Survey
OGL	Open General Licence
OIL	Oil India Limited
OM	operating expenses and maintenance
ONGC	Oil and Natural Gas Corporation
PDS	public distribution system
PSE	public sector enterprise
RBI	Reserve Bank of India
RD	rural development
RRB	Regional Rural Bank
SC	scheduled caste
SICA	Sick Industrial Companies Act
SIDBI	Small Industries Development Bank of India
SEB	State Electricity Board

SEBI	Securities and Exchange Board of India
SIL	special import licence
SLR	statutory liquidity ratio
SME	small manufacturing enterprise
SSE	small-scale enterprise
SSI	small-scale industry
SSIB	Small Scale Industries Board
ST	scheduled tribe
TB	treasury bill
TFC	Tenth Finance Commission
TRAI	Telecom Regulatory Authority of India
TRC	Tax Reforms Committee
ULCRA	Urban Land (Ceiling and Regulation) Act
UTI	Unit Trust of India
VAT	value added tax
WPI	wholesale price index

Note on lakhs and crores

We have used the Indian terms lakh, meaning hundred thousand
(10^5), and crore, meaning ten million (10^7), wherever the
number of rupees is denoted.

Note on GDP figures

Where we refer to changes or growth, GDP is measured at factor
costs. Where we express monetary magnitudes as percentages
of GDP, it is measured at market prices.

1
Introduction

The present authors' previous book on India (Joshi and Little, 1994) took her macroeconomic story only up to June 1991. Its sketch of developments from 1964 to 1991 ends with the sentence 'The new government moved swiftly and announced a programme of macroeconomic stabilization and structural adjustment'. The new government was that of P. V. Narasimha Rao, who formed a minority government after Congress (I) had won 226 seats in the Lok Sabha in the June election following the assassination of Rajiv Gandhi.

The stabilization measures taken, which are described in Chapter 2, were inevitable. India was running a current account deficit of around $10 billion. Reserves were down to two weeks of imports, despite an IMF loan of $1.8 billion in January 1991, and despite damaging import cuts. Her credibility was very low, and commercial borrowing impossible. Inflation was running at an annual rate of 13 per cent and an inflow of foreign currency from non-resident Indians had been reversed.

The crisis had been simmering since the mid-1980s, with governments relying on unsustainable levels of foreign and domestic borrowing. It was brought to the boil by the Iraqi invasion of Kuwait in August 1990 resulting in a rise in the price of oil. The Janata Government of V. P. Singh, and the successor 'lame duck' government of Chandra Shekhar, failed to take action commensurate with the rapidly growing crisis. Immediate drastic action, including a large devaluation and deflationary fiscal measures, was essential to prevent default by securing the co-operation of official donors and lenders.

Many countries have been forced to take similar measures when the borrowing that they relied on dried up. But the almost simultaneous announcement (by a new minority government) of a long-run programme of deregulation and liberalization is not so common and calls for some comment.

A crisis is an opportunity for introducing a new style of government pursuing a new model of development (new to the country, that is) when the old style and the old model can convincingly be presented as having led to disaster. But in a democracy there must also be a sufficient body of influential opinion already convinced, or very ready to be convinced, of the need for radical change.

This had come to be the case in India by July 1991. The change of mind-set, to use a fashionable cliché, during the previous five years had been remarkable, although it was also remarkably slow to come. For nearly twenty years any mention of South Korea or Taiwan resulted in signs of amazement that anyone might think that India could learn from such small economies. It was more than a decade since China's liberalizing reforms could be seen to be highly successful. But, at last, the total collapse of the Russian communist system must have convinced many people that a highly regulated economy with centralized planning was not still a model to copy.

Rajiv Gandhi had embarked on some liberalization in 1985. Although he seems to have quickly lost interest, this helped to put such reform on the political agenda. One way or another the ground was sufficiently prepared to use the crisis as an occasion for embarking on a programme of reform whose pursuit would result in a radical transformation of the Indian economy.

We are writing four and a half years after the initiation of this programme. Have we seen a radical transformation? The short answer is, of course, 'Yes and No'. Later in this book we describe in some detail what has happened, and what in our opinion remains to be done. Here we need devote only a few sentences to what has happened. Stabilization was achieved with remarkably little pain, compared with most counties that were in a similar critical situation. India now has adequate reserves and is credit-worthy, while production is expanding at a satisfactory rate. But inflation is too high, and the fiscal deficit is still too large to be sustainable in the long run. On the structural adjustment front, the derestriction of domestic production and investment has gone a long way. Foreign trade has been extensively decontrolled, but by no means completely. Tariffs have been greatly reduced, but remain high even by the standards of developing countries. Foreign direct investment is now more welcome, and has risen substantially from very low levels. Although it is still controlled, and foreign ownership is mostly restricted to 51 per cent, permits are much more readily obtainable. Useful improvements of the highly distortionary domestic tax system have also been made. Thus a good deal has been done to increase the role of the price mechanism, raise efficiency, reduce bureaucratic control, and increase the role of private initiative.

But large areas remain where almost nothing has been done. While reform of public revenues is under way, expenditure reform is shockingly neglected. Huge explicit and implicit subsidies have become a major part of Indian public finance. Their effectiveness in promoting social ends is at best abysmal and at worst counter-productive.[1] The losses of public enterprises of both the Centre and the States are a major component of the implicit subsidies. These urgently need to be tackled in various ways, by fuller cost recovery, by raising efficiency, or by closure: privatization is a means which many other developing countries have accepted, but the central government dares not contemplate. Too much is also spent on administration, especially now that the functions of administrators have been extensively curtailed. While very large savings could be made, an increase in other expenditures, most especially investment in the economic infrastructure, is a very high priority. India cannot

---

[1] See Bardhan (1984), ch. 8, and Joshi and Little (1994), ch. 3, for an earlier denunciation of these subsidies and political explanation of their provenance.

make a great leap forward with her feet tied by a lack of power, transport, and telecommunications. Company law and labour laws are other areas that cry out for reform, in vain. The same is true of agriculture, where trade is still largely controlled.

The pace of Indian reform has certainly been slow. There are good economic arguments for gradualism, and less clear arguments for a careful sequencing of reforms. But these economic arguments do not seem to explain either the pace of reform or the areas of progress and neglect. Political explanation is required.

More than two years ago, in June 1993, a conference on the reforms that had started just two years earlier was held at Merton College, Oxford. Our description of what has been achieved in four years is, sadly, not very different from what the proceedings of that conference show to have been achieved in two years.[2] There has certainly been some progress in further deregulation of the domestic economy, and further liberalization of trade and external payments. But reform slowed down, and the great areas of neglect remain untouched.

Apart from gradualness a number of political economy features of the Indian reform process to date were pointed out. There was no strategy, no clear indication of the final nature of the regime that the reformers had in mind. This was true both overall, and for most sectors. What was to be the extent of public ownership? What was the envisaged structure of the banking system, and other financial institutions? Was protection on its way out; or was continued quite high protection of the domestic market to survive? What framework was envisaged for social sector and welfare expenditures?

A corollary of the lack of definition of reform was the absence of any attempt to explain the reforms, not even to State governments let alone the mass of the people. In our opinion, the reforms were going to benefit the vast majority. Yet political opponents could, apparently with some plausibility,

[2] Cassen and Joshi (1995).

claim that they would hurt the poor. Without explaining where the reforms were leading, and what were their expected benefits, a constituency for reform could hardly be created.

At about the same time, in a paper commissioned by the Finance Minister, Jagdish Bhagwati and T. N. Srinivasan pointed to and countered a number of misunderstandings (or expressions of anti-reform propaganda?), and concluded thus:

The government needs therefore to educate the public continually about the foregoing misunderstandings, and every important Minister of the cabinet and every available occasion must be exploited to do this and thus to put the rationale and importance of the reforms before the public. If this is not done, the reforms are likely to lose support as misunderstandings multiply and acquire cogency simply because no coherent rationale and defence of the reforms is available.[3]

This was not done. The authors while recognizing the need for gradualness also suggested that the time had come for a 'change of gear' to impart fresh impetus to the reforms. The change has been to a lower gear, and support has probably been lost.

It has been pointed out by James Manor that the lack of any concerted effort to cultivate support was not due to absent-mindedness on the part of the Prime Minister.[4] He prefers to keep control of the direction and pace of reforms firmly in his own hands, and evidently believes that this is incompatible with the attempt to win widespread support through the medium of the weakened and corrupt Congress Party which he leads. He believes in stealth, small carefully controlled movements disguising what progress is being made towards some ill-defined objective. This strategy has not prevented frequent but totally unfounded attacks that the reforms were hurting the poor.

Nevertheless, Mr Narasimha Rao has managed to keep some reform moving ahead, albeit almost imperceptibly since the severe Congress Party losses in the State elections of December 1994. It is, however, argued by some that it is a fatal fault of

[3] Bhagwati and Srinivasan (1993), 10.
[4] Manor (1995).

both the Prime Minister and the Congress Party that he and it dare not challenge any of the main interest groups, even those such as the public sector trade unionists, who have little voting power, but who can cause serious short-term disruption.[5] This fault bodes ill for the eventual achievement of a liberal progressive regime.

Unlike the Prime Minister we, in this book, judge reforms already made, and recommend others, according to whether they tend towards some economic regime which we should now try to describe. This cannot be done with any precision, but let us make a suitably imprecise attempt. We favour a predominantly market economy. From this point of view the question is when the state should intervene to regulate or promote private activities, and when it should produce things itself. There are wide areas of agreement, albeit with controversial fringes everywhere.

The state should provide law and order, including the definition and enforcement of contracts, the protection of property, and the outlawing and punishment of seriously anti-social behaviour. Where necessary it should promote or create other institutions required for the operation of markets. It should regulate markets where experience has shown that *laissez-faire* may produce disorder, or where the purchaser is unable to judge the quality of what is being offered. It should provide public goods, such as defence and a stable currency.

These public goods are extreme examples either of market failure or the absence of markets. The private sector cannot profitably provide them because free-riders cannot be, or should not be, excluded. Less extreme cases arise where the private sector can provide, but only inefficiently from a social point of view, because negative externalities, such as aircraft noise or river pollution, are imposed on an unwilling public: in these cases regulation or taxation is normally the best solution. Alternatively, private operators may provide, but not enough

---

[5] For an elaboration of these points see James Manor (ibid.).

because some benefits accrue to others. Research and development, and training, are standard examples of where there may be a role for public provision, especially perhaps in some research areas, e.g. agriculture.

All of the above is common ground. How far the state should be responsible for providing education, individual health care, and a safety net for the disadvantaged, may be more controversial. We believe that the state has an important role in ensuring some provision of these basic services for the poorest people. This belief is explicit in our discussion of the social services and poverty alleviation in Chapter 6. How far the state should go depends, of course, on fiscal exigencies. There are always other deserving uses of public money. It must also be noted that these basic services are not public goods. The private sector can and does produce them. The state may ensure provision either by its own institutions, or by financing access to private ones. However, it is beyond the scope of this book to analyse and discuss these important complications.

Moving to still more controversial areas we ask in what circumstances, if any, the state should produce commodities or services beyond and apart from the basic services discussed above. Here the presumption is that production should be exclusively in the private sector. For public production to be advisable, a strong case would need to be made that private production would be inefficient or socially harmful, even after allowing for all the possibilities of public regulation. Why do we say this? There are two reasons. First, there is by now evidence not only from India but also from most other countries that the bureaucratic and political regulation of publicly owned enterprises results in an inefficient use of resources. It has proved impossible to give management the freedom to operate and the incentives required for efficiency, while preserving the idea of public accountability. Secondly, government itself has been over-extended. It has tried to do too much that requires knowledge and expertise in too many fields. This jack of all trades needs to become master of a few.

The so-called natural monopolies have long been considered to be a clear case for public ownership. These are cases where the technology is such that only a monopolist can supply efficiently. Transport by pipeline, cable, or rail provide the main examples. Here there are two points to be made. First, changes in technology have reduced the area of natural monopoly. Secondly, a monopoly can be regulated to prevent extortionate monopoly pricing. Recent experience in the UK and elsewhere seems to suggest that it is institutionally easier to regulate a private monopoly than it is to manage a public monopoly, to serve the public interest tolerably well. For these reasons we believe that there is a much stronger case for privatization in India than has yet been accepted by the government.

We turn next to the question of protection. We believe in and advocate an absence of import and export controls, and a low uniform tariff. Having regard to strong arguments in favour of simplicity we believe that this is the optimal trade regime for India. No one any longer believes in high indiscriminate protection of domestic industry as essential for general industrial promotion. It is recognized that this results in a pattern of industrialization that is biased against exports, and is inappropriate for an optimum use of the country's resources. But selective protection and selective promotion of particular industries has been strongly canvassed as an important element in the amazing late industrial revolutions that have occurred in the four East Asian tigers—Hong Kong, Taiwan, South Korea, and Singapore —followed in lesser degree by Thailand, Malaysia, and Indonesia.

We believe in the case of South Korea and Taiwan that government was very important in creating in the early 1960s the 'export-oriented' economy in which exporters operated under virtual free trade conditions, and had the assurance that government would see to it that there were many profitable export opportunities by maintaining a competitive exchange rate (or, when it threatened to become over-valued, providing compensating incentives). The government also bullied industrial leaders to export and honoured them for it. The export incentives were predominately general and non-selective. The result was an explosion of exports of labour intensive products from 1963–73.

The prime example and period of *selective* protection and promotion was the 'heavy and chemical industries' drive from 1973–79 in South Korea. Growth slowed down as real returns were reduced. In the 1980s both South Korea and Taiwan gave up the policy of selective promotion. We believe this is also true of Japan.[6] In the case of Hong Kong there never was any protection, or selective promotion.

Turning to capital movements, we believe that eventually when India has established the trade regime of very low protection that we advocate, then direct foreign investment should be allowed without restriction (unless for defence reasons). Until then, controls are justifiable in the case of investments made to supply mainly the domestic market. This is because in a highly protected market, if there are no controls, the buyer will either be subsidizing an inefficient producer or contributing to excess profits. This is always undesirable but particularly so if the producer is foreign.[7]

Portfolio investment in equities or bonds is another matter. There is probably no long-run advantage in trying to influence these potentially disturbing movements, except by orthodox macroeconomic policy measures. But in the short run, until the domestic banking and monetary systems are in good working order and inspire confidence, and the large international portfolio disequilibria that are a hangover from a highly controlled past have been absorbed, there is a case for retaining administrative controls over private foreign borrowing and lending. For further discussion of this problem see Chapters 2 and 4.

[6] Our views on industrial policy in these countries are also set out in Joshi and Little (1993). A more closely reasoned critique is in Little (1994).
[7] The way to evaluate foreign direct investment is clearly explained in Little (1982). See also Lal (1975).

The upshot is that the target at which we believe India should be explicitly, indeed vociferously, aiming is the same as that which is also the aim, now largely achieved, of all the Western industrialized countries (including Japan) and by now many developing countries. It is a market economy model with mainly private ownership, but with public intervention to deal with market failure, and to ensure an acceptable standard of living for the poorest people. Of course this target, or model, is not very closely specified. Differences arise because of differences in countries' histories and cultures. This is especially true of redistributionary and welfare policies. Sweden and the United States differ a good deal. But they are recognizably from the same mould. India would differ a good deal too! The point we are trying to make may perhaps be better put negatively. We deny that there is some characteristically different economic model which applies better to poor countries and would enable them to develop faster.

We end with a brief reader's guide.

Chapter 2 deals with the stabilization measures taken since June 1991. Medium-term stabilization has been achieved although inflation remains somewhat higher than is desirable. But public sector deficits absorb too much of the savings urgently needed for private investment, and imply levels of borrowing that are unsustainable in the long run.

In Chapter 3 the reduction of foreign trade controls and tariffs is described. Tariff reform has revenue consequences. This leads into an extended analysis of the whole fiscal scene. It is complicated because of the constitutional provisions that define the fiscal powers of the Centre and the States. The domestic indirect tax system is highly distorted, and direct taxes yield little. Some progress with reform has been made, but much remains to be done. Subsidies have become a major recognized misuse of public finance. There has been almost no success in reducing them.

Chapter 4 is concerned with financial institutions. In July 1991 the Indian financial system was collapsing. Exploitation of the banks by government, and directed credit at subsidized interest rates, had left many banks effectively bankrupt and incapable of properly fulfilling the main functions of a banking system. They were rescued by a massive infusion of public capital. The ill-designed interferences which led to their decay have been largely but not wholly rescinded. A beginning has been made to institute sound prudential regulation of both the banks and other financial institutions.

Chapter 5 deals with industrial policy. There has been a bonfire of controls. Apart from some charred remains, there are many other serious problems which have hardly been addressed. Much of the huge public sector makes losses. Public management is beset by constraints whose loosening is forever promised but never achieved. Privatization is a neglected option. Policies towards foreign investment and small-scale enterprises are discussed. Apart from public ownership, piecemeal and unco-ordinated policies over the years towards the employment of capital, land and labour, pursued with good intent and bad results, have left a welter of laws and procedures which still seriously reduce the efficiency and flexibility with which private industry operates. Prominent are those which prevent firms being closed, and so generate the sick company problem.

Chapter 6 discusses poverty. There has been much concern that reform might hurt the poor. Stabilization measures should be distinguished from the long-run structural reforms that were also initiated in 1991. Stabilization led to some increase in poverty in 1992, but we believe that this damage has been repaired. The structural reforms we advocate will benefit the poor by eliminating the bias against employment which has long been a feature of India's trade and industrial policies. But they may have some adverse distributional effects in the medium run which should be countered by improving various poverty alleviation measures. This, together with reforms of education and health policies, should anyway be part of the longer-run reform strategy.

Chapter 7 summarizes the progress and state of the reforms, and presents our conclusions. Reasons for success and failure are considered, and priorities suggested. The likelihood of a satisfactory continuation of the process of reform is assessed.

2
Stabilization Policy

2.1. Introduction

A macroeconomic crisis usually takes the form of accelerating inflation and unsustainable fiscal and current account deficits. *Per contra*, stabilization involves returning to low and stable inflation and a sustainable fiscal and current account position. Stabilization is obviously necessary in response to a crisis; but structural reform may or may not accompany stabilization measures. Since some reforms may magnify the macroeconomic problem, it has been argued that stabilization should precede structural reform. Examples are trade reforms which reduce revenue, or financial reforms which raise the cost of government borrowing. But other structural reforms help the macroeconomic problem. For instance a shift from import controls to tariffs will raise revenue, and reform of public enterprises can reduce losses and so curtail government expenditure.

India began the process of structural reform before even short-term stabilization had been achieved. In our opinion this was right. But this implies that the timing of structural reforms must be considered in the light of the macroeconomic situation, while the content and timing of the stabilization measures should as far as possible support the process of structural reform.

2.2. The Crisis of 1991

India's reform programme began in the middle of a macro-economic crisis that erupted in early 1991.[1] The crisis was brought to a head by a steep fall in foreign exchange reserves to about $1 billion (equal to two weeks' imports), a sharp downgrading of India's credit rating, and a cut-off of foreign private lending. Its basic underlying features were high inflation (12 per cent and rising), large public and current account deficits (approximately 10 per cent and 3 per cent of GDP respectively), and a heavy and growing burden of domestic and foreign debt.

External shocks played only a minor role in the crisis. Oil prices increased following the Iraqi invasion of Kuwait in August 1990, but only for a few months. This mini-shock would normally have been weathered without undue difficulty, but it impinged on an economy which was in a highly vulnerable state due to unsustainable macroeconomic policies over a prolonged period. The cut-off of foreign lending was not an exogenous shock but a reaction to the unsound macroeconomic position.

The roots of the crisis can be traced back to India's reaction to the earlier crisis of 1979–81 when world oil prices doubled. This exogenous shock changed India's current account position from near balance in 1978 to a deficit of 2 per cent of GDP (30 per cent of exports) in 1981. Remarkably, there was hardly any current account adjustment for the rest of the decade despite favourable developments such as a softening of oil prices and rising domestic oil production. The current account deficit averaged 25 per cent of exports from 1982 to 1984; from 1985 to 1990 it averaged no less than 40 per cent of exports. These deficits were covered by heavy borrowing from the IMF and from commercial sources.

From 1982 to 1985 the persistence of current account deficits was the result of the almost complete stagnation of exports

---

[1] For a detailed analysis of the causes of the crisis and an overview of Indian macroeconomic policies, see Joshi and Little (1994) and Joshi and Little (1996).

which was in turn largely the result of an inappropriate exchange rate policy. The real exchange rate was allowed to appreciate by 15 per cent from 1979 to 1981 and remained at that level for the next four years. From 1986 exchange rate policy became more flexible and the real exchange rate depreciated substantially. Exports revived strongly in response and grew in real terms at 10 per cent per annum between 1986 and 1990. But by then the export boom was insufficient to outweigh the combination of rising interest payments on external debt and the rapid growth of imports induced by fiscal deterioration.

While exchange rate policy must take part of the blame for the lack of current account adjustment and the heavy accumulation of foreign debt, the heart of the problem lay in the reversal of India's erstwhile fiscal prudence. The fiscal deficit of the central government which had averaged about 4.5 per cent of GDP in the second half of the 1970s crept up to 8.5 per cent of GDP by 1985/86 and stayed at that level thereafter. Similar increases occurred in the deficits of the consolidated government and of the public sector as a whole. This marked deterioration in the public finances was responsible both for the persistence of the current account deficit and the inflationary upsurge at the end of the decade.

The economy grew rapidly during the 1980s. GDP growth rose from the long-standing rate of 3.6 per cent per annum (1965–80) to 5.5 per cent (1980–90). Some of the growth was unsustainable, being the direct result of the fiscal deficits; but part of it was the product of desirable policy changes, in particular the deregulation of controls on industry and investment. These reforms, half-hearted and piecemeal though they were, were proving to be effective, but foundered in the macro-economic crisis at the end of the decade. More comprehensive reforms were needed but in a stable fiscal setting.

2.3. An Overview of Macroeconomic Policies and Performance Since 1991

Table 2.1 contains figures relevant to this section. The new government which took office at the end of June 1991 committed itself to a programme of structural reform, but its first priority was to stabilize the economy. Its immediate objectives were thus to reduce inflation, improve the balance of payments position, and reduce the fiscal deficit. It was also an objective to minimize the adverse impact of stabilization on real income and output, and to place the economy on a high-growth path as rapidly as possible.

In 1991/92, fiscal retrenchment and a credit squeeze were undertaken, combined with a 19 per cent devaluation of the rupee, supported by a standby credit from the IMF.[2] Severe import controls instituted in 1990/91 were kept in place. Both agricultural and manufacturing output fell, the former because of erratic weather (though it certainly does not rank as a drought year by Indian standards) and the latter because of the agricultural setback, the draconian import controls, and the fiscal contraction. Overall, GDP growth slowed to 0.8 per cent, and agricultural and manufacturing output fell by 2.5 per cent and 1.8 per cent respectively. Inflation increased further to about 14 per cent, averaged over the year. The balance of payments improved dramatically but almost entirely because of deflation and import compression. The current account deficit fell to 0.7 per cent of GDP from 3.5 per cent in 1990/91 and foreign exchange reserves increased to approximately $6 billion.

From 1992/93 onwards, there was a recovery, initially intermittent, then strong and broad based. Agricultural production was satisfactory throughout, helped by the run of good weather (and perhaps by its improving profitability following the reform measures). Manufacturing output was sluggish in

---

[2] In the event, money supply grew faster than in 1990/91 because of the significant improvement in foreign exchange reserves and an unexpected increase in the money multiplier.

Table 2.1. India: Macroeconomic Indicators

	1990/91	1991/92	1992/93	1993/94	1994/95	1995/96 [a]
GDP (annual % change)	5.4	0.8	5.1	5.0	6.3	6.2
Agriculture	4.1	−2.5	5.3	3.0	4.9	3.0
Manufacturing	5.0	−1.8	2.3	3.6	9.0	10.0
Services	4.3	4.5	4.4	5.4	6.4	6.1
Inflation (% per annum) [b]	10.3	13.7	10.1	8.4	10.8	7.5
Broad money (annual % increase)	15.1	19.3	15.7	18.4	21.2	14.5
Reserve money (annual % increase)	13.1	13.4	11.3	25.2	22.7	9.8
Gross domestic investment (% GDP)	27.1	23.6	22.0	21.6	25.2	
Gross domestic saving (% GDP)	23.7	23.1	20.0	21.4	24.4	
Real GFCF (% GDP)	21.3	20.3	19.7	20.5	22.8	
Public	8.6	8.7	7.7	7.9	8.4	
Private	12.7	11.6	12.1	12.6	13.7	
Current account deficit (% GDP)	3.2	0.4	1.8	0.1	0.7	1.6
Foreign exchange reserves ($ billion)	2.3	5.7	6.7	15.3	21.0	17.0

[a] Figures for 1995/96 are estimates. [b] Wholesale Price Index. Average of weeks.

Sources: Government of India, C.S.O. (1995) *National Accounts Statistics.* Government of India, C.S.O. (1996) *Quick Estimates of National Income 1994/95.* Government of India, Ministry of Finance, *Economic Survey 1995/96.* Centre for Monitoring the Indian Economy (1995), *Monthly Review of the Indian Economy.*

1992/93 and 1993/94 (average growth of 3 per cent) due to persisting weak demand, but grew rapidly in 1994/95 and 1995/96 (average growth of 9.5 per cent). Considering the period 1992/93 to 1995/96 as a whole, output grew at 5.7 per cent per year (composed of agriculture 4.1 per cent, manufacturing 6.2 per cent, and services 5.6 per cent), evidently a much better performance than in many other developing countries embarking on post-crisis reform programmes.[3]

Figures on saving and investment are available only up to 1994/95.[4] As a proportion of GDP, both have, broadly speaking, moved pro-cyclically. Gross domestic saving fell sharply until 1992/93 but has recovered subsequently. Since public savings have fluctuated around an extremely low level, the movement of aggregate saving largely reflects changes in private saving. Corporate saving has grown resiliently; household saving (including, somewhat alarmingly, its financial component) declined steeply until 1992/93 but has revived since, especially in 1994/95. Both public and private investment fell in 1991/92. Public investment has continued to stagnate; private investment, however, has rebounded, particularly in 1994/95 and informal evidence suggests a further increase in 1995/96. Again, it is notable that corporate investment has risen throughout, so the initial decline in private investment appears to have been in the household component.[5] In 1995/96, there has been a pronounced increase in real interest rates. As a result, there is a question mark over the future course of investment and growth (see below).

---

[3] See Acharya (1995). The figures for 1995/96 are 'advance estimates' made by the C.S.O.

[4] Table 2.1 gives only aggregate saving and investment data. A breakdown is given in Government of India, C.S.O. (1995) *National Accounts Statistics* and C.S.O. (1996) *Quick Estimates of National Income 1994/95.*

[5] The precision of the above account must be taken with a pinch of salt as saving and investment figures in India (especially the household component) are not entirely trustworthy. See Joshi and Little (1994), chapter 13 and Appendix A, and Athukorala and Sen (1995).

Inflation has proved to be stubborn. It was below 10 per cent in only one of the four years from 1991/92 to 1994/95, and the average rate was 10.8 per cent. If the year 1991/92 is excluded, the average rate is 9.8 per cent, still considerably above both the 5-6 per cent target of the government and the average rate in the second half of the 1980s (about 7 per cent). In 1995/96 inflation has fallen to 8 per cent averaged over the year, and at the time of writing is running at an annual rate of 5 per cent. But we doubt if this is an enduring change (see below).

The balance of payments improvement of 1991/92 was not merely sustained but reinforced in the three succeeding years. The current account deficit was below 1 per cent of GDP in all but one year from 1991/92 to 1994/95 and we expect it to be about 1.5 per cent in 1995/96. In addition to the current account turnaround, there was a large surge in private capital inflows in 1993/94 and 1994/95. As a consequence, foreign exchange reserves increased to $21 billion by the end of March 1995. In 1995/96, however, capital inflows slowed down and the current account deficit widened. So the year is expected to end with foreign exchange reserves in the region of $17 billion.

The rate of growth of 5.5 per cent per year in the 1980s could not be sustained without major reforms. It was based on a mountain of public borrowing which erupted in 1991. A much reduced rate of growth of output for some time was the unavoidable consequence of the essential crisis measures. However, in the past two years output has grown by more than 6 per cent per year. The critical questions are whether the stabilization measures, together with the structural reforms already made, make this rate of growth sustainable; and if not, what further measures and reforms are needed for low inflation and indefinite expansion at 6 per cent or more. We discuss the relevant issues under the headings of fiscal adjustment, inflation, and balance of payments management.

2.4. Fiscal Adjustment

2.4.1 Theory

A prime requirement of macroeconomic stability in the medium and long run is the sustainability of the fiscal deficit of the government and, more broadly, the deficit of the non-financial public sector. We define the non-financial public sector (NFPS) as the aggregation of central and State governments, public sector enterprises (PSE), and the Reserve Bank of India, excluding other public sector financial institutions such as the nationalized commercial banks.

We start from the basic identity that the deficit of the NFPS can be financed by printing money, borrowing domestically, or borrowing abroad.   Each of these methods of financing, if carried to excess, can lead to a crisis.

Growth of real income increases the demand for money issued by the central bank.   The implied monopoly profit or 'seignorage' arising from this activity provides the government some scope for non-inflationary monetization of the fiscal deficit.   This revenue can be further augmented by printing additional money and generating inflation.   This is because the public is willing to save and increase its money holdings as prices rise: in other words to pay what is, in effect, an 'inflation tax'.   But this method of raising revenue has severe limitations. First, the incremental yield of this tax falls with rising inflation since the public seeks to economize on its real money balances. At some inflation rate, the yield of the inflation tax reaches a maximum.   The revenue-maximizing rate of inflation for India has been estimated to be 50 per cent and the maximum seignorage and inflation tax 2.5 per cent of GDP.[6] This is in line with estimates of the maximum inflation tax in other developing countries.   Second, high rates of inflation increase the risk of sliding into hyper-inflation.   Third, in a substantially non-

---

[6]   Buiter and Patel (1996).

indexed economy such as India, even inflation rates of 10 per cent increase poverty and are rightly regarded as a social evil.

The second method of financing a fiscal deficit is domestic borrowing. Here the relationship between the interest rate and the growth rate of GDP is critical. If the former exceeds the latter, any primary deficit net of the inflation tax leads to a debt trap, in other words to an explosive debt/GDP ratio. This is obviously unsustainable and would lead to the government reneging on the debt either explicitly or indirectly by eventual monetization and hyper-inflation.

Even if long-run sustainability is not threatened, high fiscal deficits are undesirable because they lead to crowding out of private investment or net exports.[7] Of course the magnitude of these effects depends on whether there is output slack and whether private savings are growing. But private savings cannot grow fast enough indefinitely to absorb high fiscal deficits. If private investment is crowded out by unproductive public consumption, the growth rate of GDP is directly reduced. Even if it is crowded out by public investment there is a loss in terms of growth, if, as is often the case, private investment is more productive than public investment.[8] If crowding out takes the form of higher trade deficits, the nation's external debt increases (see below). Note that the debt sustainability issue and the crowding out issue are connected. A primary deficit is in theory sustainable if the interest rate is less than the growth rate of GDP because the debt/GDP ratio will converge to a limit (see below). But this notion of sustainability is based on assuming constant values of the interest and growth rates. If the primary deficit remains high there is likely to be a large divergence between the actual debt/GDP ratio and its theoretical limit. The growing volume of government borrowing would then drive up interest

---

[7] This implicitly (but realistically) assumes that 'Ricardian equivalence' does not hold.

[8] It must be noted that some public expenditures that are classified as 'consumption', for example those on health and education, and public investment in infrastructure, can be highly productive.

rates and reduce private investment and GDP growth. Thus crowding out could be severe enough to lead to unsustainable debt.

Finally, the fiscal deficit can be financed by borrowing abroad. But this process in turn faces similar limits to those on domestic borrowing. Debt sustainability requires that the interest rate on foreign borrowing be less than the growth rate of exports.[9] If this condition is met a primary (i.e. non-interest) deficit in the current account of the balance of payments is sustainable. Again, one has to be careful about not taking a partial view. A large primary current account deficit would imply a high terminal external debt/exports ratio. If so, it is likely (*a*) that the interest rate at which the country can borrow would rise and (*b*) that there would be credit rationing. With forward-looking lenders, these constraints can make themselves felt well before the theoretical limit is reached. Note here that public sector deficits can increase external debt in two ways: (*a*) by direct public foreign borrowing; and (*b*) by increased public domestic borrowing which spills over into current account deficits and increased private foreign borrowing. (This is not to say that external debt problems always result from fiscal profligacy. They can be also be caused by private sector incontinence as the recent Mexican example illustrates.)

We have set out the general long-run case for fiscal prudence. We now make various points which gloss the basic line taken above.[10]

(i) Early action on the fiscal deficit is especially important when economic reform begins during a macroeconomic crisis if the reform itself increases fiscal pressures, which it may (as noted in the introduction to this chapter).

---

[9] In the case of a large country like India, the external debt/exports ratio is a more relevant indicator of the burden of external debt than the external debt/GDP ratio.

[10] There is a good review of the issues surrounding fiscal adjustment in Ahluwalia (1995).

(ii) Responding to exogenous shocks—such as changes in private sector saving and investment behaviour; droughts; terms of trade changes; sudden changes in capital flows—is one of the main functions of fiscal policy, acting in concert with other macroeconomic instruments. This strengthens the case for early correction of an unsustainable fiscal position as the latter reduces significantly the leeway for a flexible fiscal policy.

(iii) The transition to a lower fiscal deficit is a task of some delicacy as it has to be dovetailed with the use of fiscal policy for cyclical stabilization. Fiscal retrenchment is deflationary and does not produce a one-for-one improvement in the budget as tax revenue falls endogenously. This problem can be eased in two ways: (*a*) by an accompanying switching policy such as exchange rate depreciation[11] and (*b*) by policies to encourage private investment. The fall in interest rates that follows from fiscal adjustment should help to 'crowd in' private investment, but this is not automatic: other conditions are important, such as provision of infrastructure and the transparency and credibility of the reform process. While the pace of fiscal adjustment has to pay attention to cyclical factors, it is obviously important to speed up fiscal adjustment during periods of boom and recovery when there is a natural tendency for the budget to improve.

(iv) The quality of fiscal adjustment is as important as its amount. A good rule of thumb is that the deficit should be cut by increasing public savings rather than by reducing public investment. Public investment in infrastructure is particularly important for growth and may be complementary with private investment. Another good rule of thumb is that public savings should be raised without cutting essential social sector expenditures such as primary education and health, as these are vital for both growth and poverty alleviation.

---

[11] If the starting position is one of excess demand, with a fiscal deficit and a current account deficit, fiscal retrenchment combined with exchange rate devaluation is appropriate. But devaluation by itself may have an ambiguous effect on the fiscal deficit.

2.4.2. Magnitude of the Required Fiscal Adjustment

As we saw above, the deficit of the NFPS can be financed by creating money and borrowing from domestic and foreign sources. We first establish safe limits for money creation and foreign borrowing and then work out the prudent levels of domestic borrowing and the primary deficit. The increase in the ratio of domestic debt to GDP can be written as follows:

$$\Delta b = (x - s - f) - b(y - r) \qquad (1)$$

where
b is the ratio of domestic debt of the NFPS to GDP
x is the ratio of the primary (i.e. non-interest) deficit of the NFPS to GDP
s is the safe level of seignorage and inflation tax as a proportion of GDP
f is the safe level of primary (i.e. non-interest) foreign borrowing of the NFPS as a proportion of GDP
y is the growth rate of real GDP
r is the real interest rate on the domestic borrowing of the NFPS[12]

---

[12]   The derivation of the formula is given below, using the notation given in the text and some additional notation to be defined.
    The budget identity of the NFPS can be written

$$X + iB + ei^*D = \Delta B + \Delta H + e\Delta D \qquad (i)$$

where X is the primary deficit, i and i* are nominal interest rates on the domestic and external borrowing of the NFPS respectively, B and D are the existing domestic and external debt of the NFPS respectively, H is base money, and e is the nominal exchange rate. Suppose P is the price level and Y is real GDP. Then, dividing equation (i) by PY (i.e. nominal GDP), we have

$$x + ib = \Delta B/PY + \Delta H/PY + (e\Delta D - ei^*D)/PY \qquad (ii)$$

In the text we work out independently the safe value of the seignorage and inflation tax $\Delta H/PY$ which we denote as s and the safe value of primary foreign

The common sense of this formula is that the increase in domestic debt as a proportion of GDP can be broken down into two components. The first is the primary deficit in excess of the safe level of the inflation tax and the safe level of primary foreign borrowing. The second is the interest payment on existing debt; but the denominator of the domestic debt ratio is GDP, so the increase in the debt ratio on this count depends on the difference between the interest rate and the growth rate of GDP.

If $y < r$, then any primary deficit greater than $(s + f)$ is unsustainable as b follows an explosive path. If $y > r$, primary deficits are theoretically sustainable. We can then calculate the implied terminal value of b (by setting $\Delta b = 0$ in the above equation) and use informed judgement to decide whether it would be sustainable in practice. In the limit, the value of b is $(x - s - f)/(y - r)$. We can also solve for the primary deficit required to achieve any specified target level of b.

We first consider what constitutes a prudent target for y. Real GDP grew at about 5.5 per cent per annum in the 1980s, but this rate turned out to be manifestly unsustainable. It would not be prudent to assume y higher than 6 per cent, even assuming a successful reform programme. So we put $y = 0.06$.

Inflation tax. Consider now the safe level of the inflation tax. Assuming that an average rate of inflation of 5 per cent is acceptable and given $y = 6$ per cent, we have a nominal growth

borrowing $(e\Delta D - ei^*D)/PY$ which we denote as f. Then equation (ii) can be written

$$x + ib = \Delta B/PY + s + f \qquad \text{(iii)}$$

Noting that $B = bPY$ and writing $p = \Delta P/P$ and $y = \Delta Y/Y$, it follows that

$$\Delta B = PY\Delta b + bPY (p + y)$$
$$\text{or} \qquad \Delta B/PY = \Delta b + b(p + y)$$

Therefore, from equation (iii) we can derive

$$\Delta b = (x - s - f) + ib - b(p + y)$$

Defining $r = i - p$, we have equation (1) in the text.

rate of GDP of 11 per cent. The ratio of base money to GDP since 1980 seems to be rather stable at around 12 per cent. (Base money is taken to be currency plus the non-interest bearing component of the required cash reserves of banks.) This implies that 11 per cent × 0.12 = 1.3 per cent of GDP is the safe limit for public revenue from seignorage and the inflation tax. Therefore s = 0.013.

Public foreign borrowing. First, we determine the safe limit for total national borrowing from abroad. Public sector borrowing must obviously be less than this. For a large country such as India, the limiting size of the debt is set not so much by the debt-to-GDP ratio as by the debt-to-exports ratio. Analogous to equation (1) we can write

$$\Delta d = z - d(g - r^*) \tag{2}$$

where
d is the ratio of the nation's external debt to exports
z is the primary (i.e. non-interest) current account deficit to exports ratio
g is the growth of export volume
r^* is the real interest rate on foreign borrowing.

If $g < r^*$ primary current account deficits are unsustainable. Assuming $g > r^*$ and given the values of z, g, and r^* the terminal value of d can be worked out by setting $\Delta d = 0$. Similarly, for given values of g and r^*, and a target value for d, the required value of z can be calculated.

The debt-to-exports ratio in India is currently about 3 but this figure includes debt on concessional terms. The ratio of discounted debt to exports is around 2 and that is the relevant figure for our purposes.[13] Since capital markets have evidently regarded India's external debt as being on the margin of the danger zone, it seems sensible not to allow d to rise above 2. It

---

[13]   See World Bank, *World Debt Tables 1994/95*.

would not be prudent to assume that India could increase export volume over a long period at more than 10 per cent per annum. What is the likely rate of interest on foreign borrowing r^*? We suggest that India cannot bank on a rate lower than 5 per cent.[14] Setting $d = 2$, $g = 0.1$ and $r^* = 0.05$, the prudent figure for z from equation (2) is 0.1, i.e. 10 per cent of exports. Exports are about 10 per cent of GDP. This then implies a prudent figure for the non-interest current account deficit of (10 per cent)(0.1) = approximately 1 per cent of GDP. For comparison, at the end of the 1980s, the non-interest current account deficit was about 25 per cent of exports or 2.5 per cent of GDP. Using equation (2), we can see that with $z = 0.25$, $g = 0.1$ and $r^* = 0.05$, the implied terminal value of d in 1990/91 was 5, clearly absurdly high.

If national borrowing should not exceed 1 per cent of GDP, this is *a fortiori* so for public borrowing. We assume that a safe limit for public primary foreign borrowing is 0.5 per cent of GDP.[15] Thus, $f = 0.005$.

Safe limits for domestic borrowing, the primary deficit and the overall deficit. We now return to equation (1). The variables remaining to be estimated are b, x, and r. The domestic debt of the NFPS is about 54 per cent of GDP so $b = 0.54$.[16] India does

[14] In the 19th century the world rate of interest on safe bonds was about 3 per cent. But the world rate of growth has risen, which would tend to raise the rate, perhaps to 4 per cent. On top of that, in India's case, allowance has to be made for a risk premium and for likely future depreciation of the real exchange rate. Note also that the real rate of interest on dollar bonds in the 1990s has been around 4 per cent.

[15] Note in this context that the average non-interest foreign borrowing of the government as a proportion of GDP in the 1990s has been around 0.3 per cent of GDP. This can be worked out from the budget documents. It might be objected that the nation's current account deficit could be covered by direct and portfolio equity investment which are not debt-creating. Even so, it would be imprudent to increase *public* foreign borrowing above the limit calculated. See also Section 2.6 below.

[16] Figures for central and State government debt are available in Government of India, Ministry of Finance, *Indian Public Finance Statistics*.

Table 2.2. Deficits of the Non-financial Public Sector   (% GDP)

	1990/91	1991/92	1992/93	1993/94	1994/95
Overall deficit	10.5	9.1	8.4	11.0	10.5
Primary deficit	5.3	3.0	2.0	4.3	3.8

Source: International Monetary Fund. See Chopra *et al.* (1995), ch. 5.

not have a satisfactory set of public accounts from which the value of x is directly available. We use here the estimates of x made by the IMF[17] as given in Table 2.2.

Interest rates on government securities and small savings have followed a rising trend in recent years, following financial liberalization. Though average real rates on government debt have not gone up much because of the outstanding low-coupon stock, marginal real rates have already risen above 5 per cent, and it is the latter that are relevant in the present context. We do not think it would be prudent to assume a real interest rate below 5 per cent. We therefore put $r = 0.05$, that is we assume that r is 1 per cent lower than y, the real rate of GDP growth. There are good grounds for thinking that this assumption is too optimistic. We return to this point below but proceed initially with the assumption made.

We first work out the implications of the fiscal situation in 1990/91, with the following parameter values: $x = 0.053$, $s = 0.013$, $f = 0.005$, $b = 0.54$, $y = 0.06$ and $r = 0.05$.

The above figure is obtained by subtracting the government's external debt and debt to the RBI from total government debt and adding the estimated debt of public sector enterprises.

[17] See Chopra *et al.* (1995). Note that this is a minimal estimate of x since the IMF's definition of the NFPS excludes State government public sector enterprises. The IMF's definition of the NFPS also excludes the Reserve Bank. We assume that its inclusion would make no difference to x, a natural assumption in the long run.

From equation (1) we have

$$\Delta b = (0.053 - 0.013 - 0.005) - 0.54 (0.06 - 0.05)$$
$$= 0.035 - 0.0054$$
$$= 0.03$$

Thus, the domestic debt ratio would be growing at about 3 per cent per year. The ultimate level of b is given by setting $\Delta b = 0$ and solving for b:

$$b = (x - s - f)/(y - r)$$
$$= 0.035/0.01 = 3.5$$

That is, the implied terminal domestic debt in 1990/91 was about three-and-a-half times GDP. This further implied interest payments on domestic debt of about 35 per cent of GDP in the steady state, assuming a nominal interest rate of 10 per cent.

This was, of course, a disastrous scenario. It is impossible to imagine that the private sector would ever save enough and want to hold enough of its savings in government bonds for such a volume of domestic debt relative to GDP to be feasible. In such a situation the interest rate would rise and the growth rate of GDP would fall and make the fiscal track strictly unsustainable. The implications of the 1994/95 level of the primary deficit (3.8 per cent) are not much better. From equation (1), $\Delta b = 1.5$ per cent per year and terminal $b = 2$, again totally unsustainable in practice.

It would obviously not be prudent to let b rise above its present level. Putting $b = 0.54$ and $\Delta b = 0$ in equation (1), we can now solve for x and thus for the required reduction in the primary deficit.

$$x = b(y - r) + s + f$$
$$= 0.54 (0.01) + 0.013 + 0.005$$
$$= 0.023$$

Thus the above calculation suggests that the primary deficit of the non-financial public sector should be reduced to 2.3 per cent of GDP.

We would regard this as the minimum reduction in the primary deficit that policy-makers should contemplate. But the prudent course would be to implement a much larger adjustment. The critical assumption made above was that the real rate of interest on government borrowing is 1 per cent lower than the rate of growth of GDP. This assumption is questionable. In India's recent experience (1994/95 and 1995/96), two years of 6 per cent growth has raised the marginal real interest rate on public borrowing to 7–8 per cent and on company borrowing to 10–15 per cent. This may be the result partly of the monetary tightening undertaken to contain inflation below the 10 per cent rate that prevailed in 1994/95. High real interest rates may come down to some extent if and when an enduring reduction in inflation brings down nominal interest rates. But it may be some considerable time before that happens if the inflation target is 5 per cent. (Note also that financial liberalization is as yet incomplete, so some further reduction in reserve ratios and upward pressure on real interest rates is yet to come.) Moreover, our judgement would be that part of the reason for high real interest rates is independent of inflation, namely the divergence between *ex ante* investment demand associated with growth of 6 per cent or more, and the available supply of domestic saving. Potentially this could lead to severe crowding out of private investment and a decline in the rate of growth.[18] Contrarily, lower public deficits, if achieved through higher public savings, would make 6 per cent growth possible.[19] Lower public deficits would also ease the pressure on real interest rates which stems

[18]   The imbalance between *ex ante* investment and saving could be eased by running higher current account deficits but only to a limited extent (see Section 2.6).

[19]   We are assuming here that it would be undesirable to reduce public investment (though its efficiency should certainly be increased) and that there are no reliable methods of increasing private savings in the short run.

from both financial liberalization and the effort to bring down inflation by monetary restriction.

The only convenient way to bring these considerations into our framework is to postulate a real interest rate higher than the growth rate. If the rate of interest is 1 per cent higher than the rate of growth, the primary deficit required to stabilize the debt at the current level is $x = b(y - r) + s + f = 0.54(-0.01) + 0.013 + 0.005 = 0.013$, i.e. 1.3 per cent of GDP. Assuming real interest rates 1.5 per cent and 2 per cent higher than the 6 per cent growth rate of GDP changes the safe value of the primary public deficit to 1 per cent of GDP and 0.7 per cent of GDP respectively.[20]

If, however, a substantial reduction in outstanding debt could be achieved by large-scale privatization, real interest rates would fall (see below). It might then be possible to regard the scenario in which y is 1 per cent higher than r as realistic. But a massive privatization programme may not be feasible in the near-term.

Note also that a reduction in the primary public deficit to 1 per cent would still leave the overall deficit of the NFPS in the region of 7 per cent of GDP. Even if sustainable, this is surely higher than is desirable from the standpoint of bringing down real interest rates sufficiently to encourage private investment. It may, therefore, be optimal to reduce the public deficit to zero or even to negative levels.[21]

We conclude that it would be prudent to reduce the primary deficit of the NFPS to no more than 1 per cent of GDP.

---

[20] The orthodox view in economic theory is that the real interest rate cannot be less than the growth rate of real GDP over a long period. It is an empirical fact that some East Asian countries have for long periods grown faster than the real rate of interest, but it is notable that most of them have had significantly lower public deficits than India. See chapter 2 of Chopra *et al.* (1995).

[21] The main difference between investment/saving balances in India and in the fast-growing East Asian economies is that India has much lower levels of public saving and private investment.

2.4.3.   Fiscal Adjustment Since 1991

We saw above that the primary deficit of the NFPS was in the region of 4 per cent of GDP in 1994/95 and needs to be reduced to 1 per cent of GDP or less. Unfortunately, India's public sector accounts do not enable us to translate this into how much of the adjustment should fall on the Centre, the States, and the public sector enterprises respectively. The role of the Centre is obviously critical because it controls the borrowing of the States and PSEs and can therefore force some adjustment on them. But there are limits to how much the Centre can squeeze without causing economic harm or hitting political barriers. There will have to be some voluntary adjustment by the States and the PSEs.

The Centre. We distinguish between the quantity and the quality of fiscal adjustment. The former refers simply to the magnitude of the change in the fiscal deficit, the latter draws attention to its composition. Tables 2.3 and 2.4 give the relevant figures.

The fiscal deficit (primary fiscal deficit) of the Centre declined from 8.3 per cent (4.3 per cent) of GDP in 1990/91 to 5.7 per cent (1.3 per cent) in 1992/93. But it rose again to 7.5 per cent of GDP (2.9 per cent) in 1993/94 and declined only slightly to 6.5 per cent of GDP (1.8 per cent) in 1994/95. According to the interim budget of February 1996, it fell further to 5.9 per cent (1.1 per cent) in 1995/96.

There are two issues of definition here which should be noted. First, the government's definition of the deficit takes credit for disinvestment in public sector enterprises 'above the line'. This practice is dubious (though sanctioned by the IMF and adopted also in the UK). Sale of assets is properly regarded as financing the deficit rather than adding to revenue; furthermore, the latter procedure and the associated optical illusion creates a temptation to increase expenditure above what it would otherwise be. Treating disinvestment as 'below the line' would increase the fiscal deficit in some years. But we

Table 2.3. Revenue and Expenditure of the Central Government

(% GDP)

	1990/91	1991/92	1992/93	1993/94	1994/95 (R. E.)	1995/96 (R. E.)
Total revenue receipts	10.4	10.7	10.5	9.4	9.4	10.2
Tax revenue (centre's share)	8.1	8.1	7.7	6.7	6.9	7.5
(Customs)	3.9	3.7	3.7	2.8	2.8	3.3
(Excise)	2.7	2.6	2.6	2.2	2.2	2.1
(Corporate)	1.0	1.3	1.3	1.3	1.4	1.5
(Income)	0.24	0.26	0.26	0.17	0.26	0.36
Non-tax revenue	2.3	2.6	2.9	2.7	2.5	2.7
Total expenditure	19.8	18.1	17.4	17.7	17.2	16.9
Revenue expenditure	13.9	13.3	13.1	13.5	13.0	13.2
Plan	2.4	2.5	3.0	3.2	3.1	2.8
Central	1.3	1.4	1.7	2.0	1.9	1.9
Assistance to states	1.1	1.0	1.3	1.3	1.2	0.9
Non-plan	11.5	11.1	10.8	10.7	9.9	10.4
(Interest)	4.1	4.4	4.7	4.6	4.7	4.8
(Subsidies)	2.3	2.0	1.8	1.6	1.4	1.3
(Defence)	2.0	1.9	1.8	1.9	1.8	1.7
Capital expenditure	6.0	4.7	4.2	4.2	4.2	3.6
Plan	3.1	2.6	2.4	2.5	2.1	1.7
(Public enterprises)	1.4	1.1	1.0	1.1	1.0	0.8
(Assistance to states)	1.3	1.3	1.3	1.3	1.1	0.9
Non-plan	2.9	2.2	1.9	2.0	2.1	2.0
(Defence)	0.9	0.8	0.7	0.8	0.7	0.7
(Loans to states)	1.4	0.9	0.7	0.6	1.0	1.0

Source: Government of India *Economic Survey 1995/96* and Budget Documents.

shall not dwell on this point, as disinvestment has not been quantitatively significant so far. The second issue is the definition of the primary deficit. Is it gross or net interest payments that should be subtracted from the gross fiscal deficit? We think the latter is conceptually the correct course. But we stick here to the government's usage.

Is the Centre's fiscal adjustment sufficient? The answer must be 'No' if it is accepted that the primary deficit of the NFPS should be reduced by about 3 per cent of GDP below its 1994/95 level and if most of the explicit adjustment has to be borne by the Centre.[22] If so, the Centre must run a primary surplus of about 1 per cent of GDP, an overall fiscal deficit of about 4 per cent of GDP, and a revenue deficit of zero (assuming some reversal in the decline of the Centre's net capital expenditure).

As worrying as the quantity of fiscal adjustment is its quality. The basic point here is that the revenue deficit is about the same in 1995/96 as it was in 1990/91. There has been a fall in the ratio of tax revenue to GDP. The fall in customs and excise receipts was an expected consequence of tax and tariff reform. Lower rates and better compliance have improved the yield of personal and corporate income taxation, but not enough to outweigh the fall in tariff revenue. There has not been much progress with widening the tax base. Non-tax revenue went up until 1992/93, largely due to one-off changes such as an increase in the Reserve Bank's dividend to the government, but has stagnated since. Current expenditure as a proportion of GDP has fallen, but only by 0.7 per cent. This is primarily because interest payments have risen sharply (as a result of the higher cost of government borrowing, consequent upon interest-rate liberalization). But the reduction in subsidies has been much less than planned. Export subsidies were abolished along with

[22]   Note that a reduction in the Centre's primary deficit does not necessarily produce an equivalent reduction in the primary deficit of the NFPS. For example, in 1994/95, the primary deficit of the Centre fell by 1.1 per cent of GDP but that of the NFPS by only 0.5 per cent. Evidently, the Centre could not prevent the States from borrowing more.

Table 2.4. Fiscal Deficit of the Central Government

(% GDP)

	1990/91	1991/92	1992/93	1993/94	1994/95 (R. E.)	1995/96 (R. E.)
Revenue deficit	3.5	2.6	2.6	4.1	3.6	3.0
Capital expenditure	5.9	4.7	4.2	4.2	4.2	3.6
Loan repayments	1.0	1.0	0.9	0.8	0.7	0.7
Net capital expenditure	4.9	3.7	3.3	3.4	3.5	2.9
Fiscal deficit[a]	8.3	6.3	5.9	7.5	7.1	6.0
Disinvestment receipts	0.0	0.5	0.3	0.0	0.6	0.1
Fiscal deficit[b]	8.3	5.9	5.7	7.5	6.5	5.9
Gross interest payments	4.0	4.3	4.4	4.6	4.7	4.8
Primary fiscal deficit[c]	4.3	1.6	1.3	2.9	1.8	1.1

[a] Revenue deficit + net capital expenditure.
[b] Government of India definition. Fiscal deficit – disinvestment receipts.
[c] Government of India definition. Fiscal deficit (Government of India definition) – gross interest payments.

Source: Government of India *Economic Survey 1995/96*.

the devaluation of July 1991. Food and fertilizer subsidies together have barely changed as a proportion of GDP. There has been some squeeze on grants to States and the governmental wage bill. Non-interest current spending in 1995/96 was 1.4 per cent of GDP lower than in 1990/91.

Such fall in the fiscal deficit as there has been has come mainly from the reduction in capital expenditure, including loans to States and public enterprises. Capital expenditure in 1995/96 was 2.4 per cent of GDP lower than in 1990/91. There is no exact correspondence between budgetary capital expenditure and public investment. Nevertheless the fall in the former is indicative of a squeeze on the latter, for which there is independent confirmation from other sources. National Accounts figures show that public real capital formation in 1994/95 was running about 1 per cent of GDP below its 1990/91 level, which in turn was 1 per cent of GDP less than the average for the decade of the 1980s. Does the fall in public investment matter? Surely it does insofar as it applies to infrastructure. Private investment, including investment in export capacity, depends on the provision of adequate infrastructure. Though private investment will have to play the major role in filling the massive gaps in power, transport, and telecommunications, public investment will also have to be increased.

Ideally, essential social expenditures should be protected during stabilization. Not much is known about what is happening on this front at the micro level. Overall, it is clear that there was severe retrenchment in 1991/92 especially by the Centre, but this was largely reversed in 1992/93; and that since 1993/94 social sector expenditures have grown rapidly (see Chapter 6). It is thus clear that stabilization has not squeezed the social sectors. However, there is a strong case for increasing social expenditure. If non-essential government expenditure cannot be cut, an unpleasant trade-off could arise between public investment, as conventionally classified, and social expenditures on health and education. So far this has been resolved in favour of the latter. But there is a danger that in the absence of fiscal reforms, State governments will cut their social spending programmes.

We have taken the view that the Centre's fiscal adjustment has been inadequate. But perhaps this conclusion should be modified by cyclical considerations? The argument would be that fiscal retrenchment and the associated fall in public investment in 1991/92 and 1992/93 caused a multiplier/accelerator downturn in industry, particularly the capital goods sector, and that the subsequent fiscal relaxation was necessary as part of a package to stimulate recovery. We would agree that the industrial downturn owed something to fiscal retrenchment, but we doubt whether the recovery in 1994/95 and 1995/96 was the product of fiscal relaxation to any large degree. Our judgement is that it resulted mainly from the recovery of exports from 1993/94 onwards (itself the result of trade reform and exchange rate policy), the reductions in the user cost of capital in the budgets of 1993 and 1994 (reductions in tariffs on capital goods and in corporate taxes), and the effects of capital inflows on both the cost of capital and the climate for investment. It should be noted also that the fiscal relaxations in the relevant years did not arise out of increases in capital spending. It appears, therefore, that the government missed the opportunity to make adequate progress with fiscal adjustment during the recent recovery.[23]

The States. Fiscal adjustment by the States has been worse than that of the Centre. The fiscal deficit has been roughly constant in the region of 3–4 per cent of GDP. (A small reduction in the initial years was reversed in 1994/95.) Most of the small revenue increase has come from increased tax devolution and

[23] The fiscal relaxation was very much in the tradition of Indian fiscal policy which tends to be expansionary when stocks of food and foreign exchange are comfortable, insuring the economy against high inflation in the short run. Long-run fiscal dynamics tend to get ignored. (See Joshi and Little, 1994, ch. 9 and Joshi and Little, 1996.) It should also be noted that expansionary fiscal policy must take some of the blame for the high interest rates of the latter half of 1995/96 which have raised fears that the recovery will be aborted.

grants from the Centre. Total expenditure has increased mainly due to interest payments outweighing a small decrease in expenditure on social and economic services.

The weakness in State finances is a continuation of a trend that was already evident in the 1980s. As compared to the early 1980s, there has been stagnation in the States' own tax revenue and a tendency for growing interest payments to crowd out expenditure in areas such as transport, power, irrigation, health, and education which are crying out for selective expenditure increases. Already, net loans from the Centre barely exceed interest payments to the Centre.

The primary fiscal deficit of the States has fallen since the reform began but by only about 0.5 per cent of GDP. In the context of overall fiscal adjustment the role of the States cannot be ignored. It is doubtful whether the States can be induced to make the desirable changes purely by a squeeze on central transfers. Such a squeeze, without the willingness to make a break with the past, could starve vital sectors of State funding.

Public sector enterprises. Public enterprises were supposed to have spearheaded India's economic development, but have in fact been a fiscal burden. Only one half of the 250-odd central public enterprises make profits. As a proportion of GDP, neither the profits of the profit-makers nor the losses of the loss-makers have shown any significant change. Budgetary support to public enterprises has been reduced; their efforts to replace that support by market borrowing have been unsuccessful so their investment programmes have been put under pressure. The performance of the 700-odd State public enterprises continues to be miserable. For example, the explicit losses of the State Electricity Boards are still in the region of 0.7 per cent of GDP.

The upshot of this discussion is that (*a*) there has to be a further reduction in the deficit of the NFPS of about 3 per cent of GDP relative to 1994/95 and (*b*) the quality of fiscal adjustment needs substantial improvement. Much more of the fiscal adjustment has to come from an increase in government and public savings. This would enable public investment, especially in infrastructure, to be maintained, and essential social expenditures to be protected. At the same time, the government needs to have a coherent programme for stimulating domestic and foreign investment to substitute for such reduction in public investment as has to occur.

2.4.4. Policies for Reducing the Public Deficit

We now turn to the options for reducing the public deficit, especially by increasing public savings. On this topic, there is often widespread pessimism arising from the fact that apparently most of government expenditure is committed. For example, in the case of the central government, the combined expenditure on interest payments, explicit subsidies, and defence was 112 per cent of tax revenue, 82 per cent of total revenue, and 59 per cent of current expenditure in 1994/95. Where then, it is often asked, is the flexibility to reduce the fiscal deficit? We think that there is considerably more room for manoeuvre than the above view suggests (and in ways which increase efficiency as well), which is not to say that there are not substantial political difficulties in so doing. The principal points are outlined below and discussed further in later chapters, particularly Chapter 3.

(i) *Taxation*: So far, tax reform has largely been concerned with eliminating distortions and improving efficiency. To this end, customs duties have been significantly reduced. There have also been reductions and rationalization in excise taxes, personal income taxes, and corporate taxes and these changes have paid dividends. From 1990/91 to 1995/96 the yield of corporate taxes has increased from 1 per cent to 1.5 per cent of GDP and of the personal income tax from 1 per cent to 1.4 per cent of GDP. But there is plenty of scope for increasing the yield of taxation further without compromising efficiency. There is more to be done as regards eliminating exemptions from customs and excise. Even more important, there has as yet been little widening of the base of the personal income tax. It is a scandal that in a country in which the middle class is estimated to be between 100 and 200 million, the number of income tax payers is about eight million. There have been some moves towards presumptive taxation but they suffer from the fatal flaw of allowing returns on a voluntary basis.[24]

(ii) *Explicit Subsidies*: Current expenditure of the central and State governments is dominated by expenditure on subsidies, defence, wages, and interest payments. We leave aside defence (for no better reason than ignorance, for there is doubtless much scope for making economies) and consider the other three briefly. As regards food subsidies, universal entitlement must surely be withdrawn and substituted by better targeting, eligibility being determined by rough and ready criteria. It is also well known that part of the expenditure on food subsidies is in effect a subsidy to cover inefficiencies in the operation of the Food Corporation of India. In any case, we doubt if food subsidies are the best way of dealing with poverty. Fertilizer subsidies do not reach the very poor. They can be reduced as part of a package to free agricultural prices and close down unviable fertilizer plants. These issues are discussed further in later chapters.

(iii)*Wages and Employment*: Public employment and wages rose rapidly over the 1980s, aided and abetted by increased indexation.[25] The States were particularly to blame. Arresting the growth of the wage bill will require a freeze on new employment and pay restraint.

[24] For a useful review of presumptive taxation schemes, see Rajaraman (1995).

[25] See Government of India, Ministry of Finance, *Economic Survey 1995/96*, Appendix table 3.4. Real per capita emoluments of public sector employees in 1990/91 were two-and-a-half times their 1980/81 levels. Real emoluments continued to increase from 1990/91 to 1993/94, albeit at a much slower pace.

(iv) *Non-tax Revenue*: The potential for reducing the primary fiscal deficit is considerably larger than suggested above if we take account of the massive hidden subsidies which permeate the provision of goods and services (leaving aside pure public goods for which free state provision is the appropriate course). It has been estimated that in 1987/88, these hidden subsidies amounted to 15 per cent of GDP.[26] We must avoid double counting. The above figure includes explicit subsidies and explicit budget support of public enterprises. But even if we subtract say 3 per cent of GDP on this count, there remains enormous scope for increased revenue through cost recovery, which is justified on efficiency grounds in any case. Free or ultra-cheap water and electricity are only the most notorious illustrations of a pervasive problem.[27] The issue is further discussed in Chapter 3.

(v) *Interest Payments*: The points outlined so far have been concerned with reducing the primary deficit. But interest payments also contribute significantly to the total public deficit and have been growing rapidly as a proportion of GDP. (For example, in the case of the Centre, they have increased from about 2 per cent of GDP in 1980/81 to about 5 per cent in 1995/96.) The increase has reflected both rising debt and higher interest rates due to financial liberalization.

Direct reduction of the interest rate on public borrowing would not be possible without bringing back financial repression and thus would also be undesirable. Interest payments can therefore be reduced only by retiring debt or curbing the growth of new debt. Assuming that primary deficits cannot be reduced beyond the levels already advocated, the only way out is sale of public assets, in particular public enterprises and land. Of course, if the primary deficit and the interest and growth rates

---

[26] Mundle and Rao (1991).

[27] By and large, these hidden subsidies cannot be justified on redistributive grounds. Scope for cost recovery also exists in the social services. It should not be imagined that these benefit mainly the poor. For example, less than half of the States' educational expenditure is on primary education.

are given, reducing outstanding debt does not lower the terminal value of debt (in the case where y > r) and cannot make an intertemporally unsustainable position sustainable (in the case where r > y). This is clear from equation (1). But interest and growth rates would not remain constant. Lower debt would reduce interest payments and hence public borrowing. This would reduce the real interest rate, crowd in private investment, and raise the growth rate of output. Naturally, these beneficial effects occur only if the proceeds from the present sale of public assets are not offset by lower public income from these assets in future. Thus sale of public assets can benefit the fisc only if profitability can be expected to rise significantly as a result of a change of ownership.[28]   But it can hardly be doubted that privatization would lead to such a rise if the enterprises sold off can be given freedom of operation with regard to investment, pricing, and employment.[29]   A well-planned programme to privatize public enterprises could thus make a large contribution to fiscal adjustment. (This is also true of the sale of other assets such as prime urban land owned by the government.)[30]

It is obvious that the measures (i) to (v) described above will require action at all levels of the public sector. The Centre is in

[28]   Even loss-making public enterprises can be sold for something. They have assets—better performance is thus always possible, given appropriate changes including the break-up of assets. Note, however, that for privatization to yield a national benefit, the improvement in future profitability must not result from exploitation of a monopoly position. Otherwise the increased profits would be at the expense of other agents in the economy.

[29]   In principle, these gains could be secured without a change from public to private ownership. In practice, this is most unlikely. Privatization is extensively discussed in Chapter 4.

[30]   The Government of India's *Economic Survey 1995/96* estimates that the book value of the central Government's saleable economic assets is approximately 26 per cent of its non-RBI marketable liabilities. This is equal to about Rs 130,000 crores, that is about three times the total annual interest payments of the Centre to entities other than the RBI. If privatization is properly handled, these assets could be sold at prices in excess of book value. In addition to the above assets, there are other possibilities such as selling urban land owned by the government.

a strong position because it can harden the budget constraints of both the States and the PSEs by restricting budget support (through direct grants and loans) and market borrowing. But there are obvious political limits to doing so. Moreover, a crude squeeze on State and PSE finances would be counter-productive if it reduces capital formation and social sector spending. In the long run, therefore, addressing the fiscal problem requires an overhaul of Centre–State financial relations to give proper incentives to resource mobilization and expenditure control by both tiers of government.[31]

In sum, India's fiscal problem is not insoluble. The extent of soft budgets and hidden subsidies is so large that the required adjustment could be achieved quite rapidly without compromising efficiency and equity. Of course, the political constraints are severe.[32] But unless they are overcome, the reform process could grind to a halt.[33]

---

[31] In this context, the recommendations of the Tenth Finance Commission are highly appropriate. Highlights are: (*a*) a proposed system of sharing all tax revenue of the Centre with the States at a uniform rate and (*b*) a proposal to tie forgiveness of the States' debts by the Centre to better fiscal performance by the States.

[32] The political economy of fiscal adjustment in the context of India's democratic institutions is discussed in Bardhan (1984), chapters 3 and 14 of Joshi and Little (1994), and Joshi (1995). Note that there have recently been some encouraging developments with regard to fiscal reform in some States (see *India: Country Economic Memorandum*, World Bank, 1995*a*).

[33] Mulji (1995) has emphasized the relevance of a well-known theorem proved by T. Sargent and N. Wallace (Sargent and Wallace, 1981). This theorem states that if r > y, financing a permanent and constant primary deficit by selling bonds is more inflationary than financing it by printing money. This is because the former eventually involves more money creation than the latter, since not only does the initial bond issue have to be monetized but also the accumulated interest. Mulji argues that reduction of the primary deficit in India is politically impossible and therefore advocates printing money to finance the deficit. We disagree. First, there is in the long run a limit to revenue from the inflation tax of about 2.5 per cent of GDP (at an inflation rate of around 50 per cent per annum) so that the Sargent and Wallace proposition cannot justify money-financing of primary deficits higher than this limit. Second, we do not believe that Indian democracy could survive inflation rates

2.5. Inflation

We saw in Section 2.3. that the government's inflation record has been less than satisfactory. India's inflation in the past has often been triggered by exogenous shocks such as droughts and adverse terms of trade changes. A disturbing feature of inflation in the 1990s is that this pattern was broken[34]. Inflation averaged 10 per cent per year from 1991/92 to 1994/95 despite a run of good harvests from 1988/89 (except for a minor setback in 1991/92). Inflation has come down significantly in 1995/96, but we doubt if this is an enduring improvement.

The course of inflation from 1990/91 to 1994/95 is not hard to explain. The basic point is that money supply grew somewhat faster than in the second half of the 1980s, but output growth was somewhat slower. When the Rao government took over, inflation was 12 per cent and rising, the result of fiscal and monetary expansion combined with an increase in the price of oil imports during the Gulf War. Inflation did not come down in 1991/92 partly because of the agricultural slowdown and partly because monetary growth was high despite fiscal retrenchment. This was the result of the accretion of foreign exchange reserves following the rapid balance of payments improvement in that year. In 1992/93, reserves stopped increasing, monetary expansion slowed down and fiscal policy continued to be tight. On the supply side, agriculture recovered. Not surprisingly, inflation fell and continued to fall until June 1993. But from 1993/94, fiscal adjustment was reversed and the money supply grew rapidly due to a surge in capital inflows. For understandable

of 20 per cent, let alone 50 per cent. Policy-makers would be acting irresponsibly if they were to throw up their hands in the effort to achieve fiscal adjustment and move systematically to money-financing of deficits. Finally, we are more optimistic about India's political economy than Mulji. We note that India has not found it impossible to reduce primary deficits since 1991 (though not by enough). Technically, the scope for fiscal adjustment is enormous. We further believe that if Indian society were faced with a Sargent and Wallace type of crisis, it would 'choose' fiscal adjustment to inflation.

[34]   For an analysis of Indian inflation see Bhattacharya and Kathuria (1995).

reasons (see Section 2.6.) the authorities chose not to let the exchange rate appreciate, preferring instead to accumulate foreign exchange reserves. While some sterilization measures were undertaken they were not aggressive enough, so that both reserve money and total money grew rapidly. It should be noted that government deficits were not monetized in this period: high liquidity made it easy for the government to borrow in the market.

While a broadly monetary explanation of inflation thus makes sense, we do not think it is the whole story. Paradoxically, price and distribution controls in the food market have also played a role. Their objective was originally to supply rationed quantities of food at subsidized prices through the public distribution system. In recent years, with a succession of good monsoons, the procurement prices paid to farmers for these supplies have become support prices. The strength of the farm lobbies is such that procurement prices have been raised even when the food supply position has been comfortable. This has led to mounting food stocks with high carrying costs and—further—to higher issue prices out of concern for the fiscal deficit. As indexation is increasing, this has added a cost-push element to the inflationary process. In the light of the above, the following facts are pertinent and clearly have a bearing on inflation in this period. From the beginning of 1990/91 to the end of 1994/95, procurement prices of rice and wheat rose at 13.5 per cent per annum and 12.8 per cent per annum respectively. From the beginning of 1990/91 to the end of 1993/94, issue prices of rice and wheat rose at 19.7 per cent per annum and 14.9 per cent per annum respectively. From January 1993 food stocks rose sharply. In January 1995, they stood at 30 million tonnes, twice the level of the 'buffer stock norm' at the time, and 18 million tonnes above their level in January 1993. Moderation of the inflationary process in India would seem to require unwinding the distortionary interventions of the government in the food market, in addition to responsible fiscal and monetary policies.

Inflation has come down sharply in 1995/96 and in January 1996 was running at an annual rate of 5 per cent. This was mainly the result of slower monetary growth (facilitated by the fall in capital inflows over most of the year) and faster growth of output. But it is also notable that in view of the impending elections, issue prices of wheat and rice have been frozen since February 1994, even though procurement prices have continued to rise, albeit at a slower rate than before. There have been large sales from food stocks. There has also been a freeze on fuel prices and administered prices generally in 1995/96, despite cost increases caused among other reasons by rupee depreciation. Moreover, monetary contraction has driven up interest rates sharply, raising fears that the economic recovery will be aborted. There must therefore be a reasonable expectation that after the elections of 1996, these tensions will be resolved by increases in administered prices and monetary relaxation.

2.5.1. *The Mix of Fiscal and Monetary Policy*

We have already referred above to the crowding-out issue. One way in which it shows up is particularly relevant in the Indian context—large fiscal deficits make it difficult to combine the objectives of high growth and low inflation.

Monetary policy is clearly a prime instrument in controlling inflation. Though inflation has many proximate causes, especially in the short run, a low trend rate of inflation requires firm control of the rate of monetary expansion. If, however, the fiscal deficit is high, real interest rates are driven up and private investment is squeezed. If high rates of private investment are necessary for rapid growth, this in effect means that low inflation becomes incompatible with high growth.[35] In that

---

[35]   It could be argued that this is a short-run problem. An enduring fall in inflation would lower inflationary expectations and hence the real interest rate *via* a lower nominal rate. But the short run could last for some time if inflation expectations do not change easily. Of course the real interest rate could also be

sense, an inconsistency arises between fiscal and monetary policy. Of course, this is not an entirely new problem in Indian policy-making. Monetary policy in India has for a long time been guided by the objective of 'making room' for fiscal deficits without letting the money supply get out of control. In the pre-reform period, this was achieved by captive government borrowing at cheap rates. Inflation stayed low but at the cost of large spreads between deposit and lending rates applicable to private sector activities.

What has happened post reform is that the inflation/growth trade-off has sharpened because of financial sector liberalization which has involved a reduction in the government's 'captive borrowing' and significant deregulation of administered interest rates (see Chapter 4). *Ceteris paribus*, these changes can be expected to increase both the level of real interest rates and their sensitivity to changes in fiscal deficits for any given rate of monetary expansion.

Another development relevant to the nexus between fiscal and monetary policy is the change in the government's access to borrowing from the RBI. In the mid-1950s an agreement was arrived at between the RBI and the Government of India that whenever the cash balances of the central government fell below a certain amount they would be restored by the creation of *ad hoc* treasury bills. This seemingly innocuous arrangement in effect paved the way for automatic monetization of large fiscal deficits. Laudably, the present government has tried to erect barriers against this automaticity.[36] In September 1994 there was a formal agreement between the central government and the RBI that monetization of budget deficits would be reduced by imposing a ceiling on *ad hoc* treasury bills for any period of ten working days, and for the financial year as a whole, and that this ceiling would be progressively tightened to phase out automatic

---

too high for reasons unconnected with inflation control (see the discussion in Section 2.4.2. above).

[36] The underlying rationale is clearly explained in Rangarajan (1993).

monetization through *ad hoc* treasury bills altogether over a period of three years.

It would be inaccurate to portray the above agreement, even if it were adhered to, as ending the monetization of deficits. Ignoring foreign borrowing, any given fiscal deficit has to be financed by printing money or by domestic borrowing. This choice cannot be avoided by forcing the government to borrow from the market in the first instance. A decision would still have to be made on whether to avoid a rise in interest rates (that is to print money by the back door through Reserve Bank open market operations) or to adhere to a monetary target and allow interest rates to rise. In India, the central bank is not independent, so this decision would be made by the government itself.

The tension between fiscal and monetary policy has been much in evidence. In 1993/94 and 1994/95 there was rapid monetary expansion as a consequence of a large, partly unsterilized capital inflow (see Section 2.6). As a result, money and credit markets were highly liquid. Interest rates came down even though there was some fiscal relaxation and government borrowing increased. Inflation rose, but so did private investment and real growth (with a lag). From the latter half of 1994/95, capital inflows slowed down. In 1995/96, the government decided to take anti-inflationary measures, perhaps for electoral reasons, and embarked on monetary contraction. (More accurately, it did not offset the monetary slowdown that followed the change in the balance of payments). By this time the recovery was in full swing and the combination of government and commercial demand for credit drove up interest rates sharply. Interest rates on 91-day treasury bills, 364-day treasury bills, and long-dated gilts rose by about 5 per cent, 4 per cent, and 3.5 per cent respectively from September 1994 to December 1995. Prime lending rates of banks rose from 14 per cent to 16.5 per cent. Only a few companies could borrow from banks, or in the market generally, below 20 per cent. Not surprisingly, in 1995/96, the government switched some of its borrowing from the market to the RBI. The government–RBI agreement referred to above was breached several times in the course of the year. The money supply remained under control, however, as the increased government borrowing from the RBI was offset by a decline in foreign exchange reserves. The tightness in the money and credit markets was exacerbated in late 1995/96 when the RBI intervened periodically to prevent a slide in the exchange rate; as a result, the RBI had to pump in money from time to time to cool the money markets.

Underlying these gyrations of policy is the fundamental problem already identified. The trade-off between inflation and growth is sharpened by high deficits, particularly in the context of financial liberalization, and can be softened only by fiscal consolidation.

2.6. Balance of Payments Management

For convenience, we divide the five-year period since the reforms began into three parts corresponding to the rather different problems confronted by policy-makers.

1991/92–1992/93. When the reforms began in 1991, there was a manifestly excessive current account deficit (3.2 per cent of GDP) and its reduction was the main focus of policy. The deficit fell sharply to 0.4 per cent in 1991/92 before widening again to 1.8 per cent in the following year. Exports were stagnant in dollar value. Imports fell sharply in 1991/92 following the deflationary policies; they rose moderately in 1992/93 but were still below their 1990/91 level. The deficits on current account were over-financed by capital inflows of the traditional variety (multilateral assistance in the first year, non-resident deposits in the second) and foreign exchange reserves increased to $6.4 billion by March 1993.

Policies relevant to the balance of payments were as follows (note that they were motivated by both stabilization and structural reform considerations). There was a fiscal squeeze in 1991/92 and 1992/93, accompanied by exchange rate depreciation. In July 1991, the rupee was devalued by 19 per cent, together with the abolition of export subsidies and the introduction of an import entitlement scheme for exporters. This was followed in March 1992 by an explicit dual exchange rate, exporters receiving the depreciated free market rate. In March 1993, the exchange rate was unified. The net result of the above changes was an effective devaluation of about 40 per cent in nominal terms and 25 per cent in real terms over this two-year period. Trade policy was kept highly restrictive during the height of the crisis in 1991/92 but eased significantly in 1992/93, when quantitative import controls were abolished for most capital and intermediate goods. Tariff reduction also began in 1992/93, but was on average less than the rupee devaluation. Restrictions on inflows of foreign direct and portfolio investment were significantly eased.

Balance of payments policy in this period was sensible and correct. Orthodox expenditure reduction and expenditure switching policies were obviously necessary, given the starting position of excess domestic demand and an unsustainable current account deficit and external debt. Some additional real devaluation was also necessary in order to secure the current account during the envisaged process of import liberalization. The exchange rate, trade, and foreign investment policies were slow to produce their intended effects on exports and private capital inflows. While such lags are quite normal, they provoked criticism and the authorities must be complimented on sticking to their guns.[37]

---

[37] Exports were also hampered by various factors such as slow growth in industrial countries and the collapse of the East European market. Note that exports were not as slow to respond as the 2 per cent average growth in 1991/92–1992/93 would suggest. This total conceals an 18 per cent rise in exports to the general currency area combined with a 75 per cent fall in exports to Eastern Europe (the rupee payment area).

1993/94–1994/95. The main feature of this period was a surge
in private capital inflows which strengthened the balance of
payments and augmented the resources potentially available for
investment, but considerably complicated the operation of
macroeconomic policy.

The current account position was comfortable. The dollar
value of exports grew at around 20 per cent per annum as the
effects of the policies already instituted came through. Imports
grew concomitantly with investment and industrial production:
sluggishly in 1993/94 and rapidly in 1994/95. The current
account deficit was only 0.1 per cent in 1993/94 and 0.8 per cent
in 1994/95. The capital account improved strongly and changed
its composition. Net inflows from external assistance, commercial borrowing, and non-resident deposits fell compared with
the past, but there was a strong surge in non-debt creating
private inflows to the tune of $4.1 billion in 1993/94 and $4.9
billion in 1994/95. About a quarter of this was direct foreign
investment; the rest was portfolio equity capital, including both
investment in Indian stock markets by foreign institutional
investors and share capital raised by Indian companies in
overseas stock markets.[38]

The slow pace of increase in direct foreign investment is not
hard to explain. Such investment normally represents a durable
commitment; it is not surprising that investors are likely to be
circumspect and want to see reforms fully entrenched before
taking decisive steps. The time taken to attract direct foreign
investment in most reforming countries has been considerable.
Portfolio capital is more mobile. In 1993 India benefited, along
with many other emerging markets, from the push factor of
lower US interest rates, the pull factor of profit opportunities
opened up by the reform process, and some bandwagon
behaviour. It must also be noted that high interest rates resulting

---

[38] The latter took the form mainly of the issue of global depository receipts
(GDRs). Note that the foreign investment figures given above do not include
foreign currency convertible bonds. These are counted as commercial
borrowing until they are converted into equity.

from India's fiscal/monetary mix created a strong incentive for Indian companies to raise capital abroad. These portfolio inflows were at their height between mid-1993/94 and mid-1994/95. There was some cooling off in the latter half of 1994/95, especially after the Mexican crisis broke. The resulting capital account surplus led to a large accumulation of foreign exchange reserves which increased from \$6 billion in March 1993 to \$21 billion in March 1995.

The main and unfamiliar policy issue confronted by the authorities in this period related to the conduct of macroeconomic policy, in particular exchange rate policy, in the face of the large capital inflow.[39] The two extreme options available were (*a*) to float the nominal exchange rate and allow it to find its market-determined level and (*b*) to fix the nominal exchange rate by buying foreign exchange and to allow the money supply to increase, in other words to practise unsterilized intervention. There is an essential similarity in these two approaches. Both involve an appreciation of the real exchange rate, a worsening of the current account deficit, and an acceptance of market forces in effecting the transfer of capital. But there is also an important difference. In alternative (*a*), the real appreciation follows from the appreciation of the nominal exchange rate. The effect on trade and current account payments is rapid, with a real transfer of resources. There is no inflationary effect: indeed the deterioration of the trade account will be deflationary. In alternative (*b*), the real appreciation is brought about by inflation consequent upon money supply expansion; and the transfer is effected slowly as the initial accumulation of reserves is run down.

The Indian authorities decisively rejected alternative (*a*). The rupee–dollar exchange rate was kept at \$1 = Rs 31.37 for more than two years from March 1993. This was a sensible decision, in view of the possibly transient nature of the capital

---

[39]   This issue is discussed in Joshi (1994).

inflow. The authorities rightly feared various consequences of allowing a nominal (and hence real) exchange rate appreciation.

(i) It could have aborted the export recovery, an outcome that could not be regarded as benign if the inflow turned out to be temporary. Exports, once discouraged, cannot easily revive, being subject to lags and hysteresis effects.

(ii) It could have created resistance to import liberalization, an important aspect of the reform process.

(iii) Even if the inflow were reasonably long lasting it was important that the associated increase in the current account deficit should reflect an increase in investment, not a reduction in saving. The absorption of foreign inflow into investment was more likely if it took place at a measured pace rather than in a rush. In this context, it is also relevant that the inflow began when investment and industrial growth were significantly below normal. It was hoped that economic recovery would increase the current account deficit and absorb the inflow without inflation and real appreciation.

Thus, while alternative (*b*), if carried through in its pure form, would have been similar in essential respects to (*a*), it did have the advantage of delaying the transfer and buying time. The government decided to accept the inflationary risk associated with this alternative, but attempted to reduce it by the use of sterilization policies to break the link between reserve accumulation and monetary expansion. This effort was limited by the costs involved. Pure sterilization by the sale of government bonds (including both switching the government's normal borrowing from the Reserve Bank to the market, and conducting open market operations) involves a quasi-fiscal cost since the interest rate on government securities is higher than that on foreign exchange reserves. Other methods of sterilization, such as raising the cash reserve ratio, do not involve a fiscal cost but have the unwelcome effect of reducing bank profitability. Capital flows into India in 1993/94 and

1994/95 were about 2 per cent of GDP per annum. Assuming a 7 per cent differential in the interest rate on government bonds and foreign exchange reserves, the cumulative fiscal cost of pure sterilization of the entire inflow would have been (.04)(7) = about 0.3 per cent of GDP. (The fiscal cost would have been lower if other methods such as a rise in the CRR had been employed.) In the event, the government sterilized the inflows in these various ways, but not fully. Consequently, reserve money and the money supply accelerated and so did prices with some lag. This led to some appreciation of the real exchange rate, but luckily not by much since the US dollar was weakening. The current account deficit increased but no more than was desirable and expected in the light of economic recovery.

Arguably, sterilization policies should have been more aggressive despite the associated costs. Unarguably, stronger fiscal adjustment, desirable in any case on other grounds, would have helped in preventing inflation and real appreciation by reducing the pressure of demand in the goods market. It would also have exerted downward pressure on interest rates and thereby (*a*) reduced the fiscal cost of sterilization and (*b*) helped to deter those capital inflows which were caused purely by the inappropriate fiscal/monetary mix in India.

The Indian government also operated various price and quantity measures to prevent excessive inflows such as limits on external commercial borrowing and equity funds raised abroad; stipulations requiring that the latter should be kept outside the country until they were committed to a specific investment use; and measures to reduce the attractiveness of non-resident deposits. Given the macroeconomic difficulties created by excessive inflows, these measures were not inappropriate.

Stronger fiscal adjustment should have formed part of the package of measures to respond to the capital inflows problem. Subject to that caveat, our judgement is that the response was, broadly speaking, appropriate.

1995/96. The payments position remained comfortable in 1995/96. Exports again grew at an estimated 20 per cent in dollar value, imports faster. The current account deficit is expected to be in the region of $6 billion (c. 1.5 per cent of GDP). Aggregate inflows of foreign investment were lower than in 1994/95 though, encouragingly, disbursements of direct investment are estimated to have increased to about $1.5 billion. Portfolio equity inflows were lower for most of the year in the aftermath of the Mexican crisis, but revived strongly in early 1996. The higher current account deficit and smaller capital inflows reduced foreign exchange reserves to about $17 billion.

As in the previous two years, the main policy issue confronted was the management of the exchange rate, but this time in reverse. From the beginning of the year there was some downward pressure on the exchange rate due to shrinking capital inflows and a widening trade deficit, and the rate was maintained only by selling foreign exchange reserves: they fell by $2 billion between April and August 1995. The government formed the view that some depreciation of the nominal exchange rate was desirable in order to offset the real exchange appreciation of about 7 per cent between 1993/94 and August 1995. It therefore tried to engineer a depreciation by the expedient of shifting its own debt-service payments to the market. This effort went out of control as speculative pressures both exacerbated the downward movement in the exchange rate and increased its volatility. In the next few months, the rate moved in the range of $1 = Rs 34 to $1 = Rs 38, but appears to have stabilized around Rs 34 in March 1996, close to where the government wanted it to be. There were some anxious moments in the interim. The authorities in general followed the policy of guiding the market by emphasizing their view of the appropriate level of the exchange rate. They intervened in the market to the tune of $2 billion but wisely refrained from committing themselves to defending any particular rate.

Two features of the flurry in the exchange market stand out:

(i) the authorities eventually succeeded in stabilizing the rate, but it was critical to their success that they were trying to stabilize around a level which took account of the inflation differential between India and the rest of the world.

(ii) the episode showed that the thinness of the foreign exchange market can make the exchange rate highly sensitive to small disturbances, thus emphasizing the need to open up and deepen the foreign exchange market over time.

2.6.1. *Balance of Payments Outlook and Issues*

Without doubt, the balance of payments position in 1995/96 constitutes a large improvement over five years earlier. The current account deficit is about 1.5 per cent of GDP, even though GDP has grown rapidly for two years. The external debt position has improved quantitatively and qualitatively. The debt/GDP ratio and the debt/service ratio have come down from 41 per cent and 33 per cent respectively in March 1991 to 35 per cent and 27 per cent respectively in March 1995. Over the same period, short-term debt has fallen from 10 per cent of GDP to 4 per cent and foreign exchange reserves have increased from $2 billion to $17 billion. There has been significant progress towards current account convertibility for everyone, and capital account convertibility for non-residents. This is not to say that the balance of payments position is completely secure. Oil imports are expected to increase rapidly as India's oil production levels off in the next year or two. There is a sizeable hump in debt repayments over the next three or four years. Non-resident deposits which are potentially volatile still constitute 15 per cent of the total external debt of $99 billion. Even so, the fundamental balance of payments position should remain healthy provided export growth stays robust. This will require an appropriate macroeconomic/exchange rate policy, continuation of trade reform, and the easing of the currently severe infrastructural constraints.

Three questions concerning future balance of payments policy are of some interest. We give below our judgements on the issues involved, without any pretence at an exhaustive discussion:

(i) Should the level of the current account deficit be a matter of policy concern?

(ii) Should the rupee be made fully convertible on capital account?

(iii) How should the exchange rate be managed in the context of volatile capital flows?

Should the current account deficit be an object of policy concern? Indian policy-makers are concerned to limit current account deficits to safe levels, even though the country's large infrastructure requirements would seem to call for a significant recourse to foreign savings. Are they right?

There is a fashionable view that the size of the current account deficit should be a matter of indifference so long as it corresponds to a private rather than a public deficit. The rationale is that the former would be self-correcting since the private sector can be expected to respect its own intertemporal budget constraints. But India's public accounts are not yet in good order; and even if they were, international experience shows that unsound private borrowing and lending followed by crises and crashes can and do occur. Experience also shows that the pool of internationally mobile net long-term funds is limited and that countries which have successfully run current account deficits of 6 per cent of GDP or more are the exception rather than the rule.[40]

---

[40] See Feldstein and Horioka (1981). Canada, Australia, and Argentina ran large current account deficits in the 19th century but long-term capital was not then constrained by exchange risk. Some East Asian countries are currently running current account deficits in the region of 6–8 per cent of GDP but they have considerably higher growth rates of exports than India. Moreover, they are far more open: in their case, a deficit of 6–8 per cent of GDP corresponds to

We suggest that India should be wary of running current account deficits higher than 3.5 per cent of GDP unless long-term real export growth can be stepped up significantly above 10 per cent per year. This is so even if capital inflows are not debt creating. While such inflows have better risk-sharing character-istics they do require a rate of return considerably higher than the interest rate on bonds, taking one year with another.

Should there be capital account convertibility? The benefits of capital account convertibility are principally microeconomic, arising from the opportunity to use the world capital market for risk diversification. Is there also a macroeconomic case for convertibility? It has been argued that this is so, because it would enable aggregate saving and investment to be optimized. Here it is important to distinguish between inflows and outflows. Typically, a developing country should invest more than it saves, in other words run a current account deficit. Liberalizing inflows should be sufficient to enable a country to draw on foreign savings to the optimum extent. Of course, capital will not come in unless it has the assurance that it can go out. But it should be sufficient to meet this point that there be freedom of repatriation for capital inflows; it does not follow that controls on other capital outflows should be abolished.

We have already discussed some of the problems created by liberalization of inflows. Inflows can be volatile not only because of irresponsible domestic policies or unsound and ex-cessive borrowing and lending, but also as a result of exogenous international developments. Volatility can impose costs; if inflows suddenly slow down or reverse, a very painful adjust-ment may have to follow, involving severe deflation and large depreciation. Therefore, while India can and should have larger inflows (and current account deficits) than in the past, some monitoring of the overall size of inflows is desirable, and

25–30 per cent of exports; in India's case it would correspond to 60–80 per cent of exports.

instruments to moderate inflows (such as reserve requirements and taxation of profits) should be kept in reserve.

Liberalization of outflows by residents, over and above the very necessary freedom to repatriate inflows, would be risky until fiscal adjustment is complete and there is a strong enough political commitment to convertibility to rule out its abandonment. Without these conditions, large capital outflows in a crisis are a potential danger; if they occur, they can impose heavy costs in terms of the export of domestic savings, reduction in the domestic tax base, and dislocation of the financial system. But are capital controls feasible? We agree that capital controls are leaky, but we do not believe they are completely ineffective. Capital mobility is undoubtedly increasing but India still has a few years' leeway in which to establish the desirable pre-conditions for capital account convertibility. We would thus advocate moving towards capital convertibility, but gradually, in concert with fiscal stabilization, trade liberalization, and domestic financial sector reform.

How should the exchange rate be managed? The exchange rate regime is now a managed float with the nominal exchange rate targeted, broadly speaking, to achieving the real exchange rate which yields a sustainable current account deficit. We think this will continue to be a sensible strategy over the medium-term future in which capital movements are likely to be volatile.

We briefly examine two contrary views. One view is that the exchange rate should be floated in a clean manner because it is impossible to distinguish between temporary and permanent real shocks, including those caused by changes in capital flows. We think this is too nihilistic: in many cases, policy-makers *can* make such judgements. We think also that 'benign neglect' of the exchange rate could lead to serious misalignments of the real exchange rate whose eventual correction would prove very costly. Of course, our views are entirely compatible with non-intervention in certain situations: we would certainly be against the authorities fighting the market to try and impose their view of the exchange rate. Management of a flexible exchange rate is an art that policy-makers have to learn: in this respect, India is no different from other countries.

A different and diametrically opposite view is that the nominal exchange rate should be fixed to serve as an anchor against inflation. First, as India has recently discovered, a fixed exchange rate offers no insulation from inflation if there are balance of payments surpluses. Second, devaluation is not an important factor in causing inflation in a large and largely un-indexed economy like India. India's inflation is driven mainly by agricultural production, money supply growth, and fiscal deficits, not by the exchange rate.[41] This has, however, the important implication that nominal exchange rate devaluation becomes essential if there are adverse shocks that require in response an improvement in trade competitiveness: it is very hard to imagine that a fixed nominal exchange rate could achieve the appropriate real exchange rate by bringing about changes in India's inflation relative to her trading partners. One example of such an adverse shock would be a slowing down or reversal of capital inflows judged by the authorities to be more than purely temporary.

On none of the three issues adumbrated above do our views differ markedly from those of India's present team of economic policy-makers.

2.7. Conclusion

When the Narasimha Rao government assumed office, the country was facing an acute macroeconomic crisis. In a short-run sense, the stabilization policies that were adopted must be judged a reasonable success. The inflation record is indifferent, but the balance of payments has been a success story. For three years there was a slow-down in the growth of investment and

---

[41]   See Joshi and Little (1994), ch.11.

output, particularly in the manufacturing sector. Even so, the growth performance was better than that of many countries undergoing stabilization and structural adjustment. Moreover, in the last two years, there has been a rapid recovery.

Stabilization cannot, however, be judged a success in the medium-run sense. The principal shortcoming is the inadequacy of fiscal adjustment. A substantial increase in public savings is essential to deliver rapid growth and low inflation, indeed even to avoid another crisis.

3
Fiscal Policy and Trade Policy

3.1. Introduction

Taxes are used to raise revenue: but they are also imposed (and this includes negative taxes) for redistributive reasons, to correct market distortions, and to persuade people not to consume what is bad for them. In these respects taxes on international trade are no different from any other taxes. Trade policy consists both of imposing such taxes on trade, and of other restrictions and regulations which prevent or control trade. In India, as in many other developing countries, international trade has long been dominated by regulations and controls. But throughout much of the developing world since the mid-1980s there has been an important policy reversal in favour of eliminating most of these controls.

Since June 1991, India has shared in the policy reversal referred to above, but to a lesser degree than many countries in Asia and Latin America. In June 1991 India was the most autarkic non-communist country in the world. Despite a little liberalization in the 1980s all imports were subject to licensing or were prohibited. Licenses were in general granted only on proof that there was no source of indigenous supply ('indigenous clearance') and they were granted only for own use (i.e. not to commodity traders for resale).[1] All 'bulk' items (e.g. cereals, petroleum, ores, metals, fertilizers) were 'canalized', that is they could be imported only by a government monopsony. Over most of the period since independence, it has been controls

---

[1] The exception is that from time to time export subsidization has taken the form of giving exporters import licences that could be sold at a premium.

rather than tariffs which limited imports—in other words there was excess demand for most imports. But with the massive increases in tariff rates in the 1980s and the devaluation of 1991, excess demand was probably eliminated for most products.

We believe it is by now widely agreed that, emergencies apart, trade should not be regulated by quantitative restrictions on imports or exports. Exceptionally, a few prohibitions may remain for reasons of defence, health, or morality. When this liberalization is achieved exports and imports will be regulated only by taxes and subsidies, and trade policy mostly becomes part of fiscal policy. Trade taxes must be considered in the light of other sources of revenue, and the social value of the various forms of public expenditure.

Trade may be taxed primarily for the revenue, or to protect the domestic market. Protective tariffs, or export taxes, are those that make production for the domestic market more profitable than production for export. We shall show later that protective trade taxes can be greatly reduced, perhaps even to zero, without causing a fiscal problem. Here we discuss trade taxes as means of protection.

The standard reason for protection is that it may improve the terms of trade by influencing world prices. We believe that India has nothing to gain on the import side: she is too small a part of the world market in any commodity she normally imports for one to think otherwise. There could be a reason for a few export taxes, on commodities where India has a large share of the world market, but probably only if they were co-ordinated with other countries. The only good terms of trade reason for any protective tariff would be to allow for some generalized inelasticity of foreign demand.[2] A uniform protective tariff of

---

[2] The so-called new trade theory, propounded by P. Krugman and others, calls particular attention to the case of internationally oligopolistic increasing return industries (the prime example being large passenger aircraft), where government intervention may help to capture supernormal profits for one country rather than another. We do not think this theory is very relevant for India.

10 per cent was suggested for this reason in Little, Scitovsky, and Scott (1970). It is important to note that if this is the reason, then agriculture should be as much protected as industry. We ourselves make the same proposal of a low uniform protective tariff, of not more than 10 per cent. The reason for the stress on uniformity is brought out later.

But what about the various asserted reasons for protection of manufacturing on grounds of external economies or factor price distortions? No one in the past thirty years has seriously undermined the finding of Bhagwati and Ramaswami (1963) that domestic taxes and subsidies, not trade taxes, are the best way of correcting domestic distortions. Some may feel that there is still a fiscal problem in implementing an optimum system of subsidies and taxes. Yet, if a subsidy to a particular industry is justified by some distortion, then it surely cannot be optimal that domestic consumers of the product should pay the whole cost of the subsidy (the tariff method) rather than general taxation, or taxation of other polluting industries, or a reduction in other expenditures.

Is there not still a case for an active governmental industrial policy? There is a running debate on this issue, especially in relation to the amazing industrial revolution that has occurred in the past thirty years in South Korea and Taiwan. We cannot here comment in depth on this issue.[3] We believe that government was very important in creating the 'export-oriented' economy in which exporters operated under virtual free-trade conditions, and had the assurance that the government would ensure that there were profitable export opportunities by maintaining a competitive exchange rate (or, when it threatened to become over-valued, by providing compensating incentives). We do not believe that the 'heavy and chemical' industries that government (in particular, President Park) promoted from around 1973 played a leading role in Korea's success. Growth

---

[3] Many references can be found in *The East Asian Miracle*, World Bank (1993). Our own views are given more fully in Cassen and Joshi (1995), ch. 4. See also Little (1994).

slowed after 1973 despite higher investment. Previously, from 1963–73, Korea experienced a decade of astonishing growth manifestly based on exports of clothing and other textile products, footwear and hats, cutlery and tools, and light electrical equipment and instruments.

Before leaving the subject of protection, it should finally be noted that the domestic excises and VAT, which we shall be recommending, should always be charged on imports, by way of so-called (in India) 'countervailing duties'. Small manufacturers cannot, for administrative reasons, be usefully subjected to these taxes, and they therefore enjoy protection both from imports and from the products of larger domestic enterprises.

3.2. The Reform of Trade Controls

The balance of payments crisis which the incoming government of Narasimha Rao faced in June 1991 necessitated some temporary increase in the stringency of import controls. But at the same time the intention of moving from a regime of quantitative restrictions to a price based mechanism was announced. The rapid recovery of the reserves after the devaluations of July 1991 permitted progress in this direction by the end of the year. A blow by blow account of the process of liberalization would be tedious. We simply ask how far the process had gone four years down the line (that is by July 1995).

The major change in import policy has been the introduction of a negative list. All other goods may now be imported freely, except those still reserved for import by the government's canalizing agencies. The negative list consists not only of the usual security or health items, but also almost all consumer goods.[4] Some capital goods and producers goods are also on the

---

[4] The exceptions are mainly items which are largely producers' as well as consumer goods, e.g. computer software, but also include contraceptives and Braille typewriters. Licences for consumer goods are rarely obtainable, though

negative list and still require licences, usually for protectionist reasons: examples are newsprint and a number of items reserved for production by small enterprises. Gems are a special case: polished stones and jewellery are large export items, and imported stones are presumably controlled to reduce domestic market sales. Canalized imports as of March 1995 had been much reduced to seven items including crude oil and most petroleum products (excluding kerosene), nitrogenous fertilizers, oil seeds and most edible oils, and cereals. The reasons for this list are the complex subsidies and administered prices that are in force on the domestic market.

The virtual ban on the import of consumer goods has been a major policy defect. Yet there were strong fiscal and monetary reasons why imports of consumption goods should have been allowed in the past three years. The balance of payments was embarrassingly strong, with an inflow of foreign currency which threatened either to make the rupee appreciate with damaging effects on export profitability and production, or to result in excessive increases in the money supply with inflationary effects. At the same time the fiscal deficit was embarrassingly large. Some imports of consumer goods paying high duties (including countervailing duties) would have relieved the problems of the Minister of Finance on both counts.

Only very recently, in 1995, have there been a few concessions. A few consumer goods were removed from the negative list, and put on OGL, under the Exim Policy of 1995/96. The list of items which could be imported under the special import licence (SIL) scheme was broadened.[5] More important perhaps is that parts of consumer durables are now freely importable, and the actual user condition has been removed. This may enable some manufacturers of durable

---

special import licences (SILs) are given to some large exporting firms: these can be sold and constitute a minor export incentive.

[5] Some textile and clothing items were included in the SIL list in February 1995.

consumer goods to improve the quality of their products and enter export markets.

The still quite prevalent attitude in India to consumption good imports seems to stem from a more general attitude to foreign goods, going back to the Swadeshi movement. Some imports have to be allowed when essential to India's own production. But what purpose, it is said, can consumption good imports serve—except perhaps for 'essentials', such as food when there is a drought? However, the antipathy is not just to 'inessentials', for Indian-made candyfloss is not so vehemently damned. It is quite difficult to get people to understand that it is better to import candyfloss if one is not good at making it, and instead to make and export something one is good at making. Alternatively if candyfloss should be discouraged, whether imported or produced at home, this can be achieved by high taxation of such luxuries.

Of course, the ban on consumer good imports might have been continued for simple protectionist reasons. For fifty years the home market has been totally protected with limited internal competition. This has proved to be a recipe for high-cost, low-quality production, and lack of innovation. The Tax Reform Committee (TRC), whose book we discuss later, did not investigate any consumer good industry. However, a World Bank study based on data collected in November–December 1993 suggests (*a*) that the nominal tariff protection of 85 per cent was never realized, and (*b*) that high protection of inputs resulted in negative effective protection for about half the thirty products for which it could be calculated. About half of these products were being exported. This does not suggest that there was any good temporary protective reason for continuing the ban on consumer good imports.

In the long run import competition helps to solve problems arising from insufficient domestic competition, as when the number of producers of optimum size is limited by the size of the domestic market. Permitting import competition also encourages the absorption of international standards of design and quality which is useful for thriving exports. Finally, from a macroeconomic point of view, it is an advantage to have some imports that are inessential. Crises cannot be ruled out, and in a crisis it may become necessary again to restrict imports. With a cushion of relatively inessential imports this will cause less harm to domestic production.

Despite assertions concerning the importance of exports, that go back for thirty years, a good many important quantitative restrictions remain in force even after the derestrictions made since 1991. The restrictions relate mainly to agricultural and livestock products, and ores and minerals. It is claimed that 'food security' is the reason in some cases—that is to prevent food prices rising with world prices. Pulses, rice, vegetable oils, and some small fish require licences. But the main reason has been to keep indigenous raw material prices low and thus protect domestic industry. Timber, hides and skins, and leather, are the main remaining restrictions imposed for this reason. Some items fall under neither of these headings e.g. horses and vintage cars. Canalized items include petroleum products, most mineral ores, and onions. In the case of some products, there are also certain export requirements, such as registration with an export promotion council or trade association. One hopes these are not restrictive. Finally, even if a good is on neither the banned nor the negative list for export, nor canalized, the Director General of Foreign Trade may nevertheless specify through a Public Notice the terms and conditions under which exports can be made.[6]

Apart from certain export restrictions there is also a number of export promotion schemes. As already mentioned, certain large exporters are granted special import licences (SILs) permitting imports of some consumer goods.[7] These licences can be sold at a premium. There is an export promotion capital

---

[6]   See Government of India (1995a), para. 123.

[7]   There is an impressive hierarchy of Export Houses, Trading Houses, Star Trading Houses, and Super Star Trading Houses. There are also Export Oriented Units, and units located in Export Processing Zones.

goods scheme (EPCGS), under which capital goods may be imported at concessional rates of duty (including zero duty) against an export obligation. There is a duty exemption scheme, giving exporters access to duty-free import of materials and components: advance licences for such imports are available. Certain rupee sales are deemed to be exports and get export-linked concessions. These complicated schemes were no doubt intended to mimic South Korea's and Taiwan's trading regimes, which created virtual free trade conditions for exporters while maintaining a protected home market.[8] They go a long way towards doing so, and are indeed essential until such time as India has very low protection and a domestic fiscal system under which exports are exempt from all domestic indirect taxes. However, their complexity, administrative cost, and the inevitable persistence of some anomalies, are strong arguments for a trading regime which requires no such complications to render it free of bias against exports. We look forward to the demise of all these export promotion schemes.

3.3. The Reform of Tariffs and Protection

We turn now to tariff reform. In 1990–91 the unweighted average nominal tariff was 125 per cent, with a peak rate of 355 per cent. In 1993/94 the corresponding figures were 71 per cent and 85 per cent.[9] In the budget of 1994 the peak rate was reduced to 65 per cent, probably bringing the average down to 50–55 per cent. In 1995 the peak rate was further reduced to 50 per cent, together with reductions in almost all other rates.

Reductions in the rates have not been uniform. There has been a concentration first on reducing the very high rates (little if anything can have been imported at the highest rates), and

---

[8] These schemes also gave domestic supplies for exporters a level fiscal playing field with imported supplies. We do not think India has fully achieved this desirable situation.

[9] GATT (1993).

secondly on reducing the rates on capital equipment for certain sectors. In 1991/92 the general rate for capital equipment was 85 per cent. By 1994/95 this had come down to 25 per cent for a number of sectors including coal, petroleum, electronics; and recently a number of successful exporting industries such as leather, watches, and gems have also been favoured. Power and fertilizers are especially favoured with import duties of 20 per cent and nil respectively. At the same time many capital goods for other industries were still apparently paying the maximum rate of 65 per cent in 1994/95. However, the budget of 1995/96 further unified the rate of duty on almost all capital goods at 25 per cent.

The concentration on emphasizing an early reduction in tariffs on capital goods was probably intended to avoid discouraging investment because of the expectation of a later reduction in tariffs. Capital intensive and infrastructural industries were favoured, where high project and capital costs would cast a long shadow of high costs ahead.[10] This policy appears to have some justification. Assume that we are considering an industry which will be normally profitable at some low rate of effective protection planned for, say, five years ahead. An investor who buys a capital good now, paying a high tariff that will raise his capital input costs for the whole life of the equipment, could suffer a loss for many years after low protection has been inaugurated; while someone who delays investment until the time when low protection prevails will *ex hypothesi* make a normal profit. However, this does not imply that an early reduction of tariffs on capital goods is always correct. It may not be so in the case of an industry which will not be viable given the low rate of effective protection planned. The early reduction of the tariff on capital equipment raises the

---

[10] Low tariffs (15 per cent) on imports of capital goods by exporters of manufactures who accept an obligation to increase exports have been available since April 1990 under the Export Promotion Capital Goods Scheme (EPCGS), the sectoral coverage of which has since been extended to mining and agriculture.

rate of effective protection in the transitional period. This could be enough to cause investment in an industry which will not be viable when the tariff on its output also comes to be reduced to a low rate.

India was probably unique in having very high protection of capital goods, and the early reduction of high tariffs on such goods was in general justified.[11] However, the selectivity of the reductions until 1995/96 can be criticized. It implied a philosophy of selective protection of some industries by government which we believe to be unjustified. The result was a very marked bi-modal distribution of tariff rates for different capital goods.[12] However, the budget of 1995/96 seems to have largely restored uniformity.

With a large reduction in tariffs on the output of some capital goods (together with delicensing) it was necessary also to reduce tariffs on their inputs. This was done, but probably not by enough to prevent the emergence of negative protection in some cases. For instance, the main material inputs of capital good industries are steel and non-ferrous metals. Tariffs on these inputs were 50–60 per cent in 1994/95 while many capital goods paid a tariff of only 25 per cent. This anomaly was reduced but not eliminated in 1995/96 when tariffs on the metals were reduced to 40 per cent. At the same time, the aim of not discouraging investment during the transition period may have missed. Private investment was quite sluggish until 1994/95 when it revived.[13]

Apart from capital goods, we believe that a more rapid general reduction of duties would have been desirable, at least from the protection point of view (we consider the fiscal problem below). The Tax Reforms Committee (TRC) produced evidence that even after the 1993–94 duty reductions the tariff rate of protection would still be far higher than it was in 1986–87 when allowance is made for the change in the exchange

---

[11]   Ettori (1992).
[12]   World Bank (1994*a*), vol. i, chart 2.2.
[13]   Government of India, *Economic Survey 1994–5*, 3.

rate.[14]   Even if Indian industry is now beginning to feel the pinch after the further tariff reductions of 1994/95 and 1995/96, it remains true that a more rapid reduction in protection could have been made without undue hardship.   There is no doubt that a good deal of Indian industry, after 40 years of almost total protection and limited domestic competition was in poor shape in 1991 to survive international competition with only very limited protection.   Everyone agrees that time for adjustment was needed—say seven years.   But the need to adjust was not made sufficiently apparent in the first three years of the reforms. The worry is that this adjustment should by now be more advanced than it is.

However, the above argument assumes that the target for Indian industries is to achieve international competitiveness in both the domestic and export markets with very limited protection of the former, and very limited disadvantages in producing for the latter; or to go under.   Unfortunately this does not yet seem to be an accepted target.

The course of tariff reduction has been loosely guided by the Tax Reforms Committee (TRC) chaired by Raja J. Chelliah, which was appointed in August 1991, and whose interim report came out in December of the same year.   It was warmly welcomed by the Finance Minister in his Budget speech of February 1992.   In its Final Report (Part II) of January 1993 the Committee recommended tariff rates of 5, 10, 15, 20, 25, 30, and 50 per cent, to be achieved by 1997–98.   The lowest rate was to apply to inputs for fertilizer and newsprint, the 10 per cent and 15 per cent rates to other 'basic' inputs such as metals, 20 per cent to capital goods, and 25 per cent to chemical intermediates. Other final products (not being inessential consumer goods) would attract 30 per cent.   Inessential consumer goods when allowed to be imported (evidently not necessarily by 1997–98) would attract the highest rate of 50 per cent.

---

[14]   Government of India (1992*b*), pt. ii, tables 2.1, 2.2.

This structure of rates was proposed in answer to the Committee's own question 'What should be the structure of rates at the end of the reform period and what economic principles should determine this structure?'[15] So far as principles go it referred to the Long Term Fiscal Policy Document (1985), and provided its own endorsement of such a multi-rate structure whereby the degree of protection rises with what is thought to be the degree of processing. To quote, 'tariff policy should have some relation to the stage of development and in a developing country, while the market should have a large role to play, the structure of import duties should be used to achieve the longer-term goals of industrialization and to further the strategy of dealing with the world market'.[16] Apart from their seven basic rates (referred to as a very limited number of rates) it was suggested that additional or special protection might be given for a limited period to new industries, new products, or new technologies.[17]

The reference to special protection clearly endorses the so-called infant industry argument for protection. But what of the other seven protective rates? What reasons can there be for this escalation? It surely cannot be thought that industry can be reliably divided into seven groups distinguished by their varying net external benefits, thus meriting seven different degrees of protection. Indeed, externalities are not mentioned by the TRC as reasons for protection.

Part of the reason for suggesting so many rates seems to have been some degree of acceptance of the principle that higher stages of manufacturing should have higher rates of nominal protection than lower stages. But this is a totally unprincipled principle, for it has no foundation in economic principles. It is, of course, a simple fallacy that a higher stage of production must have higher nominal protection than a lower stage in order to

[15]   See Government of India (1992*b*) *Final Report of the Tax Reforms Committee*, pt. ii, para. 2.1.
[16]   Ibid. para. 2.9.
[17]   Ibid. para. 2.20.

achieve the same level of effective protection. Identical nominal protection yields identical effective protection at all stages.

It is, however, almost without exception in developing countries that higher stages of production get higher protection. It is fairly easy to see how this comes about. The belief in industrialization as the road to independence and riches, and in protection as the obvious stimulus to industrialization, implies that manufacturers should be protected, but not the hewers of wood and drawers of water who supply materials (and anyway materials were often mainly imported). It seems to follow quite plausibly that the more processed is a good, the better it is to make it (and the 'higher' the technology the better!).[18] Not only that, but the makers of intermediates face the countervailing power of the makers of final goods, while the consumers of the latter are most unorganized and impotent. The fact that almost every country has institutionalized the fallacy in all this, is not a good reason for following the herd. The main argument given by the TRC for not endorsing a single low rate of customs duty is that only Chile has done so (with much success in recent years).

[18] The Indian representative at GATT's trade policy review (GATT, 1993, vol. ii) asserted that developing countries need an escalating tariff structure to promote domestic value added industries. This assertion by the Indian representative from the Ministry of Commerce suggests that this Ministry is still imbued with erroneous protectionist ideas that diverge from the main thrust of policy reform. It is very confused and confusing. First, effective protection *means* the promotion of domestic value added above what it would be under free trade: under a uniform tariff all industries have equal effective protection. So evidently the thrust of the statement is that some industries should have more effective protection than others, i.e. their domestic value added should be more promoted than that of others. Why? No reason is given. In place of any reason the wording manages to suggest that some industries are good and should be promoted because they have high domestic value added. High value added per what? Per man? Per rupee of investment? And if without protection they have high domestic value added per rupee of investment (say), or relative to value added at world prices, then why do they need to have it raised further by an escalating tariff structure? The truth is that high protection is generally given to uncompetitive industries—that is to industries with *low* value added relative to value added at world prices.

This processing fallacy goes some way towards explaining the allotment of industries to the seven different levels of protection, for inputs are generally allotted to the lower rated slots. But there are still five different rates for these inputs. The TRC to a considerable extent calculated in the manner of old-fashioned tariff commissions which enquired into domestic and cif costs, and tried to find a rate of duty which would bridge the gap to the extent of permitting at least the more efficient domestic units, or a 'representative firm', to make a normal profit. The TRC enquired into the costs of seven different industries, all producing intermediates. They tried to allow for the disadvantages of each industry. This approach is indeed necessary for the adjustment period: industries must be effectively protected to the degree required to avoid any immediate drastic loss of output or employment, but not over-protected. Multiple rates and changes in the assignment of industries to particular bands in the tariff spectrum may also be necessary *in the reform period* to see that desired rates of effective protection for one industry can be maintained when changes (reductions) are made in its output tariffs. But an approach which forever compensates for present disadvantages denies the validity of all the work of the past thirty years on optimizing the benefits to be derived from trade (and the earlier work of David Ricardo). It amounts to a policy of promoting industries with a comparative disadvantage. Lastly, we therefore question the TRC proposal of a 50 per cent tariff on consumer goods when the ban on their import is finally removed. With input tariffs of 25 per cent or less this would often give rise to an absurdly high rate of effective protection of around 100 per cent. There is no good reason why the tariff on consumer good imports should be higher than that on any other imports (apart from countervailing duties corresponding to domestic taxation of some luxury or 'demerit' goods).

The TRC did not recognize that its approach was defensible only for a transitional period of reform. If they had presented their targets as essentially interim, to be followed by a further period working towards a single low uniform tariff, we would have no complaint. But if the Committee's tariff structure is to be maintained for the long run, then India will probably still have the most protected industry in the world, with effective rates of protection ranging up to 100 per cent or more. Unfortunately, the Ministry of Finance discussion paper on economic reforms 'Two Years After and the Task Ahead' seems to accept the TRC's proposed structure as valid for the long term.

The TRC recognized in principle the advantages of simplicity. In 1991 the complexity of the Indian tariff structure with its multiplicity of rates, and its web of exemptions from those rates, was indescribable. Following the TRC, the Finance Minister is to be congratulated on making some important simplifications, especially by reducing the exemptions which have lent themselves to much lobbying and rent-seeking. However, seven rates of duty, even with no exemptions, would still leave plenty of room for lobbying and corruption to determine which rate should be applied to particular products. These seven pillars of folly would serve little or no purpose beyond benefiting members of the customs administration itself.

We must also recall that the TRC endorsed the possibility of further infant industry protection—presumably at rates up to 50 per cent or more. This supposes that the government can spot infant industries whose eventual high social returns would more than compensate for the very high early social losses implied by the need for effective protection of 50 per cent or more. Even if this were the case, it is widely agreed that such industries should be promoted by subsidies financed by general taxation, rather than making domestic users of the product alone finance the initial losses (assuming also that private entrepreneurs would not take the initiative).

3.4. The Fiscal Deficits[19]

The fiscal aspect not only of tariffs but of all other revenues and expenditures has to be seen against the background of the fiscal deficit of both the central and State governments. In 1990/91 the central fiscal deficit was 8.3 per cent of GDP. This deficit coming at the end of the series of deficits approaching 8 per cent of GDP was the prime cause of the crisis of 1990/91. It had to be drastically reduced. The primary deficit (i.e. excluding interest payments) was 4.3 per cent. With government debt already at the high level of about 65 per cent of GDP, India could no longer afford primary deficits of around 4–5 per cent of GDP—a level she had enjoyed for many years. It has been suggested that the primary deficit would probably have to be reduced to zero with a central government fiscal deficit of 4–5 per cent.[20] Indeed with a probable rise in the interest cost of servicing the debt, a primary surplus may well be needed.

Good progress in deficit reduction was made in 1991/92 and 1992/93 when the central fiscal deficit was reduced to 5.7 per cent, with a primary deficit of 1.3 per cent. 1993/94 was a grave disappointment. The budget estimate was for a deficit of 4.7 per cent implying a primary deficit of roughly zero. But estimates of both revenue and expenditure were too optimistic, and the deficit turned out to be 7.5 per cent with a primary deficit of 2.9 per cent. For 1994/95 the actual fiscal deficit was reduced to 6.1 per cent, with a primary deficit of 1.8 per cent. For 1995/96 the revised estimates are for a fiscal deficit of 5.9 per cent, and a primary deficit of 1.1 per cent.

The States also incur fiscal deficits, 2.6 per cent in 1990/91 rising to an estimated 4.0 per cent in 1994/95. The overall public sector fiscal deficit in 1990/91 was 10.5 per cent, and the same in 1994/95. The corresponding primary deficits were 5.3

---

[19]   For the Centre, figures in this section are taken from Government of India (1996). For the public sector and the States they are from Chopra *et al.* (1995).

[20]   Joshi and Little (1994), esp. ch. 9.

and 3.8 per cent. The latter may have been somewhat reduced in 1995/96 as the Central primary deficit fell by 0.7 percentage points. There is no doubt that the States should reduce their own deficits, a major contribution to which are subsidies largely given to agriculture by way of very low water and electricity charges. However, it must be said that the deficits of the States are ultimately under central control since they can borrow only with the consent of the Centre. The Centre can thus force a reduction in States' deficits if it has the political will to do so. For this reason and also because any deep analysis of States' finances is beyond the scope of this work, we concentrate on the Centre's revenue and expenditure. The argument of Chapter 2 implies that the overall public sector primary deficit should at least be limited to the amount that can be covered by seignorage and inflation tax (1.3 per cent), implying a reduction of about 2.5 percentage points. In view of the level of the debt, more might be desirable. It is arguable how much of this improvement should be the Centre's responsibility. A rough target for the Central fiscal deficit might be 4.0 per cent, a reduction of about 1.9 per cent from the revised estimate of 5.9 per cent for 1995/96.

3.5. The Fiscal Aspect of Tariffs

It is not entirely clear whether it has been the political need to reduce protection very slowly, or whether it is the loss of revenue which has governed the speed of reform. Naturally the budget speeches reflect both concerns. The Finance Minister himself may not know which has been the more powerful influence, though the consumer good import ban rather suggests that protectionism may have outweighed the fiscal argument. Customs revenue stood at 3.9 per cent of GDP in 1990/91, and was reduced to 2.9 per cent in 1993/94. In the budget of 1994/95 further reductions amounting to about 0.3 per cent of GDP were made. But the Finance Minister argued that the total loss of about Rs 4,000 crores implied by his proposed tax changes (of which the customs duty loss was about Rs 2,300 crores) as conventionally calculated, could be ignored since it would be made up by improved collection resulting from the simplifications of structure that he was proposing and the improved administration and compliance which he would promote and pursue.   The revised estimates for 1994/95 again give customs revenue as 2.9 per cent of GDP, vindicating the Finance Minister.

In the long run tariff revenue, excluding countervailing duties corresponding to internal taxation should be reduced to about 1.5 per cent of GDP.   Imports as a proportion of GDP will rise as a result of the fall in the tariffs and the removal of the ban on consumer good imports.   Supposing the proportion of imports rises to 15 per cent from the present figure of 10 per cent, then customs revenue of 1.5 per cent of GDP implies an effective tax on imports, excluding countervailing duties, of 10 per cent.   We have already suggested that this is about right.[21]   But countervailing duties corresponding to internal indirect taxation might amount to another 15 per cent, so that the total revenue collected on imports would amount to about 3.75 per cent.

The speed with which customs duty can be reduced depends both on expenditure reforms and on other elements of (positive) taxation, notably direct and indirect domestic taxation.   We deal first with taxation.

3.6. Direct Taxes

Direct taxes yield little in India, accounting for only about 15 per cent of total tax revenue, whereas the developing country

---

[21]   Although it is dangerous to look to other developing countries for norms (since their tax structure is often very far from ideal) it may be worth noting that most other large developing countries collect less than 2 per cent of GDP in import duties, including Bangladesh, Brazil, Indonesia, Mexico, Nigeria, and Turkey (1987 data from Burgess, Howes, and Stern, 1993).

average is about 30 per cent. Only about eight million people pay income tax, less than one in a hundred. As a proportion of GDP direct taxes hit a low of 2.3 per cent in 1990/91, much less than customs revenue. Their part of total tax revenue has fallen from about 40 per cent in the early 1950s to 30 per cent in the early 1960s, and about 15 per cent in the last decade.[22] Admittedly total tax revenue rose from about 10 per cent of GDP to 20 per cent over the whole period. Even so, direct taxes as a proportion of GDP have fallen since the early 1960s as real GDP per capita has risen: it is normal to expect the reverse.[23] There has been no reduction in direct tax rates until the late 1980s, and in 1992/93, since when the percentage of direct tax revenue to GDP has *improved* a little.

It is clear that the dismal performance of direct taxation has been due to increasing inefficiency, evasion, and corruption. The reasons for this have been considered at length by the TRC, and a great many detailed reforms suggested.[24] We do not know the extent to which these administrative reforms have been accepted and implemented in the past two years. However, the burden on administration has been somewhat reduced by reducing the number of rates to three, and by reducing the top marginal rate to 40 per cent from the absurdly high marginal rates that have been applied in the past.

It is to be hoped that much better administration, fiercer penalties for evasion, and a broadening of the tax base by closing legal loopholes, will eventually result in a large rise in the revenue from direct taxes. Voluntary presumptive taxation for small traders was introduced in 1992/93. Unsurprisingly it has yielded extremely little. Compulsory presumptive taxation should be tried for certain classes of citizens and undertakings.

---

[22] These rough figures come from Burgess and Stern (1993), table 1 and fig. 2.
[23] There is a clearly positive cross-country correlation between GNP per head and direct taxation as a percentage of GDP.
[24] Government of India (1992*b*), pt. i, chs. 5 and 6.

3.7. Domestic Indirect Taxes

We turn to indirect domestic taxation—that is to central excise duties and States' sales taxes. As the Finance Minister has remarked, 'Normally, the revenue loss from customs duty reduction could have been made up through higher excise duties. However, there are compelling reasons for rationalising and reducing excise duties over a wide range of industries'.[25] The compelling reasons are that the domestic tax system (including the States' sales taxes) consisted of an extremely complex maze of more than a hundred different rates of tax on (mainly) industrial products whether they were current inputs, capital goods, or final consumption goods. It was a major research task to calculate the effective tax rate on different consumption goods resulting from these cascading taxes. [26] The multiplicity of rates bore no relation to any good social or economic purpose. The extensive taxation of inputs, both current and capital, has constituted a serious bias against both investment and exports.[27] No other country relies as much on excise taxes as India. Excise taxation (i.e. taxes on the domestic *production* of commodities) is normally reserved for alcohol, tobacco, and petroleum products. But in India the Centre was constitutionally barred from sales taxes on final consumption. Decades of lobbying must account for the large number of rates, and the hundreds of exemptions granted (which also account for the very high rates, reaching 100 per cent, on some products). Much the same applies to the States' sales taxes which constituted 21 per cent of total tax revenue in 1992/93 and are mostly levied on the first point of sales, and thus use the same base as the union excises (except that the tax base for the sales tax includes the union

[25] Budget speech 1993/4. Union excise duties accounted for 4.4 per cent of GDP in 1992/93 and 27 per cent of total tax revenue.
[26] Ahmad and Stern (1991).
[27] To some degree commodities used as inputs have been exempted under MODVAT (see below), and from sales taxes in certain States.

excise tax).[28]   Together excise and sales taxes account for almost half total tax revenue.

In view of the above, no-one could be happy with an increase in union excise taxes. Nevertheless in 1991/92 and 1992/93 the Finance Minister did raise excise taxes mostly on final consumption goods, to compensate for loss of customs revenue. At the same time, some simplifications were made, and some specific duties were converted to *ad valorem* (as recommended by the TRC). In 1993/94 many of the earlier increases were reversed, and in the 1994/95 budget a major reform of the excise tax structure was adumbrated. A start was made with extending MODVAT, with substituting specific for *ad valorem* taxes, with reducing the number of rates and halving the number of special exemptions. A few services were also brought into the tax net for the first time. The 1995/96 budget extended the process of excise tax reform along similar lines with many reductions of rates. The detail of the changes is necessarily as complex as the structure they are designed to reform.

The fiscal reforms of the Manmohan Singh era have been cautious, but always in the right direction. Comparing 1994/95 revised estimates with 1990/91, the Centre's revenue has fallen by 0.5 per cent of GDP, a tax revenue fall of 0.9 per cent being offset by a rise of 0.4 per cent in non-tax revenue. Within tax revenue, customs has fallen by almost 1.0 per cent and a fall in excise of 0.7 per cent has been offset by a rise of 0.7 per cent in direct taxation. These reforms were seen as paving the way for an eventual adoption of a value added tax (VAT). The possibilities of a VAT for India cannot be discussed without also considering the States' sales taxes, and the whole relation of the central and States' finances. This is reserved for Section 3.9 below.

---

[28]   The almost incredible irrationality of the domestic indirect tax system is well described by the TRC, and also by Burgess, Howes, and Stern (1993).

3.8. Expenditure on Central Subsidies

Of course, the fiscal deficit depends also on current expenditure. Among expenditure items, subsidies are, from an economic point of view, negative indirect taxes. In 1990/91 the explicit subsidies for which provision is made in the Centre's budget amounted to Rs 10,728 crores, about 2 per cent of GDP. [29] In effect, they subtracted 25 per cent from the Centre's tax revenue (net of the States' share). Fertilizer subsidies were the biggest (0.83 per cent), followed by export subsidies (0.52 per cent) and food subsidies (0.46 per cent). The devaluations of 1991 permitted the elimination of cash subsidies for exports, so that the total expenditure on export promotion fell to Rs 700 crores (0.1 per cent of GDP) in 1993/94 (revised estimate). As a result, net trade taxation (customs less export subsidies) has fallen only from 3.4 per cent to 2.8 per cent of GDP. This supports the view that tariffs should have been reduced more rapidly than they have been.

Apart from exports, there has been no progress in reducing subsidies. Fertilizer subsidies were Rs 4,400 crores in 1990/91, and Rs 5,194 crores in 1993/94 (revised estimate).[30] Rs 4,000 crores had been budgeted. For 1994/95 the Finance Minister again budgeted Rs 4,000 crores. In the budget speech of March 1995 it was announced that this had to be revised to Rs 5,166 crores (about 0.6 per cent of GDP). For 1995/96 Rs 5,900 is budgeted.

It is important to note that fertilizer subsidies are partly subsidies to the fertilizer industry (including the producers of feed stock). They are subsidies to farmers only insofar as the farmer pays less than the cif price (plus internal transport

---

[29]   From Government of India, *Indian Public Finance Statistics, 1994*. Debt relief to farmers is not included.

[30]   World Bank, *Country Economic Memorandum* (1995), table A 4.11.

costs).[31] They are subsidies to the fertilizer industry insofar as the 'retention' prices paid to fertilizer plants exceed the cif price. Which is the more subsidized depends on the cif price and varies considerably. During the 1980s roughly half went to the industry and half to farmers.[32] A bold start to subsidy reduction was made in July 1991 when controlled fertilizer prices were raised by 40 per cent. But back-tracking began almost immediately, for in August the rise was reduced to 30 per cent and small farmers were exempted from the increase: and in August 1992 the controlled price of urea (accounting for half of fertilizer sales) was further reduced by 10 per cent. In that year imported inputs for phosphatic fertilizer production were decanalized, and price controls were removed. The price of di-ammonium phosphate almost doubled and imports were then freed with no tariff, which brought the price back to cif levels. But this was still higher than before, and so a subsidy of Rs 1,000/ton was introduced. Finally, since most domestic producers could not compete with imports, the subsidy was limited to domestic production, thus reintroducing protection. This has been a sorry story, which shows the political strength of the farming lobby, reinforced no doubt by that of the fertilizer industry.

The fertilizer subsidy has no sound economic or social justification. As we have seen, it partly protects the fertilizer industry. Thus nitrogenous fertilizer plants in India receive a 'retention' price which for many is above the import price (and for some, double the import price). Imports of nitrogenous fertilizers are canalized, and fill the gap between domestic supply and demand. There are no tariffs either on fertilizers, or on capital goods or feedstock imports for the industry (this includes phosphates and potash). There is no reason why the fertilizer industry should in the long run receive any more protection than that afforded by the low general tariff of 10 per

---

[31] The subsidy to the farmer may partly accrue to the consumer of his produce if the government's procurement price is reduced because of the subsidy.
[32] Pursell and Gulati (1993).

cent that we advocate. In the reform period some protection has to be retained, for probably about half the industry would otherwise collapse. But the subsidy should certainly be limited and greatly reduced: the industry must be restructured and a beginning made with closing down some high cost plants. There is also no good argument for subsidizing fertilizer to the farmer—prices should rise to import parity. This increase would, however, have wide repercussions: we consider it in Section 3.9 where we deal with agricultural pricing more generally.

It is also true that no progress has been made with reducing food subsidies. These represent the difference between the 'procurement' prices paid by the Food Corporation of India to farmers, and the 'issue' prices of the public distribution system (PDS). In 1990/91 they amounted to Rs 2,450 crores, and in 1993/94 to Rs 5,537 crores. For 1994/95 the Finance Minister budgeted Rs 4,000 crores, raised to 5,100 crores in the revised estimates. For 1995/96 Rs 5,250 crores is budgeted. The justification for food subsidies is poverty relief. However, it is widely acknowledged that the PDS has proved to be a very cost-ineffective way of dealing with poverty. We revert to this problem in Section 3.11 after considering agricultural prices including food in Section 3.10.

These two explicit central government subsidies will probably amount to close on Rs 11,000 crores for 1994/95, or about 1.2 per cent of GDP. In 1990/91, they were 1.3 per cent of GDP. These subsidies are, however, the tip of an iceberg. In the case of public services or products which could be sold to persons or firms one should include as subsidy the difference between the cost and what is actually recovered. Going back to 1987/88 central subsidies in this sense were about 5.5 per cent of GDP.[33] The social sectors that some may consider should be fully subsidized accounted, very roughly, for 1 per cent and the explicit subsidies for 1.5 per cent, leaving subsidies of about 3

---

[33]   Mundle and Rao (1991).

per cent of GDP going mainly to industry, transport, and communications. We do not have up-to-date figures except for the losses of non-departmental central enterprises which came to 0.7 per cent of GDP in 1993/94. Even if there has been considerable improvement, there is no doubt that there is plenty of room for improving cost recovery and reducing losses.

Subsidies are also a large part of this expenditure of the States. In 1987/88 the States' subsidization of the social sectors, mainly health and education, amounted to about 4.9 per cent of GDP. But another 4 per cent went on economic services. These include the most criticized and socially unjustifiable subsidies for irrigation, power supply, and transport. Since then there seems to have been little or no improvement. Non-development expenditure has risen by almost 1 per cent of GDP, while development expenditure has fallen by 0.6 per cent, social and economic services falling equally (by 1993/94).

3.9. Other Current Expenditures (Centre and States)

We have considered the subsidies inherent in the public provision of social and economic services, but not the full cost of these services. In 1990/91 current expenditure on the social services was 5.5 per cent of GDP, and that on the economic services 5.3 per cent of GDP. [34] In 1993/94 (revised estimates) these figures were a little lower, 5.3 per cent and 5.0 per cent respectively. Other current expenditures rank as non-developmental. Excluding food subsidies, they amounted to 11.6 per cent of GDP in 1990/91. This had risen to 12.4 per cent in 1993/94. The rise was more than accounted for by a rise in interest payments (plus 1.0 per cent). Defence was slightly down at 1.9 per cent, and so also was general administration and 'others'. We consider the problem of interest in Chapters 2 and 4 and have nothing useful to say about defence.

---

[34]   See Mundle and Rao (1991), tables 2 and 4.

We have no particular observations to make about the efficiency of all these government services. But two general comments must be made. First, it is notorious that government departments are grossly overstaffed at all levels (and there are too many overlapping departments). Secondly, governmental pay rates are relatively high and have grown excessively. In the period 1974/75 to 1989/90 per caput income rose by 2.5 per cent per annum, while government pay for employees rose by 5.7 per cent per annum to a level that was 6.3 times per caput income.[35] Government employees have been a powerful factor in the level and growth of governmental expenditures.

3.10. The Reform of Agricultural Incentives

We have seen that the Centre has been spending large sums on fertilizer subsidies, some part of which is a subsidy to agriculture. The central fertilizer subsidy is only a small part of the total massive subsidization of agricultural inputs, much of which is the responsibility of State governments. The farmer pays only a small fraction of the long-run marginal cost of the irrigation and electricity which he uses. Agricultural credit is also subsidized. The irrigation subsidy may be of the order of Rs 10,000 crores, that of electricity Rs 4,000, and credit subsidization Rs 3,000 crores.[36]

These subsidies not only contribute to the overall fiscal deficit, both directly and indirectly, but they also threaten the actual supply of irrigation and electricity as they undermine the financial viability of the State irrigation authorities and electricity boards. Credit subsidies have also contributed to the weakness of the banks that threatened the whole financial system of India in 1990/91.

[35]   See Rao and Sen (1993), 22.
[36]   This whole section owes a great deal to Pursell and Gulati. (See Pursell and Gulati, 1993.)

In a sense, however, agricultural subsidies, though politically influenced to a high degree, have been an essential part of the whole agricultural system of India. The prices of all major agricultural products have been largely determined by the central government's total control of foreign trade in them. The prices of cereals—rice, wheat, and coarse grains—and cotton, have been held below world prices in most years by controlling exports. Except for fertilizers, farmers have had to pay more than world prices for inputs, e.g. machinery and pesticides. In contrast some crops, notably sugar and edible oils, have been protected, but the value of these is dwarfed by cereals and cotton, so that on balance agriculture has been heavily disprotected.[37]

The input subsidies offset this negative protection, but only partially, so that a considerable bias against agriculture remains. They are also a very inefficient offset. The extreme under-pricing of water and electricity unduly favours water-intensive crops such as sugarcane, and also results in excessive use of water for these and other crops. The fertilizer subsidies which favour nitrogen relative to phosphates and potash have also resulted in inappropriate usage. The input subsidies (and protection of edible oil and sugar) can also be criticized in that they favour the richer irrigated areas relative to the poorer rain-fed areas, richer farmers relative to poor farmers, and capital intensive relative to labour intensive crops (e.g. edible oils and sugar relative to cotton and rice).

Clearly agriculture must be compensated for the loss of input subsidies. The obvious compensation would be to allow free trade in agricultural products.[38] Indeed the finding that

---

[37] We lack space to deal with lesser crops such as tea, coffee, and tobacco. In these, as well as cotton, sugar, and oilseeds, government intervention in trade and domestic marketing has caused serious damage. For a powerful indictment of agricultural policies in these areas see Desai (1993), ch. 17.

[38] The low general tariff (10 per cent) which we advocate should apply to agricultural imports. But it would be redundant in most years for the main products, cereals, and cotton.

agriculture has been negatively protected even allowing for the input subsidies implies that free trade would more than compensate agriculture.

The price of cereals and cotton would rise, while production and exports would increase. Exports of many minor agricultural products would also be likely to rise. The biggest sufferer would be edible oils. Here India has a clear comparative disadvantage. Consequently the government instituted a major import substitution drive in 1986. Something near self-sufficiency has been achieved largely at the expense of wheat production, as a result of which three million tons of wheat were imported in 1992/93. The domestic price of edible oils was about double that of imports, while the domestic price of wheat was much below that of imports. In some areas sugar production would also become unprofitable, especially if irrigation charges were raised as they should be.

The price of agricultural outputs would need to rise by 11–12 per cent to compensate farmers and agricultural workers for the total loss of input subsidies.[39] Actual prices could rise a good deal higher on integration with world prices for the major tradable crops, though much would depend on the real equilibrium rate of exchange that became established. The price of food would rise significantly, since falls in the prices of edible oils and sugar would be more than offset by rises in the prices of cereals. Even although we would expect employment and rural wages also to rise, this rise in the price of food would be serious for the very poor—especially those unable to work, in both rural and urban areas. In advocating free trade in agricultural products we presume that this would be preceded or accompanied by a strengthening of anti-poverty programmes. These are discussed at length in Chapter 6.

Even if an increase in poverty programmes were to take up the whole of the savings from reducing input subsidies, the

---

[39] Subsidies to agriculture were 11.4 per cent of agricultural GDP in 1989/90. See Cassen, Joshi, and Lipton (1992).

change would be highly beneficial. First, the poverty programmes would be far better from a distributional point of view than the input subsidies. Secondly, the price reforms accompanying the removal of the subsidies would change agricultural incentives in such a way as greatly to improve the efficiency of production. However the saving in public funds (central and State) would be of the order of 3 per cent of GDP, and it is not anticipated that more than a fraction of this would be spent on targeted poverty programmes. Some of the rest could go to increasing public agricultural investment which has been falling in recent years: this could be directed especially to the poorer regions.

Whatever the long-run benefits of free trade in agricultural products and the removal of input subsidies, it has to be recognized that the change would cause some large disturbances, and a good many people might suffer, or fear they would suffer, for some time. Exports of cereals may have to be controlled for a few years more, while improvements are made in the PDS or other 'safety net' arrangements. Tariffs on the highly protected items—edible oils, sugar, and rubber—may be brought down only gradually to the general level of 10 per cent, and so on. Further temporary protection of handloom weavers and small-scale leather workers might or might not be justified in the face of a rise in the domestic price of their inputs. These transitional problems must be dealt with in the context of a fairly rapid move towards free trade. Uneconomic activities in both agriculture and industry should not be preserved indefinitely.

Some people argue that the domestic prices of food in a very poor country cannot be allowed to vary with world prices. This could result in severe hardship, even starvation. We believe that this argument has some force. But if the poorest sections of the population (say the poorest 25 per cent) can be protected from large temporary rises in cereal prices we would think that is all that is needed. For this purpose the government may hold buffer stocks as at present, and be ready to import and subsidize. We do not think that any elaborate system of variable import levies and export taxes would be advisable.

The reform of agricultural trade policy and pricing is as important as that of industrial policy and pricing, and financial reforms. But it has attracted less attention. Much less has been done, and no accepted framework of reform has been accepted, such as that provided by the Tax Reform Committee in the case of industrial tariffs. It is notable indeed that the TRC ignored agricultural tariffs and trade. It implicitly assumed that agricultural trade would remain controlled.

Indeed, to date it has remained almost wholly controlled. Some exports of the major products have been allowed from time to time, but they remained controlled. The controls over cotton have been especially unpredictable, and hamfisted. Only minor items have been decontrolled—with some notable increases in export. A great many restrictions on internal trade remain, though these are largely operated by State governments. In short, there appears to be no coherent policy on agricultural reform.

To some extent this is because agriculture is a States' subject. For instance, the electricity and irrigation subsidies are determined by the States (but the fertilizer subsidies and credit subsidies mainly, though not entirely, by the Centre). Only the States can tax the land or agricultural income. Much public agricultural and rural investment is decided and implemented by the States. And the States regulate and control the ownership and use of land. Nevertheless the broad lines of agricultural policy are determined by the Centre's control of agricultural trade, and by its lack of a rational fertilizer policy.

3.11. Centre and State Indirect Taxation, and VAT Possibilities

In 1990/91 States' sales and excise taxation came to 4.2 per cent of GDP, and central excise to 4.1 per cent. However, 47.5 per cent of the latter is paid to the States.[40]   We have seen that central excise taxation is highly illogical and economically inefficient. The States' taxation compounds the inefficiency. It falls predominately on the same base, that is ex-factory quantities or values, and suffers from the same faults of multiple rates and multiple exemptions. Except for a few States, sales taxes are not rebated at subsequent stages of manufacture or distribution. Interstate sales are also taxed under the Central Sales Tax Act of 1956 at a rate of 4 per cent with the States retaining the proceeds.

It is clear that a rational and tolerably efficient national system of indirect taxation must involve reform at both the central (federal) level and that of the States. Such a reform obviously requires the agreement of the States, and this is complicated by the revenue sharing of the different taxes.

The taxation powers of the Centre and the States are laid down in the Constitution. Broadly speaking, the taxes assigned to the States are land tax, agricultural income tax, alcohol excise, and sales taxes. The rest belong to the Centre, and consist of customs and central excise, and personal and corporation income tax (and wealth tax). But the Centre must share the revenue from some taxes (excluding trade taxes) with the States in proportions decided by quinquennial Finance Commissions. At present, 47.5 per cent of central excises go to the States, and 77.5 per cent of personal income taxation. Such a division of revenues produces a crazy set of incentives for levying and collecting the different taxes.[41] Only a very naive economist might think that this does not matter, since the central government is concerned only with the national interest. There is no doubt that the stagnation of personal direct taxation and the burgeoning of customs revenue, which has risen since 1970 from about 10 per cent to over 20 per cent of the total tax take, owe

---

[40]   45 per cent from 1990/91 to 1994/95.

[41]   The percentages given are those recommended by the Tenth Finance Commission.   They are a slight improvement on those of the previous quinquennium, 45 per cent and 85 per cent.

much to the fact that the Centre until recently retained only 15 per cent of the former and 100 per cent of the latter. There is also no doubt that this cock-eyed growth of the tax system has harmed the development of the whole economy.

It was accepted by the Tenth Finance Commission, reporting in December 1994, that a pooling of central taxation with a proportion devolving to the States would be desirable; but this would require an amendment of the Constitution, and its recommendation for 1995/96 was bound by the Constitution. However, it devised a pooling scheme under which the States would get 29 per cent of all central taxation, and suggested that this be brought into force from 1st April 1996. It also suggested that the agreed proportion for the States should be reviewed only after fifteen years. It is devoutly to be hoped that these suggestions will go through.

It is now accepted policy (in New Delhi at least) that the Centre and the States should work towards some form of value added taxation to replace excise taxes and sales taxes, except for the excises on alcohol, petrol (gasoline), and tobacco, and possibly a few other 'luxury' consumption goods, excise taxes on which are prevalent in all countries. Much good work has now been done on the difficult problem of devising the best system that (1) preserves the fiscal autonomy of the States, (2) permits the inter-state redistribution that stems from the division (determined by the Finance Commissions) of the shared portion of central taxes between the States, (3) maintains the desirable economic qualities of the VAT, and (4) is administratively efficient, discouraging leakages and corruption.[42] We discuss the various options in the light of the above considerations.

There seems to be no disagreement as to the best type of VAT. First it should be based on consumption, which means that tax paid on capital goods can be recovered by the purchaser just as is the case with other inputs. Secondly, it should be

---

[42]   We refer to the Chelliah Committee (TRC); and to Burgess, Howes, and Stern (1993 and 1994).

destination based. This means that imports are taxed in the same way as domestically produced goods, while an exporter charges no VAT to his customer but can reclaim the tax paid on his inputs.[43]

Difficult problems arise for a federal state such as India over the assignment of the powers to levy and administer the VAT or VATs. In most federations the VAT is levied and controlled by the centre, though administration and the proceeds are shared. This applies, for instance, to Argentina, Austria, Germany, and Mexico. From the point of view of economic efficiency, there is no doubt that this is the best option. It avoids the problem of different rates applying in different states (and thus of tax competition to attract industries). It avoids also the problems of taxation of inter-state trade, for the centre would insist on the destination principle under which inter-state (and international) trade is exempt. It is only via a central-only VAT that the minimum distortion of economic incentives can be achieved. The revenues could be shared just as central income and excise taxes are presently shared. However, all observers agree that there is no possibility of getting the States' agreement to the constitutional changes that would be required for a central VAT. The States jealously guard such fiscal autonomy as they have.

Paradoxically, the extreme opposite solution is also very attractive. The States would run their own VATs, and the Centre would deny itself all indirect taxation except customs duties and excises on a few specified 'demerit' or luxury consumption goods—alcohol, tobacco, petrol and diesel fuels, and perhaps motor cars. There would be no revenue sharing. There are very strong advantages. The end of sharing would give the Centre more incentive to improve the direct tax regime. The States would gain fiscal autonomy and responsibility. The incentive to bring State subsidies under control would be increased, since they could no longer look to the Finance Commissions to fill the

---

[43] This is the meaning of 'zero-rated'. Being 'VAT exempt' means that the operator charges no VAT but cannot reclaim tax paid on inputs.

gap in their finances by ordaining that ever-increasing slices of centrally collected revenues should devolve to the States. There would remain certain disadvantages that are the counterpart of the already discussed advantages of a central VAT. Problems could arise because of variations in the coverage, rates and forms of different State VATs. We discuss these problems below when considering an interim or compromise solution, since they arise also in that context.

It has been argued, however, that the above separation of the Centre's and States' powers is neither politically possible nor morally desirable. The point is that the devolution of the Centre's revenues to the States permits the Finance Commissions to decree more for the poor and economically disadvantaged States than they could possibly raise from their own resources. Furthermore the Centre at present retains enough revenue to give subsidies to the States, and these subsidies form a high proportion of the revenues of the small poor States. In short, there is a strong reason for the Centre to be able (or be required by the Finance Commissions) to play a redistributory role. This problem is recognized by Burgess, Howes, and Stern (1993) who favour State VATs as a solution for the long run, but who tend to suggest that redistributive taxation of the richer States would be necessary. The NIPFP (1994) did not rule out the State VAT solution for the very long run. But it rejected (no doubt rightly) the idea of interstate redistributory taxation as impractical given the realities of the Indian political scene. It considered that a viable solution to the redistributive problem would constitute such a drastic change in the system of devolution and grants as to require consideration by a Finance Commission.

We agree that in the interest of achieving desirable reforms quickly the radical solution of exclusive State VATs should be ruled out for the next few years. But we do not consider that the redistributive problem is as difficult to solve satisfactorily as Burgess, Howes, and Stern (1993) and NIPFP (1994) suggest. Our reasons are given in the Appendix to this chapter, where we suggest that it is possible for the Centre to retain enough revenue to deal with the problem of the poor States with very low taxable capacity while giving up all indirect taxation except customs and a few 'luxury' excises on alcohol, tobacco, gasoline, and cars. We believe, however, that it would be necessary for the Centre to retain some control over the forms and coverage of the State VATs.

We turn next to the NIPFP preferred solution,[44] which has the great advantage of not requiring a constitutional amendment. It enables important progress to be made towards a more rational indirect tax system,, and does not preclude the eventual adoption of the exclusive States' VAT system described above.

The suggestion is for an independent dual system. The Centre would extend its present MODVAT to all manufactures, turning it into a MANVAT with full rebate of the tax paid on all inputs including capital goods for all VAT-registered manu-facturers. Existing exemptions would be withdrawn. The number of MANVAT rates should be greatly reduced, eventu-ally to one. MANVAT would be shared with the States, roughly as at present.[45] It would not be rebatable against State VATs which would be levied on the ex-factory price including MANVAT.[46] The Centre could retain special (non-shared) excises on some 'demerit' or 'luxury' products, and also initiate taxation of some services.

States' sales and other minor taxes should be replaced by VATs. But if this reform is to achieve an important improve-ment in economic efficiency, some agreed harmonization of the independent State VATs will be necessary in order to create a common market within India, and to avoid undue tax

---

[44] The NIPFP examined other variants of a dual or concurrent system under which both the Centre and the States impose indirect taxes. Since we concur with their reasons for rejecting these we do not examine them.

[45] Our brief description does not try to deal with every problem that arises. See also NIPFP especially Appendix 1 for many essential improvements needed in the MODVAT scheme.

[46] NIPFP correctly argues (para. 6.2–2-3) that the small tax on tax (pyramiding) element involved is not an example of undesirable cascading.

competition and other distortions. Agreement is needed with respect to (1) the type of VAT, (2) its product and service coverage, (3) size exemptions, and (4) a permissible band or bands within which the tax rate or rates may fall.

We agree with NIPFP that the type of VAT should be destination-based consumption. There is very general agreement that this is the most desirable type, and it is also the most widely implemented.[47] It means that the tax on capital inputs should be rebatable. This presents no special difficulty. It should also mean that both international exports, and exports from one State to another, are zero rated. Interstate trade presents a problem. At present India is not a free-trade area. The States levy sales tax on inter-state sales. Powers to tax inter-state sales belong to the Centre under the Constitution, but under the Central Sales Tax (CST) Act of 1956, the States were authorized to levy CST on inter-state sales originating in their territories. The Centre lays down a ceiling rate which stands at 4 per cent. This applies only to sales to a registered dealer. If the sale is to an unregistered dealer or a consumer the local tax rate or 10 per cent, whichever is higher, applies. Even if administration and compliance were simple, this system would constitute a serious economic imperfection. Administration and compliance are very complex.

Unfortunately it is not easy to ensure that zero rated 'export' sales actually go to another State. In other words, it is hard to prevent fraudulent evasion. In the European Union this is possible at least for sales to a VAT registered trader. But European arrangements might be administratively impossible in India. There are various possibilities, all of which would at least greatly reduce the highly undesirable incidence of inter-state taxation.[48]

---

[47]   But it seems that State officials and politicians in India are loth to give up imposing sales tax on exports to other States. In the world at large, taxing exports is now recognized to be usually harmful for the exporter. It is quite surprising that Indian States cannot understand this.

[48]   See Bagchi (1995); also NIPFP (1994).

The product coverage should be total except for specific exemptions. We would suggest that unprocessed food should be the only exemption. This agrees with NIPFP. Services should be covered so far as possible, though some may be better taxed by the Centre.[49]

Everywhere very small producers and dealers are VAT exempt because it is not worth trying to collect very small parcels of tax (and also perhaps because it would be vote-losing). This exemption protects the small operator from larger firms, and also from imports which bear countervailing duty. In India small manufacturing enterprises (SMEs) are already heavily protected and subsidized. Apart from the reservation of products for SMEs, they are exempted from central excises, and often also receive tax favours or input subsidies from state governments. Initially (1978) sales below Rs 5 lakhs were exempt. For various reasons this exemption limit has been greatly increased, and is now 20–30 lakhs (depending on the number of goods produced). On top of this, reduced rates are allowed up to Rs 3 crores.[50]

These exemptions are of a different order of magnitude to those proposed for VAT exemption on fiscal grounds. The NIPFP suggests Rs 3 lakhs. This seems rather low given the NIPFP's own figures which claim to show that dealers with turnover of less than Rs 5 lakhs constitute 68 per cent of the total but pay only 8 per cent of State sales tax collected, and those with less than Rs 10 lakhs constitute 76 per cent of the total and pay 17 per cent of the tax. We would suggest a VAT exemption threshold of Rs 5 lakhs of turnover—still far lower than the central excise exemption and concession limits (and presumably MODVAT limits). Clearly these latter exemptions are made on protective, not on fiscal, grounds. The primary season for thus favouring SMEs was supposed to be that they were labour-

---

[49]　Services present some special difficulties too detailed for us to examine. The reader is referred to NIPFP (1994), Section 7–2.

[50]　The limit was raised from Rs 2 crores to Rs 3 crores in the budget of 1995/96.

intensive. But it has been argued that this promotion of SMEs was a very ineffective way of encouraging labour-intensity in manufacturing, and had other undesirable effects.[51] We believe that the large fillip given to labour demand by the reforms advocated in this study (especially favouring exports and agriculture) would amply justify the eventual removal of the protection of SMEs larger than the VAT registration threshold. It would be a great simplification, and would benefit the revenue, to have a single exemption limit or threshold for VAT registration (though the states might be allowed to set their own thresholds within an agreed range, say 5–10 lakhs).

Lastly we turn to the rates. It would be highly advantageous for each State to have a single VAT rate (apart from exemptions or zero rated products). These need not be the same. Indeed the States must be allowed some flexibility in this respect. Apart from differing needs, their sense of autonomy would be reduced to vanishing point if they could not diverge from a single rate. Anyway, it would be too difficult to reach agreement on a single rate. But too much divergence could also create problems. A permissible band should be negotiated, with a width of, say, 3 percentage points. All this would be hugely complicated if each State had two or more VAT rates. Then agreement would have to be reached on the assignment of different products to different rates, otherwise large variations between particular product-rates in different States could occur which would cause production distortions especially between neighbouring States.

We think that NIPFP erred in suggesting a low rate (4–5 per cent), a standard rate (12–14 per cent) and a high rate (20 per cent or more). Their low rate consisted of some minor items of processed food and spices, and kerosene. We believe these items should bear the standard rate (but kerosene is always a special case, and might be exempted if agreement could be reached on this). Their list of high rate items typically includes

---

[51]　See Little, Mazumdar, and Page (1987), ch. 16; and Suri (ed.), (1988), pt. ii.

those normally subject to high excise taxes (petrol, narcotics, tobacco, alcohol). They should pay the standard VAT rate, with an excise tax on top (either a central excise or a States' excise depending on the final configuration of central and State indirect taxes).

The biggest problem with State VATs will be securing agreement. The NIPFP has suggested the creation of an all-Indian VAT Council which would also supervise the extensive training of officials, and the public education needed. The Council would need powers to discipline States which broke the agreed rules. Most large Asian and Latin American countries have now successfully introduced a VAT. There is plenty of experience and expertise to draw on in planning this major project, which probably needs two to three years of preparation. While the Centre has gone quite far towards turning central excises into a MANVAT, progress towards replacing sales taxes by States' VATs has been very slow.

3.12. Conclusions

This chapter has been concerned (1) with the fiscal con-sequences of introducing a near free trade regime with almost no restrictions and with a uniform protective tariff of 10 per cent, and (2) with domestic tax reforms that are highly desirable in themselves but which need to be considered in the context of trade reforms, and (3) with the economic and distributional consequences of the regime we propose.

We cannot give full reasons for our preference for a low uniform tariff. A complete set of relevant references would itself fill many volumes. We confine ourselves to the idea of uniformity, since there may be some confusion here. Several Indian documents, including the TRC reports, state their recognition of the theoretical case for uniformity. In fact the theoretical case in general suggests non-uniformity wherever import prices could be affected by tariffs (assuming no retaliation from foreign governments), although there is no case for non-uniformity on protective grounds as we argued in Section 3.3 above. The case for uniformity is a practical one advanced more by institutional and political economists than by theoreticians. First, it is suggested that economic bureaucrats are highly unlikely to realize the small theoretical gains that might be extracted from foreigners by tariff (or quota) manipulation. Secondly non-uniformity raises problems of classification, invites lobbying and rent seeking, results in an economically irrational structure of rates, and in prosecutions and litigation. The amazing complexity of tariffs and exemptions that has evolved in India and other countries bears witness for our case. We would advocate a single rate for everything including cereals (the domestic production of which would be exempt from VAT), especially as we believe that there would usually be no cereal imports!

Before examining the fiscal consequences of a low uniform tariff it is convenient to consider uniformity of domestic indirect taxation. Here the reasons for non-uniformity are stronger than in the case of tariffs. The well-known Ramsey theorem suggests that the more inelastic the good the higher should be the tax. Distribution considerations suggest that the more essential the good the lower should be the tax. British administrations taxed salt. They might have appealed to Ramsey. Distributional considerations later won the day. For similar reasons, but also because the complex elasticities required for 'optimal' Ramsey taxation are inestimable, we ignore the theory.[52] Moreover, all the political economy and administrative arguments that favoured a single rate of taxation in the case of imports apply just as strongly to domestic indirect taxation. In the case of a VAT we would exempt only unprocessed food on distributional grounds (and perhaps salt, for old times' sake!). On top of this one would have non-rebatable excises on the usual items— alcohol, tobacco, gasoline—which qualify for high taxation on

[52]   See Deaton (1987).

all counts—inelastic demand, undesirable externalities, and distribution.

We go along with the NIPFP's proposals for concurrent central and State VATs as the best way of achieving a major rationalization of India's indirect tax system in the next few years. We also concur with all that the NIPFP has to say about the kinds of VAT needed and about the manner in which progress towards agreement may be made. We disagree only with the multiplicity of rates proposed. The aim at least should be for a single rate (apart from the exemption of unprocessed agricultural products, and the zero-rating of exports). We think however that the withdrawal of the Centre from all indirect taxation except customs (and the collection of countervailing duties for the States) and a few special excises should ultimately be possible, and would be the best long-run solution to the federal fiscal problem.[53]

We have already noted in Section 7 the considerable progress made in reforming central indirect taxation. We applaud the conversion of the Tenth Finance Commission to the idea of a single rate of sharing all central tax revenue with the States as a whole. Unfortunately, we are unaware of any significant progress made in the direction of educating and persuading the States to reform their own taxes and subsidies, and to move towards a harmonized set of VATs.

We are now in a position to examine the fiscal consequences of a low single external tariff. In 1990/91 customs revenue was 3.9 per cent of GDP. This was reduced to 2.9 per cent in 1994/95 (revised estimates). We guess that liberalization will result in an increase of imports to about 15 per cent of GDP, so that a uniform tariff of 10 per cent would yield customs revenue of 1.5 per cent (a reduction of 1.4 per cent of GDP from 1994/95). To set against this we consider that a rise of one per cent of GDP in direct taxation is both feasible and desirable.

---

[53] We here agree with Burgess, Howes, and Stern (1993).

Domestic indirect taxation is likely to amount to VAT plus excise duties at an average rate of at least 15 per cent.[54] This would of course be levied on imported goods as countervailing duties. Special excise duties at high rates would need to have their own corresponding countervailing duties. But for the rest there should be a single countervailing rate, which should correspond to a single rate MANVAT and the average of States' single rate VATs.[55] In all about 25 per cent of the cif cost of imports would be charged at the frontier (probably equal to about 3.75 per cent of GDP) assuming that very few exempt goods (unprocessed food only) are imported. But only 10 per cent of this is protective for VAT registered producers and dealers since the other 15 per cent corresponds to similar taxation of domestic production. Small-scale enterprises which are VAT exempt gain the full protection of 25 per cent of their own value added.

The above calculations may be summed up roughly as follows. Using 1994/95 revised estimates as a base, a reduction of 1.4 per cent of GDP in customs revenue should be partly offset by a rise in direct taxation of 1 per cent. This leaves a rise of only 0.4 per cent of GDP in domestic indirect taxation to leave total tax revenue unchanged. There is thus certainly no fiscal reason why tariffs should not be reduced to the uniform 10 per cent we advocate.

The above assumes that positive taxation should remain about the same with the same division between the Centre and the States. But we have seen that the central fiscal deficit needs to be reduced by about 1.9 per cent of GDP. This could be achieved by cutting the explicit central subsidies. Increases in

---

[54]   It is to be noted that revenue neutral VAT rates for the Centre and States are estimated to be 8.1 and 7.5 per cent respectively, assuming taxation of services, and no exemptions except for primary agricultural commodities and those below a threshold of Rs 5 lakhs. The usual special excise duties are also assumed to be in force. (See NIPFP, 1994, table 8.1.)

[55]   NIPFP initially recommends four rates 5, 10, 15, and 20 per cent for MANVAT. We would hope this could be unified initially at about 12 per cent, reducing to 10 per cent or less.

non-tax revenue by eliminating public enterprise losses; reductions in implicit subsidies to industry, transport, and communications; and greater economy in general government by reducing excess employment and limiting rises in real pay, should yield large economies, permitting greater expenditure on social services and investment in infrastructure. Some reduction in States' deficits is also required. In their case large savings can also be made by reducing subsidies, and by greater economy in administration, this in turn permitting more expenditure on social services and investment.

Finally we turn to the economic and distributional consequences of the trade and fiscal reforms proposed. Prices ideally reflect the true costs and benefits of different products and activities, and economic efficiency requires this. There is no doubt that the Indian trade and fiscal systems have been a major cause of divergences from this ideal, that is of distortions, and hence economic inefficiency. But there are many other sources of distortion, including much industrial and labour legislation, and the many controls that remain despite three years of liberalization. There must be reform in these areas, which are discussed in Chapter 5, if great benefits from the fiscal and trade reforms are to materialize. We are confident that almost all Indians will gain in the end from the whole reform process.

But every reform has distributional consequences. Even if the vast majority will eventually gain, there will always be losers who never gain if only because they die too soon. And in the short and medium run, there will be many losers who fear they may never gain—even if they will. Many of the losses and gains will be quite small: and we should not worry about some of the losers because they are rich enough to be ignored. All we should do is to try to identify significant losses among the very poor, and look for ways to compensate them. We need not warn politicians of other less deserving potential losers who may be able to mount opposition to the reforms.

On the industrial front, much restructuring of Indian industry is surely required. That this should not cause much short-term loss of output and employment is the reason why the government rightly believed that several years should be allowed before the full competitive thrust of near-free trade was felt. In addition, a National Renewal Fund was created in 1992 for the compensation and retraining of workers affected by industrial restructuring. But the major redistributional effects will be felt in agriculture and as a consequence of freeing trade in agricultural products. There will be some restructuring as production of oil seeds and, probably, sugar cane and a few other crops is cut back in favour of cereals, cotton, and some other agricultural exports. But the major distributional effect will come as a result of price rises of rice and wheat. Some compensation for the sufferers will be required. This is fully discussed in Chapter 6.

Appendix

It is accepted that the Centre should be able to give grants to the States in such a way as to reduce the disparity in their abilities to provide social and economic services. It has been held by Burgess, Howes, and Stern (1993) and NIPFP (1994) that a fiscal system under which the Centre would give up all domestic indirect taxation except for a few 'luxury' excises, and under which there would be no revenue sharing, would leave the Centre with insufficient revenue to fill its essential redistributive role. We suggest that this fear is groundless. If we are correct this is important because a solution of the federal fiscal problem under which the States would have complete fiscal autonomy, relieved only by current grants for the very poor States, has many advantages.

Table 3.1 shows the revenue as a percentage of GDP accruing to the Centre and the States from various taxes, both before and after tax sharing, for the year 1993/94 (revised estimates): it is an updated and amended version of table 4 in Burgess, Howes, and Stern (1993). It further shows a plausible scenario after a reform in which the Centre gives up to the States all domestic indirect taxation, except for a few 'luxury' excises, and in which there is no tax sharing.

This scenario retains the same total taxation and virtually the same level of central grants to the States as in 1993/94. It includes a raising of direct taxation from 2.86 per cent of GDP to 4.00 per cent. This is surely both desirable and achievable. It also includes the fall in customs duty to 1.5 per cent of GDP which we have advocated in the text. The only item which may be questionable is the retention by the Centre of 1.8 per cent of GDP as special excises on luxury or 'demerit' commodities. At present total indirect taxes on petroleum products for transport, tobacco, alcohol, and cars come to just about the required 1.8 per cent of GDP. The States would have to concede all taxation of alcohol, gasoline, and diesel oil, to the Centre. That might not be too high a price for the greatly increased autonomy which such a reform would give to the States.

Table 3.1 Tax Revenues as a percentage of GDP in 1993/94 (revised estimates)

	Combined Centre and States	Before sharing		After sharing		After reform—no sharing		
		Centre	States	Centre	States	Combined	Centre	States
Total	15.51	9.76	5.75	6.93	8.58	15.51	7.00	8.51
Direct	2.86	2.70	0.16	1.71	1.15	4.00	3.60	0.40
Personal	1.52	1.36	0.16	0.37	1.15	2.00	1.60	0.40
Corporation	1.34	1.34	0.00	1.34	0.00	2.00	2.00	0.00
Customs	2.86	2.86	0.00	2.86	0.00	1.50	1.50	0.00
Domestic indirect	9.76	4.20	5.59	2.36	7.43	10.01	1.90	8.11
Union excise	4.04	4.04	0.00	2.20	1.84	1.80	1.80	0.00
State excise	0.86	0.03	0.83	0.03	0.83	0.00	0.00	0.00
Sales/VAT	3.51	0.09	3.43	0.09	3.43	6.71	0.00	6.71
Other	1.37	0.05	1.33	0.05	1.33	1.50	0.10	1.40
Grants				−2.12	2.12		−2.19	2.19
Total with grants				4.81	10.70		4.81	10.70

4

Financial Sector Reform

4.1. Introduction

In assessing India's financial sector reform, we bear in mind both recent developments in the theory of finance and the experiences of financial liberalization in other countries. In the early 1970s, the writings of Mckinnon and Shaw challenged the wisdom of government intervention in the financial sector.[1] They argued that 'financial repression'—high reserve requirements, interest rate controls, and direction of credit to favoured sectors—is harmful for resource mobilization and resource allocation. For example, artificially low interest rates discourage savings and distort the choice of investment projects. Financial liberalization, it was suggested, would eliminate these distortions and therefore increase efficiency and growth.

This view has been subject to challenge in recent years. The theoretical challenge has come mainly from the 'economics of information' which has emphasized market failures arising from asymmetric information. It has been argued that adverse selection and moral hazard permeate unregulated financial markets and lead to major inefficiencies in the allocation of resources.[2] It is further claimed that government intervention in credit markets can offset these distortions. Experiences of financial liberalization have also dented the optimism underlying the Mckinnon–Shaw view. In some countries, financial

---

[1] Mckinnon (1973) and Shaw (1973).
[2] For example, see Stiglitz (1993). Mckinnon too has shifted his position: see Mckinnon (1989, 1991).

liberalization has exacerbated macroeconomic imbalances and created financial distress, at least for a while.

Rather than embarking on an extended examination of these considerations drawn from theory and experience, we shall discuss them selectively in the context of Indian financial sector reform.[3] Our main focus will be on the reform of the banking system which accounts for two-thirds of the assets of the formal financial sector. The rest of the financial sector is treated fairly briefly. The plan of the chapter is as follows. Section 4.2 deals with the banking sector. It begins with a brief description of the state of Indian banking *circa* 1991 and is followed by a critical examination of changes that have taken place since then and of what remains to be done. Note that in the section on 'directed credit', we go beyond the commercial banking system and appraise the overall framework of lending to agriculture and small-scale industry. Section 4.3 is concerned with the non-bank financial sector, with a particular focus on capital markets. Section 4.4 is a brief discussion of external financial liberalization. Section 4.5 contains our concluding remarks.

4.2. The Banking Sector

4.2.1. The Indian Banking Scenario in 1991[4]

Government intervention in the banking sector had its origin in nationalist thinking. Colonial banking was perceived to be biased in favour of working-capital loans to trade and large

---

[3] Readers interested in overviews of India's financial sector and its reform may wish to consult the following papers and reports: Government of India (1991*a*), Government of India (1993*a*), Nayak (1993), Khatkhate (1993), Mistry (1995), Rangarajan (1994*a*), Rangarajan (1994*b*), Sengupta (1994), World Bank (1995*b*). For inter-country experience, reference may be made to Cho and Khatkhate (1989) and Caprio, Atiyas, and Hanson (1994).

[4] For a critical evaluation of Indian banking prior to the reforms, see Reserve Bank of India (1985), Joshi and Little (1994) and the works cited in n. 3 above.

capitalist enterprises, and against rural areas and 'the common man'. This legacy combined with socialist ideology culminated in the nationalization of all the large banks in 1969. The nationalized banks were explicitly set quantitative targets to expand their network in rural areas and to direct credit to priority sectors. Over time, they also became a major source of lending to the government and thus of financing fiscal deficits.

Considering the post-independence history of Indian banking, the surprising thing is not the evident weaknesses of Indian banking but the fact that there were nevertheless some notable achievements. There was a dramatic expansion of banks throughout the country and while many bank branches were unprofitable, they did play a positive role in increasing financial savings. The worst elements of 'financial repression' were avoided, largely because inflation remained reasonably low and real interest rates were only mildly negative. But while perform-ance was satisfactory in resource mobilization, it was very unsatisfactory as regards resource allocation. The low produc-tivity of investment in India has many causes, but inefficient credit allocation by the banking sector was undoubtedly one of them.

By 1991, the country had erected an unprofitable, inefficient, and financially unsound banking sector. A few facts will suffice. The profitability of Indian banks was extremely low in spite of the rapid growth of deposits. The average return on assets in the second half of the 1980s was about 0.15 per cent, an extraordinarily low figure by world standards. Return on equity was higher (about 9.5 per cent) but that was simply a reflection of the low capitalization of Indian banks. Capital and reserves averaged about 1.5 per cent of assets, compared to 4–6 per cent in other Asian countries. The true picture was even worse because these figures were not based on applying the correct income recognition and provisioning criteria.[5] Not only were

---

[5] 'Income recognition' rules specify what counts as 'income'. For example, income on a loan may be defined as interest actually paid or as interest that is due, whether or not it is paid. Obviously, it can make a big difference to

the banks financially unsound but, by universal agreement, they also provided an abysmal quality of service.

What led up to this state of affairs? The following list contains some external causes, i.e. those pertaining to the regulatory environment in which the banks functioned, and some internal causes, i.e. those pertaining to shortcomings of internal organization. The distinction is convenient, albeit superficial, because most of the internal shortcomings were a perfectly natural response to the institutional and regulatory environment.

- *Pre-emption of bank resources.* Indian banks are obliged to satisfy two reserve ratios: the cash reserve ratio (CRR) and the statutory liquidity ratio (SLR). The CRR requires banks to hold part of their deposits in the form of cash balances with the RBI. In the 1960s and 70s, the CRR was around 5 per cent but since then there have been steep increases. In early 1991, the CRR stood at its legal upper limit of 15 per cent. The SLR stipulates the proportion of deposits that banks must hold in the form of government and other approved securities. The trend in the SLR was also firmly upward. By law, the upper limit of the SLR is 40 per cent. Starting from 25 per cent in 1970, it was increased over time to its 1991 level of 38.5 per cent. Both the impounded cash balances and the government securities carried considerably lower interest rates than were available on commercial advances. Thus more than 50 per cent of deposits had to be invested in investments that barely covered the cost of funds.[6]

---

declared profits which of the two definitions is adopted. A 'provision' is money set aside out of current profits to cover the possibility of partial or total non-recovery of a loan. Provisioning rules specify what proportion of a loan has to be provided for, depending on how long the asset has been 'non-performing', i.e. how long interest payments have been in arrears.

[6] In fact pre-emptions at the margin were often higher since the government stipulated marginal CRR requirements in addition to the average. In 1991, there was an incremental CRR of 10 per cent in addition to the average CRR of

- *Directed credit.* The banks were also required to direct a sizeable part of their lending to certain 'priority' sectors at concessional rates of interest. After nationalization, the priority sector target was 33 per cent of advances, but it was later raised to 40 per cent. In addition, there were sub-targets for agriculture, small farmers and 'the weaker sections of society'.

- *Administered interest rates.* Virtually all interest rates offered and charged by banks (and other financial institutions) were stipulated by the government.

- *Portfolio quality.* The quality of the banks' loan portfolio deteriorated steadily due to a combination of factors. (*a*) Accounting rules for income recognition and provisioning were very soft. For example, income was booked on an 'accrual' rather than a cash basis; in other words, even if no interest was actually paid on a loan, it was shown as 'income'. (*b*) The focus on quantitative targets for credit allocation diverted the energies of the banks away from screening and monitoring of borrowers and debt recovery. (*c*) The credit market was subject to political influence. The clout of influential borrowers and the periodic loan-waiver schemes encouraged a culture of non-repayment. (*d*) The procedures of the legal system made loan recovery extremely difficult. These factors took a heavy toll. The application of new accounting criteria revealed that on average 24 per cent of the advances of public sector banks were non-performing in 1991.

- *Lax regulation and supervision.* The supervisory system was lax (though ironically the degree of interference was very high). This was partly because of the absence of clear, internationally comparable accounting norms for banks, so the essential elements of financial discipline were missing.

15 per cent. Since the SLR was 38.5 per cent, a staggering 63.5 per cent of bank deposits were compulsorily captured by the RBI and the government.

The banks too did not have the incentive to set up their own internal control systems.

- *Low internal and organizational efficiency.* The low profitability of Indian banks was the result not only of the restrictions on their income-earning opportunities but also of their own high operating costs. Contributory factors included rampant overmanning, bad industrial relations, and inadequate incentives for managerial competence.

- *Lack of competition.* There is a large number of banks in India but there has been little competition between them. The public sector banks had no incentive to compete. Competition was inhibited by regulated interest rates and by the activities of the Indian Banks Association. Non-price competition was not particularly active either. It was difficult for customers to shift from one bank to another. Lending to large borrowers was subject to consortium arrangements in which banks shared in inflexible proportions.

- *Political interference.* As with any system of controls, bank credit was subject to political manipulation. The consequence was a further erosion of the banks' ability to judge credit-worthiness or manage portfolio risks.

The result of the above factors was a banking system that was virtually bankrupt and ill-suited to the task of allocating credit or performing ordinary banking functions efficiently.

Banking sector reform (and reform of the financial sector more generally) were regarded from the very beginning as priority areas by the Rao government. Some thinking had already been done by the Chakravarty Committee, but that was now somewhat out of date.[7] A new Committee on the Financial System under the chairmanship of M. Narasimham was appointed in August 1991 and delivered its report within three

---

[7]   See Reserve Bank of India (1985).

months.[8]   This was a landmark document and strongly influenced government thinking and action.

4.2.2. Prudential Regulation and Supervision

It is generally accepted that financial markets need supervision not merely to prevent criminal fraud but to prevent financial panic. It is in the nature of a fractional reserve banking system that it is subject to the danger of large-scale withdrawal of deposits. A run on an individual bank may be rationally or irrationally based, but in either case it can spread to healthy banks and cause major disruptions in the payments system. Governments have responded to this both by setting up explicit deposit insurance schemes and by establishing lender of last resort facilities (which can be thought of as implicit deposit insurance).   These devices have reduced significantly the emergence and spread of bank runs, but like any insurance scheme they are subject to the problem of moral hazard. They reduce the care with which depositors monitor the behaviour of banks and the care that banks exercise in making loans.

Bank supervision and regulation can be seen as an answer to the moral hazard problem.[9]   What is the scope of desirable supervision and regulation? Controls on interest rates and credit allocation and micro-monitoring of bank decisions are, in general, undesirable. The current international consensus favours imposing minimum capital requirements. The underlying idea is simple: not only is adequate capital a cushion against unforeseen losses but banks are less likely to take risks the greater the loss that shareholders might suffer. But capital adequacy

---

[8]   See Government of India (1991a).

[9]   It would be wrong to conclude that the need for supervision would disappear in the absence of deposit insurance. Both managers and owners of banks in trouble have an incentive to 'gamble for resurrection' at the expense of depositors. Depositors are typically far too dispersed and uninformed to monitor effectively. But deposit insurance clearly exacerbates the problem.

requirements are not enough because bank managers may not act in the interest of shareholders. (Ironically, this may be particularly true in a nationalized banking system where there is a single shareholder with 'deep pockets'!) It is therefore generally agreed that banks must also be subject to rules concerning income recognition, provisioning, and portfolio concentration.[10] Audit and disclosure requirements are also necessary so that the accounts of banks are transparent to outsiders. It is clearly important that bank supervisors should be independent and possess adequate enforcement powers. Of course, they cannot check everything and most of the work has to be done by the internal control systems of the banks themselves. So, an important part of improving the regulatory system consists of putting in place satisfactory internal procedures in banks as regards accounting and lending.

Strengthening supervisory systems is especially important in the process of financial liberalization. In this context, the danger is that the removal of restrictions, the entry of new players and the possible weakening of bank portfolios in the short run can lead to a competitive scramble for deposits and loans in which excessive risks may be taken, given the existence of deposit insurance and/or lender of last resort facilities. This has been the experience in several liberalizing countries, especially in Latin America. In retrospect, lack of adequate regulation clearly played a major role in causing their financial crises. It is also worth noting that public support for liberalization can be severely dented if there is inadequate supervision. An example is the scam in India in 1992 in which illegal bank advances to stockbrokers were used to fund stock market purchases that led to a stock market bubble which eventually collapsed. Losses arising from these irregularities were estimated at Rs 5,000 crores. No doubt banks were tempted to undertake these illegal activities because of various government restrictions which

---

[10]   Caprio and Summers (1993) argue that in addition there should be restricted entry into banking. This would encourage banks to avoid risky behaviour because they have a franchise value to protect.

severely reduced their profits. But weak supervision and enforcement of regulations also played their part. The scam spoiled the image of the reform programme for some length of time.

It has been clearly recognized in the Indian reform programme, following the report of the Narasimham Committee, that (*a*) banking supervision had to be strengthened and (*b*) its character required drastic change, away from intrusive micro-intervention over credit decisions towards prudential regulation. To this end, the RBI issued guidelines in April 1992 for income recognition, asset classification and provisioning, and adopted the Basle Accord capital adequacy standards. These norms began to be applied in the accounts of the year ending 31 March 1993, but they reached their full force on 31 March 1995 (in the case of capital adequacy on 31 March 1996). Banks can no longer treat as income the putative 'income' from non-performing loans, the latter being defined as a credit facility in respect of which interest has remained unpaid for 180 days. Non-performing assets are classified as sub-standard, doubtful, and lost, depending on how long they have been non-performing—up to two years, more than two years, or certified as 'lost' by external auditors. Provisioning is on the basis of 10 per cent for sub-standard loans, 20–50 per cent for doubtful loans and 100 per cent for loss loans. As for capital adequacy, banks were expected to reach a 4 per cent capital to risk–assets ratio by 31 March 1993 and 8 per cent by 31 March 1996.

In terms of organizational structure, the government's response has been to constitute a supervisory authority, the Board of Financial Supervision (BFS), functioning within the RBI. In our opinion, it would have been better to set up a completely separate institution. Such an institution would have had the advantage of starting from scratch in terms of staffing, recruitment, and ethos. It would have had a better chance of being independent and not crossing wires with the RBI's monetary policy functions.

Inadequate bank regulation has been the source of many dramatic failures (such as the collapse of BCCI and Barings) even in the advanced countries. An important lesson of these episodes is that designing early warning systems is as necessary as *ex post* monitoring. India has a long way to go in devising appropriate structures. The RBI has recognized this and put in motion a programme to strengthen its monitoring techniques. Previously, the RBI's emphasis was on on-site inspection, but it had inadequate off-site backup because the information system was archaic. It is now planned to streamline and automate the returns made by the banks to the RBI, so that off-site analysis can be deployed to support on-site monitoring. The supervisory operation will also have to become more sophisticated. Liberalization will increase the complexity of the financial environment and the use of instruments such as swaps, forwards, and options.[11] It is clear that both the RBI and the banks have to make a massive effort in terms of training and improvement of skills. Technical assistance will have to be sought from foreign central banks and financial institutions.

4.2.3. Rehabilitation of Public Sector Banks[12]

Major alternatives and the approach of the government. We saw above that by 1991 the banking system had become

---

[11] It is now widely recognized that the Basle Accord capital adequacy standards are an inadequate protection in the new environment in which market risk (the risk of loss due to unexpected market price and interest rate developments) is even more important than credit risk (the risk that a counterparty may default on its position). The Basle Committee is currently exploring setting up more complex standards which mesh with the banks' own risk-management systems.

[12] For facts on and analysis of this topic, in general, and in the Indian context, see Khatkhate (1993), Tarapore (1993), Bery (1992), Bery (1993), Sheng (1991), Government of India (1993a), R. B. I. *Annual Reports* (various years), R. B. I. *Trend and Progress of Banking in India* (various years), and Indian Banks Association (various years).

extremely fragile as a result of the large overhang of non-performing assets (NPA). Under proper accounting procedures, the latter result in lower income, higher provisions, lower net profits, and erosion of capital and net worth.[13] The new norms introduced in 1992 exposed the true state of the banking system. The highlights, relating to the public sector banks in 1992/93, were as follows: (i) NPA amounted to 24 per cent of the total loan portfolio[14] albeit with significant variation among banks. In the relatively stronger banks, this ratio was around 8–10 per cent; in the weaker banks, it was 25–40 per cent. (ii) Only 15 out of 28 public sector banks declared a net profit; 13 banks made overall losses of which eight made operating losses. The loss-making banks constituted one-third of the public sector banking system measured by size of deposits and assets. (iii) Public sector banks made an aggregate loss of about Rs 3,500 crores. The net profit to assets ratio of public sector banks varied between minus 6.8 per cent and plus 0.5 per cent. (iv) Half of the public sector banks had negative net worth.

Clearly, a clean-up operation was an urgent priority. In theory, many banks could have been liquidated; in practice, this was obviously not an option. Liquidation involves allocating the loss from bank insolvency to shareholders and depositors. In India's nationalized banks, the government was the sole owner; and imposing losses on depositors was clearly impossible if the integrity of the payments system was to be preserved. Even if selling off banks to private owners could be contemplated politically, it clearly required as a precondition the restoration of the net worth of banks. It was thus natural that rescuing the banks became a charge on the budget, i.e. on present and future taxpayers.

---

[13]   The reader should note the following definitions:
        operating profits = income − expenditure
        net profits   = operating profits − provisions
        capital = equity + reserves + net profits.
[14]   This was an underestimate because the application of the norms was not yet fully phased in.

It was recognized that a viable rescue required both a 'stock' and a 'flow' solution. Without fundamental changes to improve the future profitability of banks, the restoration of net worth would clearly be only a temporary palliative. But without a rapid restoration of net worth, it would be a Sisyphean task to return the banking system to health purely on the basis of measures to improve profitability. Restoration of net worth can be carried out in one of two principal ways. The recapitalization route involves a direct capital infusion to the banks from the budget, leaving non-performing assets on their books. Another alternative that has been adopted in some countries is to carve out the bad assets from the banks and place them with a tailor-made institution dedicated to recovery. The Narasimham Committee favoured setting up such an institution, which they dubbed the Asset Reconstruction Fund (ARF), as an accompaniment to recapitalization. The scheme may involve the banks selling the non-performing assets to the new institution at a discount or at book value. If they are sold at a discount, the problem of banks' negative net worth remains; if they are sold at book value, net worth is restored but it adds to the cost of establishing the new institution. The initial cost to the government is the same to a first approximation in all these variants; the choice essentially revolves round which scheme maximizes the chances of recovery of bad loans. The case for an ARF is that removing contaminated assets from the banks' books enables bank managers to concentrate on the future and to delegate the problem of recovery to specialists. The argument against an ARF is that the process of transfer of the bad assets to another institution destroys the 'information capital' that is critically important for recovery—banks know their clients much better than a new institution is likely to.

Faced with the above alternatives, the government chose the route of recapitalization from the budget. This involved the danger that government help may impair the incentives of the banks to undertake restructuring; the government sought to overcome this by making capital injections conditional upon performance agreements. Generalized asset exchange with an ARF was rejected. It was felt that the banks should not be let off the hook too lightly and moreover that the large expanse of the country would create difficulties for the reach of a new institution. It was recognized, however, that the banks needed legal support in their recovery efforts; this was to be provided by special recovery tribunals which could dispose of cases expeditiously.

The Narasimham Committee also proposed that during the process of rescue, the banking system should be rationalized in a top-down manner into a four-tier system comprising three to four large international money-centre banks; eight to ten national clearing banks performing universal banking functions; a number of regional banks; and a rural banking network. The government did not favour this strategy, preferring, rightly in our view, to enable most banks to achieve a reasonable starting point and then leaving it to the market to pick winners. A problem with this strategy concerned the four or five weakest public sector banks which were making large operating losses. It was decided that these would be dealt with on a case by case basis.

Bank restitution: a progress report. By 1995 the banking system was looking much healthier. The recapitalization process has proceeded fairly smoothly. Initial estimates had put the cost of the operation at Rs 18,000 crores. So far, the government has put in or pledged about Rs 12,500 crores (Rs 700 crores in 1992/93, Rs 5,700 crores in 1993/94, Rs 5,300 crores in 1994/95, and Rs 800 crores allocated in the budget of 1995/96). At the end of March 1995, 13 banks had achieved a capital adequacy ratio of at least 8 per cent, another 11 between 4 per cent and 8 per cent; that leaves three banks below 4 per cent. It appears that the government is hoping to limit its capital contribution below the original estimate. It is encouraging the stronger banks to tap the capital market and some have already done so successfully.[15] But the weaker banks will not find this possible, so the scale of the government's eventual contribution is still an open question.[16]

In 1993/94, banks made an overall net loss of Rs 4,700 crores, bigger than in 1992/93, but this reflected the full phasing-in of the new accounting norms. In 1994/95, there has been a significant improvement and the aggregate net profit is about Rs 1,100 crores. More significantly, only three banks have made an overall net loss and only one bank shows an operating loss. The factors that contributed to this turnaround were: (*a*) lower provisions than in the previous two years; (*b*) improved spreads—the cost of funds fell in the earlier part of the year due to the increased liquidity generated by foreign inflows; while lending rates both to the government and the private sector rose sharply in the second half as the economic boom gathered momentum; (*c*) somewhat better recovery on outstanding loans. The critical question is whether this improved performance represents a durable and fundamental change. We remain to be persuaded. The macroeconomic situation in 1994/95 has been exceptionally favourable from the viewpoint of the banks.[17] The effect of marking government securities to market is yet to be absorbed. Even more important, there is as yet no convincing evidence of cost-cutting (operating costs as a proportion of working funds did not fall in 1994/95) or of a substantial reduction in NPA. The overall level of NPA was in the region

---

[15] Legislation has been enacted to enable dilution of government ownership: see below. Ironically, in tapping capital markets, some banks have faced the difficulty that infusion of government funds has made their equity base over-sized in relation to earnings. Some recent infusions have therefore taken the form of Tier II capital.

[16] It should be noted that the original estimate of the government's capital contribution included compensation of the banks for the losses they would suffer on 'marking to market' their holdings of government securities. ('Marking to market' involves valuing the securities at market prices rather than at par.) So far, the government has not asked banks to mark to market more than 40 per cent of government securities.

[17] 1995/96 is likely to be a much more testing year for banks than 1994/95.

of 20 per cent in March 1995.[18] This is still far too high; in an efficient banking system, it should be less than 5 per cent, ideally 1–2 per cent. There is as yet insufficient evidence of reduction in incremental NPA, and of successful recovery since 1992, to conclude that credit management has decisively improved.

Recovery was to be facilitated by special tribunals. The Recovery of Debts Act was passed in 1993 and tribunals were set up in several major cities. But they have not functioned because their constitutionality has been challenged in both the Delhi and the Madras High Courts. Hopefully, some way will be found to strengthen the legal recovery process. If the banks are not able to speed up recovery, NPAs will remain on the banks' books and make it difficult to access the capital market. There may be life in the ARF yet!

The NPA problem is also intimately connected with the issue of lending to sick industries. At the last count (March 1993), total bank credit locked up in sick units was Rs 13,100 crores, constituting 9 per cent of total bank credit and 16 per cent of bank credit to industry. Only a quarter of this represents lending to small-scale industries which are part of banks' directed credit requirements. The rest is not formally directed but is often the product of arm-twisting of banks (sometimes by the BIFR) and politicized lending. The process of winding up and restructuring of sick companies is painfully slow and is hampered by cumbrous procedures and by counter-productive labour and land laws (see Chapter 5). Reform is urgently necessary not only to deal with the stock of bad debt but to prevent the NPA problem from resurfacing in future. Further discussion of this issue is postponed to Chapter 5; here we only draw attention to the intimate connection between banking reform and reform of the real economy.

[18] See Tarapore (1995). Eleven banks had NPA above 20 per cent in March 1995.

The weakest banks still remain a serious problem. One of them, the New Bank of India has been merged with a stronger bank. But that still leaves two or three very difficult cases. They suffer from manifold problems: surplus manpower, high NPA, low productivity per employee, and a high incidence of fraud. The RBI has received reports on them from 'turnaround experts' but the revival strategies involve a wage freeze and redundancies. The difficulty is that they are basically union-run banks. They therefore encapsulate all the difficulties of an exit policy (discussed further in Chapter 5). The courage and political skill of the government will be severely tested in finding a satisfactory solution to their problems.

In sum, there has undoubtedly been a good beginning in the restitution of banks. The financial health of banks has improved faster than many observers had feared and there have been some favourable attitudinal changes as regards asset management and credit allocation. But it is too early to say that there has been a fundamental improvement. Spreads in banking are still very high and add substantially to the cost of capital. There is still a long way to go in achieving an efficient banking system.

The following four sections examine progress in various aspects of deregulation of the banking sector.

4.2.4. Pre-emption of Bank Resources

High reserve ratios were a central feature of government intervention in India's banking sector. The system was driven by the object of capturing bank deposits for government use. While pre-emption of bank deposits at below-market rates reduced the cost of government borrowing, it was directly responsible for low profitability and high spreads in the banking system. Alteration of these arrangements was thus an urgent priority, as recognized by the Narasimham Committee which recommended both a reduction in the SLR to 25 per cent by 1996 and a progressive but unspecified reduction in the CRR.[19]

The government has acted decisively as regards reducing the SLR. By March 1995, the incremental SLR was 25 per cent and the average SLR was down to 29.5 per cent (compared to 38.5 per cent in 1991).[20] This reduction was achieved smoothly because it went in tandem with paying market rates on central government debt (see below). A recognized problem with such a move is the effect of higher interest rates on the fiscal deficit. But until the latter half of 1994/95, even this difficulty was not too serious. Industrial demand for credit was weak during the recession and banks were flush with funds as a result of foreign capital inflows. Demand for government securities was therefore high without any element of compulsion. Recently, due to industrial recovery and slowing down of inflows, interest rates have risen sharply (see Chapter 2). Reduction of the SLR is no longer painless and cannot be effected without increased pressure on the budget. This underscores the importance of medium-run fiscal adjustment. (For further discussion of this point, see Section 4.2.5 below.)

The RBI has taken a different attitude to the CRR and has been in no hurry to reduce it consistently. In 1991, the CRR was 15 per cent, with an incremental 10 per cent on top. By mid-1993, it had been reduced to 14 per cent and the increment abolished. But it was raised again to 15 per cent in 1994 in order to sterilize foreign capital inflows.[21] We find this perfectly acceptable. The CRR is a distortionary tax on the banking system but it is also an instrument of monetary policy proper. Such is the importance of monetary control that it may be necessary to pay some price in terms of efficiency to achieve it. Progressive

---

[19]   In a discussion paper issued in June 1993, the Ministry of Finance included in a list of 'measures that need to be taken over the next three years' a phased reduction in the CRR to 10 per cent. See Government of India (1993*b*).
[20]   See Reserve Bank of India, *Annual Report*, 1994/95.
[21]   At the time of writing (end of 1995), it has been lowered to 14 per cent in response to the credit crunch in the current financial year.

reduction in the CRR may have to be postponed until the government securities market has achieved sufficient depth to enable open market operations to become the prime instrument of monetary policy.

4.2.5. Deregulation of Interest Rates

We begin with some theory. Interest rate control is a cardinal feature of government intervention in financial markets, and financial liberalization is motivated by the belief that this control reduces both the quantity and the quality of investment. However, arguments have been recently advanced, based on the economics of information, that appear to support the case for interest rate controls. We start, therefore, with our view of this controversy.

The basic point made is that in the presence of asymmetric information, competitive credit markets may not clear, equilibria being characterized by credit rationing.[22] The reason is that the interest rate plays a dual role: it affects the excess demand for loans but it also affects the average quality of a lender's loan portfolio. As the interest rate rises, the quality of the portfolio worsens because (*a*) sound borrowers are discouraged relative to unsound borrowers (the adverse selection effect) and (*b*) all borrowers have an incentive to undertake riskier projects (the moral hazard effect).[23] Hence, a divergence can arise between the interest rate that clears the credit market and the interest rate that maximizes the lender's return. If the latter is less than the former, there will be credit rationing and some borrowers (including some good borrowers) will not receive loans.

So far there is no dispute. But does this constitute a case for administered control of interest rates? The argument so far has

[22]   Stiglitz and Weiss (1981).
[23]   This assumes (realistically) that enforcement and foreclosure are costly and that there are difficulties in screening borrowers and monitoring their actions.

shown that in the presence of asymmetric information, the free market outcome is inefficient relative to a situation where the information constraint is absent. But the operational question is whether it is possible to improve the situation. Prima facie, this seems very doubtful since the government usually faces the same or worse constraint.[24] Moreover, the government clearly can worsen the situation by imposing an interest rate ceiling lower than the loan rationing equilibrium.

The credit-rationing literature can, however, be employed to construct a case for interest rate control in the following way.[25] The above argument presupposed that moral hazard applies to borrowers but not to lenders. But this assumption may not hold in the case of banks if there is free deposit insurance or government assurance of bailout (widely prevalent in modern economies) and if, in addition, prudential supervision and regulation are weak or absent. Banks can then become risk-lovers. If outcomes are favourable, they stand to make large profits since they do not face the costs imposed by provisioning and capital requirements or high deposit insurance premia; if outcomes are unfavourable, they can walk away from the losses as these are borne by the monetary authority. (This is true *a fortiori* if there is implicit protection of *both* deposits and equity. But the danger exists even if bank owners bear their share of the losses. Indeed, in a nationalized banking system, equity losses are borne by the state and may not constrain the behaviour of managers.) These dangers are exacerbated during liberalization since banks have increased freedom with regard to interest rates and the direction of credit, and all the more so if the

---

[24] Greenwald and Stiglitz (1986) have shown that in the presence of asymmetric information the free market equilibrium is not 'constrained Pareto efficient'. But the magnitude and even the direction of optimum government intervention—whether to have an interest-rate tax or subsidy—is ambiguous and depends on factors such as the relationship between the mean and variance of projects which are impossible to identify (see DeMeza and Webb, 1987). It would be idle to pretend that this theory provides any useful guideline for intervention.

[25] Mckinnon (1989).

macroeconomic environment is unstable and the variance of project outcomes is higher than in more stable times. In such circumstances, temporary imposition of ceilings on deposit and loan interest rates may well be desirable.

It should be noted that the above is not an argument for interest rate control in a 'long run' equilibrium but a sequencing argument about the order of liberalization, particularly in the context of macroeconomic instability. A particular worry along these lines is that real interest rates may rise excessively during financial liberalization, leading to acute difficulties for companies in the real sector, and eventually distress and even collapse of financial institutions. This phenomenon has been observed in several Latin American liberalizations. But it was the product not only of bankers' moral hazard in the presence of weak regulation but also of high inflationary expectations, exchange risk, oligopolistic financial markets, and wrong sequencing as regards opening of the capital account. One would have to be careful in drawing lessons for India. A material difference is introduced by the fact that India is not a high-inflation country in the Latin American sense. Nor does India suffer from the close ownership links between banks and firms as was the case in, for instance, Chile. Even so, India's regulatory apparatus is currently in its infancy. So the moral hazard/weak regulation argument for interest rate ceilings is not devoid of relevance.

Interest rates in India. Until the mid-1980s, interest rates in India were almost entirely administered and their structure was heavily influenced by the requirements of financing fiscal deficits and making bank credit available to favoured activities at concessional rates. The effect of these twin compulsions was that deposit rates had to be kept low and general lending rates had to be kept high. Deposit rates ruled around zero in real terms; extreme financial repression was thus avoided. But interest rates did not perform any significant allocative function on the asset side of banks' balance sheets. Credit was mostly allocated by non-price means, a system which naturally resulted in inefficiency and corruption.

These weaknesses of the financial system were highlighted by the report of the Chakravarty Committee in 1985. Since then, there have been liberalizing moves in line with the Committee's recommendations. The Committee correctly identified the arrangements for government borrowing as the key to reforming the system. It recommended both a reduction in the government's recourse to compulsory borrowing and an improvement in the terms offered. The former recommendation was not adopted until 1992, as we saw above. The latter recommendation has been gradually implemented since the mid-1980s. Coupon rates on government bonds were increased (for example the rate on government bonds of 20 years maturity went up from 9.5 per cent in 1984/85 to 11.5 per cent in 1989/90). Some changes were also instituted in the treasury bill (TB) market. A 182-day TB, sold by auction and non-rediscountable with the RBI, was introduced in 1986 alongside the traditional tap TB which yielded a fixed 4.6 per cent. Rates in the call money market were freed in 1989.

Interest rate deregulation has been much faster since 1991 though not in the first year which was taken up with stabilization.[26] The market for government paper has seen substantial changes. A 364-day TB replaced the 182-day TB in April 1992; like its predecessor it was sold by auction and was not rediscountable with the Reserve Bank. In January 1993, a 91-day TB, sold by auction, was introduced. Since then, about 30 per cent of the government's TB sales have been auctioned, the remaining 70 per cent representing *ad hoc* and tap bills eligible for rediscount at the fixed rate 4.6 per cent. The changes in the market for dated securities have been equally large. Since April 1992, the central government borrowing programme in dated securities has been conducted by auction with, however, an

---

[26] Information on interest rate deregulation can be found in Rangarajan (1994*a*), Government of India *Economic Survey* (various years); and Reserve Bank of India, *Annual Report* (various years).

informal cap set by the coupon on State government securities. These changes, along with the reduction in SLR pre-emptions have breathed some life into the previously moribund market in government securities.

Parallel with the changes in the market for government paper, the process of liberalization has also gone forward in commercial-bank deposit and loan rates. Prior to 1990/91, progress in the direction chalked out by the Chakravarty Committee had been very slow. As recently as 1989/90, the interest rate structure was still very complicated with 50 lending categories and a large number of stipulated interest rates depending on loan size, usage and type of borrower. Starting in April 1992, the structure has become much freer and simpler. By the end of 1993, there were only two restrictions on deposit rates: a fixed rate on savings deposits of 5 per cent and a maximum rate of 10 per cent on term deposits (defined as deposits with maturities above one and a half months). On the lending side, there was a minimum lending rate of 15 per cent for loans above Rs 2 lakhs and a concessional rate of 12 per cent for very small loans. Since then, there has been further deregulation. The lending rate for loans larger than Rs 2 lakhs has been totally freed, though two concessional rates (13.5 per cent and 12 per cent) are now in place for loans of smaller size. The cap on the deposit rate (now 12 per cent) applies only to maturities of one and a half months to two years; the deposit rate for deposits longer than two years is unrestricted.[27]

We now offer some comments on the above changes.

(i) The market determination of interest rates on government debt has been a great step forward. So has the abolition of the multitude of administered rates, including concessional rates. The latter are still present, however, and apply to a sizeable

---

[27] Towards the end of 1995, unrestricted deposit rates were around 13 per cent. Most of the restrictions on issuing certificates of deposit have also been removed. Interest rates have also been freed on company debentures and bonds issued by public sector enterprises.

proportion of bank credit. Their merits are highly questionable (see section 4.2.6 below).

(ii) Inter-country experience points to two main concerns regarding interest rate deregulation. The first is that deregulation can lead to a rise in the cost of government borrowing and consequently to destabilization of the budget. Until recently, this was not a major problem in India because unsterilized foreign capital inflows lowered interest rates despite high fiscal deficits. But the sharp rise in interest rates following the monetary tightening and slowdown in inflows in 1995/96 highlights the potential dangers. The inconsistency between tight monetary and loose fiscal policy could lead to spiralling fiscal deficits (see Chapter 2). Fiscal consolidation is now essential for the success of further interest rate liberalization. The second concern is that high interest rates consequent upon interest rate deregulation can lead to financial crises. As discussed earlier, this provides a valid ground for some interest rate regulation. Indian policy-makers have shown awareness of this point. For the first three years, there was both a cap on the deposit rate and a floor to the general lending rate.[28] This was primarily to protect banks from strong competition while their financial soundness, internal controls, and asset-liability management capabilities were still in doubt. When banks' balance sheets strengthened, the minimum lending rate was abolished but the deposit rate cap was left in place. Recently, the latter has been slightly loosened. Clearly, the authorities have moved forward with some caution.

As deposit rates are freed, the danger of deposit-rate competition leading to unsound lending and excessively high lending rates will have to be carefully monitored. The current (end of 1995) environment of liquidity shortage and rising interest rates

---

[28] Some critics argued that the RBI had got it precisely wrong and there should have been a floor to the deposit rate and a cap on the lending rate, e.g. see Khatkhate (1993). But when the criticism was made, the banking system was highly liquid and lending rates were most unlikely to spiral upwards. The worry about a cap on the deposit rate leading to lower deposit growth and disintermediation from the banking system was, however, quite legitimate.

is not favourable for full deregulation of deposit rates as this may give a further upward twist to lending rates. Excessively high lending rates could lead to a reduction in borrower net worth (particularly if the economy is already slowing down) which in turn could weaken the banking system. At this juncture, it would be wise (*a*) to put deposit rate deregulation on hold until further progress is made with fiscal adjustment and (*b*) when deposit rates are fully deregulated to keep in reserve the power to impose a ceiling on the lending rate and to use it in good time if it becomes necessary.[29]

(iii) The arrangements in the market for government paper still have various shortcomings. There is some way to go in ending the involvement of the RBI in the primary market for government debt. At present, TBs (other than tap and *ad hoc* TBs) are auctioned but the volume is not preannounced 'for fear that the government may not meet its funding target' (presumably at an acceptable price). In the market for dated securities, the quantity is preannounced but there is no published calendar (which would be highly desirable to encourage market development). Furthermore, the RBI reserves the right to participate in the auctions to absorb 'unclaimed securities' (again presumably unclaimed at an acceptable price). RBI participation was extremely limited in 1993/94: this is unsurprising as the market was flush with liquidity due to foreign capital inflows. But this hands-off stance was substantially modified in 1995 when the government had to compete more actively for funds.[30] Finally an informal ceiling on coupon rates still exists. Abolishing the ceiling involves the delicate question of marketing the debt of State governments. The worry is that if

---

[29]   Countries which have made a success of interest rate deregulation such as Korea and Malaysia have not adopted a big bang approach. They have varied the pace of deregulation in the light of macroeconomic circumstances. See Caprio, Atiyas, and Hanson (1994).

[30]   In 1995, money and credit markets were tight and interest rates rose sharply. Several issues of dated securities were bought by the RBI in order to prevent an even sharper rise in interest rates.

this debt is not placed in the classic way (effectively by the compulsion inherent in SLR obligations), there will be wide differences between the market acceptability of the bonds of different state governments.[31]

We do not believe that total withdrawal of the RBI from the primary market for government debt can be accomplished without a reduction in the huge borrowing requirement of the public sector. Some institutional strengthening will also be required. The government will have to give more attention than it has done so far to the structure of the market. An active debt market needs both depth and liquidity. Substantial quantities of securities of varying maturity should be available in a market environment in which the holdings of market participants are easily tradable. Achieving this will require a network of market-makers, dealers and brokers, preferably with a separation between those who operate in the primary and the secondary markets. Naturally, this is difficult to arrange at the present stage of development of India's debt market because of the limited number of players (banks, insurance companies, and provident funds). This issue is further discussed in Section 4.3.

4.2.6. *Directed Credit* [32]

One of the main features of state intervention in the Indian banking sector is the institution of directed credit, consisting of

---

[31] But in the long run, financial discipline in State governments would surely be furthered if individual States had to borrow in the market at interest rates which reflect their credit-worthiness.

[32] We suggest the following background reading for the issues dealt with in this chapter, in addition to the general surveys referred to in n. 3: Reserve Bank of India (1989), Hulme and Mosley (1996), Mudgil and Thorat (1996), Binswanger and Khandker (1992), Drèze (1990), Copestake (1996), Dandekar (1993), Yaron (1994), Calomiris and Himmelberg (1993), Goldar (1988), Tarapore (1994), Little, Mazumdar, and Page (1987), Seabright (1992), Rao (1994), Pulley (1989), and National Bank for Agriculture and Rural Development (1993, 1994).

arrangements whereby the end-use of a specified portion of bank lending is laid down by the government. Active steps to direct bank credit began after bank nationalization in 1969. In 1974, banks were asked to direct 33 per cent of their credit at concessional interest rates to 'priority sectors' comprising agriculture, small-scale industry, small transport operators, small business, and professional and self-employed persons. Directed credit soon received a pronounced egalitarian impetus. Banks were asked to finance various credit-based poverty alleviation programmes within the overall priority sector targets. Foremost among these was the Integrated Rural Development Programme (IRDP) which was introduced in 1980. The overall target for priority sector lending was gradually raised to reach 40 per cent of bank credit in 1985. Various sub-targets were also introduced; in particular, the share of agriculture was specified as 18 per cent of bank credit. Formally, these targets have not been altered since 1991 though there was for a time a policy of benign neglect. By March 1995, credit to agriculture and directed credit as a whole had fallen to 13 per cent and 33 per cent of bank credit respectively. This occasioned some concern and in the budget of 1995 banks were asked to contribute an amount equal to their shortfall from the 18 per cent target for agriculture to a new Rural Infrastructural Development Fund for on-lending to State governments to hasten completion of unfinished irrigation projects.

Agriculture and small-scale industry are served not only by directed credit of commercial banks but also by other institutions such as regional rural banks and co-operative banks. In this section we take a critical overview of the directed credit system broadly construed.

The object of directed credit is to alter its allocation from what it would otherwise be on the ground that banks would not direct credit in socially desirable directions. A case for intervention has been argued on both efficiency and equity grounds. A traditional reason for the provision of institutional credit in India is the presumed monopoly power of money-lenders. State provision of finance would break this monopoly and bring down the price and increase the volume of credit.[33] Another supposed justification for state intervention is that financial markets are informationally imperfect. Since lenders lack the information to screen and monitor borrowers and since poor borrowers cannot provide collateral and there are difficulties in foreclosure, lenders will tend to ration credit. This means inevitably that some worthwhile projects that should get finance will not. As discussed in the previous section, this does not constitute a valid ground for state intervention (other than in improving the legal framework for loan repayment). Ameliorative directed credit is hampered by the fact that the state faces an even more severe informational (and enforcement) constraint than informal sector lenders. Externalities of financial infrastructure and the high fixed costs incurred in setting it up have been put forward as another reason for intervention. Extending banking to rural areas would yield social benefits but may not be undertaken by banks because they cannot capture the benefits. Finally, it has been argued that the provision of cheap credit is an important means of redistributing income and wealth.

We discuss below whether directed credit in India can be justified on efficiency and equity grounds. But we preface that with an examination of the commercial profitability of directed credit operations and the financial viability of the institutions involved. This is important particularly with regard to the efficiency-oriented arguments. Whether it is breaking the monopoly power of money-lenders, or identifying promising ventures overlooked by the private sector because of information problems, or subsidizing rural networks to pay for non-recoverable private costs, the financial viability of the state institutions within a reasonable time-horizon is surely one test of their success in overcoming these market imperfections.

[33] Ironically, if money-lenders carry exploitation to the limit (i.e. if they operate a perfectly discriminating monopoly), the outcome would be no different from the 'efficient' competitive outcome.

Directed agricultural credit: financial viability. Commercial banks have met directed credit targets but at the cost of cross-subsidies and bad debts. Before 1991, the interest rate structure was enormously complicated in addition to being concessional. Since then, there has been significant rationalization but differentiation by size remains and cross-subsidies continue on a substantial scale. Currently, loans smaller than Rs 25,000 carry a stipulated interest rate of 12 per cent and loans between Rs 25,000 and Rs 2 lakhs of 13.5 per cent. Interest rates on loans larger than Rs 2 lakhs are unregulated; in the prevailing market conditions (end of 1995), prime lending rates are 16.5 per cent and most borrowers pay around 20 per cent. The maximum two-year deposit rate is 12 per cent; higher, unregulated rates are available for longer maturities. It should be noted that the average agricultural loan is well below Rs 10,000 in size and the average loan to small-scale industry and transport operators is at the lower end of the Rs 25,000–Rs 2 lakh range. The average loan to medium- and large-scale industry is larger than Rs 10 lakhs. Thus, it is evident that loans to agriculture still carry a significant subsidy especially if allowance is made for administration and overheads (higher than average for the typical small agricultural loan) and for the greater risk. The same conclusion holds for loans to small-scale industry though the subsidy is somewhat smaller.

The overdues picture with regard to commercial banks' directed credit is also worth noting. In 1992, directed credit accounted for 35 per cent of lending but 55 per cent of overdues.[34] For comparison, medium- and large-scale industry accounted for 40 per cent of lending and 29 per cent of overdues. Another indicator is the higher share of 'sick' firms in lending to small-scale as compared to large-scale industry.[35] Thus, the data show that while overdues, arrears, and non-performing

---

[34] See Khatkhate (1993).

[35] In 1990, 17 per cent of bank credit to small-scale industry was locked up in 'sick' units, compared to 12 per cent for medium and large industry. See Reserve Bank of India, *Trend and Progress of Banking in India 1992/93*.

assets are a systemic problem, the performance of directed credit is worse than that of non-directed credit. Concessional directed credit has been an important factor in vitiating the financial performance of commercial banks and raising the cost of capital to non-priority sectors.

We now turn to the performance of regional rural banks (RRBs). Regional rural banks were set up in 1976 as a result of disappointment with the progress of co-operative and commercial banks in extending credit to agriculture. Each RRB is capitalized to the tune of 65 per cent by the central and relevant State government and 35 per cent by a 'sponsor' bank. RRBs were mandated to lend solely to people below the poverty line at concessional interest rates applying to small loans, significantly below a break-even rate.[36] Their deposit rates were controlled. Their freedom of operation was severely restricted even with regard to providing incentives to borrowers to repay on time. They could survive only with 'refinance' from the National Bank for Agriculture and Rural Development (NABARD) and their sponsor commercial banks.[37] Refinance from NABARD is available at heavily subsidized rates of 6.5–8.5 per cent. In 1994, refinance from NABARD and sponsor banks was about 37 per cent of advances. Even so, 43 RRBs defaulted with respect to their payments to NABARD.[38]

The network of RRBs grew rapidly, and currently there are 196 RRBs with approximately 15,000 branches. Spread has not been matched by strength. At the beginning of 1994, 171 out of 196 banks were making losses and about three-quarters of them had negative net worth. Their overdues performance was even

[36] Hulme and Mosley (1996) have worked out that the break-even rate for RRBs would be between twice and three times their actual lending rate, allowing for administration, overheads, and default.

[37] NABARD is the apex institution in the field of agricultural credit and refinances lower-level institutions such as RRBs and co-operative banks. In its turn it receives refinance from RBI.

[38] For factual background on the financial state of RRBs and co-operative banks, see Reserve Bank of India (1989), NABARD (1993), (1994), Mudgil and Thorat (1996).

worse than that of commercial and co-operative banks: in 1992, overdues were 60 per cent of debt-service due. The basic reason for the financial collapse of the RRBs is their total lack of commercial orientation. Their administration costs are high; particularly important in this context is the fact that their employees have been given parity of wages with commercial banks. Identification of borrowers and projects is both lacking in care and highly politicized. Overdues are a pervasive problem, with wilful default playing a major role.

These facts have been known for a long time, but there has been little action. Recently, some steps have been taken to improve the financial viability of RRBs. They have been given more flexibility both in managing their funds (the restrictions regarding lending to target groups have been diluted) and in relocating loss-making branches. Since the government has not bitten the bullet of interest rate deregulation, the above change has apparently led to RRBs reducing their lending to poor farmers and increasing their lending to the government! The budgets of 1994 and 1995 also announced that 100 RRBs would be taken up for clean-up and restructuring with the government contributing its share of Rs 450 crores for the operation.[39]

At the grass-roots level, co-operative banks are still very important and account for 37 per cent of all rural advances in 1994. (Their share in short-term rural advances is considerably larger.) Unfortunately, their financial state is dismal except in a few states such as Punjab, Kerala, and Maharashtra. The low margins allowed on lending have been quite insufficient to cover the servicing of a large number of small accounts. The performance with regard to overdues is miserable. Overdues accounted for 34 per cent of advances and about 50 per cent of debt service in 1992. Surveys have found that a substantial proportion of default is wilful. Co-operative banks are co-operative only in name. Their deposit mobilization is grossly inadequate and their

---

[39]   Note that the government had previously estimated that cleaning up of the balance sheets of RRBs would cost about Rs 2,000 crores (Government of India 1993*a*).

dependence on outside agencies such as NABARD very heavy. They are largely co-operatives of borrowers using their political muscle at State and local levels to secure subsidized credit.

Does directed agricultural credit promote efficiency and equity? We saw above that all the financial institutions involved in agricultural lending are weak or insolvent. This in itself indicates that the system is unhealthy. But this is not conclusive as regards the effects of directed credit on economic efficiency and a more direct test of the issue would obviously be desirable. Such a test is difficult to conduct, in part because it is difficult to set up the counterfactual case. In the absence of directed concessional credit, would the investments that took place in agriculture have been deterred? No empirical study that we know of has faced up to this question. Even the excellent econometric work of Binswanger and Khandker using data for 85 districts proceeds on the *assumption* that directed credit has overcome credit constraints. Moreover, the results of this study are no more than modestly favourable to directed credit. Directed credit is shown to have only a mildly positive effect on output and a zero effect on employment. (Tractors were substituted for bullocks and labour without increasing output significantly.)[40]

The effects of directed credit on equity have been extensively studied. The conclusions are far from encouraging. At the aggregate level, the facts were surveyed by the Agricultural Credit Review Committee (RBI 1989) at the end of the 1980s and confirmed what many people already knew. Institutional credit to agriculture has expanded rapidly and rural households as an aggregate obtain 61 per cent of their credit requirements from institutional sources (as against only 12 per cent in 1951). But there is a clear and dramatic correlation between household wealth and reliance on institutional credit. For example, the poorest households (households with assets less than Rs 1,000)

---

[40] Binswanger and Khandker (1992).

meet only 9 per cent of their credit requirements from institutional sources. Just as striking is the fact that only 30 per cent of rural families have obtained access to institutional credit. It is clear that medium and large farmers (those with holdings above 5 hectares) have pre-empted a large part of such credit and have consequently received large subsidies.[41] It is also notable that the incidence of overdues is just as bad among the large as among the small farmers. Indeed, one of the reasons for overdues among the large farmers appears to be that they corner agricultural credit and re-lend it on the informal market.

Further evidence comes from studies of the operation of the IRDP, a national programme launched in 1979 whose aim is to enable households to cross an income-based poverty line by investing in income-generating assets. The investments are financed by a financial package, half of which is a government grant and the rest is a non-collaterized bank loan. The targeting of eligible households is done by local government officials while a commercial or regional rural bank co-operates with them and the recipient in selecting or purchasing the asset bought with the loan. Loan collection is the responsibility of the lending bank. The loans carry a government-stipulated concessional rate of interest and they are eligible for both refinance and insurance cover.

Many careful field studies have provided a damning indictment of IRDP.[42] Even government evaluations of IRDP do not show it to be a success. Some of the identified problems are as follows.

(i) The targeting of beneficiaries is poor. The 'income criterion' on which households are chosen can be and is manipulated. In his careful study, Drèze found that the poorest

---

[41] Bhagwati and Srinivasan (1993) write, 'The World Bank estimates that farmers cultivating over 5 acres receive an interest rate subsidy on term loans of about Rs 1 billion per annum'. We have not seen the details of this estimate but think that it is plausible.

[42] For example, see the excellent study by Drèze (1990). For an overall review of IRDP see Copestake (1996).

households were largely excluded and many rich households were included.[43]   Targeting is particularly bad in backward states such as UP and Bihar, but it is bad even in progressive states like Gujarat (West Bengal is an exception).

(ii) Even government studies which give a favourable view of targeting agree that the viability of the investments and the repayment record are extremely poor and the effect on living standards is uncertain. Not only is it difficult to find projects with high rates of return but there is also price discrimination against poor households.[44] For example, there appears to be a systematic tendency for the poor having to pay excessively high prices for livestock. Moreover, experience suggests that many poor households do not have a comparative advantage in livestock investments, perhaps because they have no land.

(iii) An important dimension of the problem is that the income generated by IRDP is insecure and risky and poor households do not have the required debt capacity—IRDP borrowing often gets them deeper into debt than they were to start with.

Thus, the evidence regarding IRDP is unfavourable. Poverty alleviation objectives are likely to be more effectively furthered by other types of intervention, for example, public employment programmes (which have the merit of incorporating a self-selection element) and social security schemes that directly target vulnerable groups such as the handicapped, the aged, or the widowed. Policies to improve health and education are also likely to improve living conditions and earning capacity. All these measures have the additional advantage, as compared to the IRDP, of enhancing security and reducing risk. (See Chapter 6.)

---

[43]   Government-sponsored studies of IRDP give a more favourable view of targeting but these studies contain various flaws. See Drèze *ibid.*
[44]   See Drèze *ibid.* and Seabright (1992).

Directed credit to small-scale industry. As with agricultural credit, directed credit to small-scale industry was motivated by the belief that small firms were discriminated against by banks, due to risk aversion and informational imperfections. It was felt that correcting such discrimination would improve both aggregate output and the distribution of income (given the presumption that small-scale industries are labour-intensive). Concessional credit to small-scale industry comes from two sources. It is part of the banks' priority sector target and currently (March 1995) accounts for 14.3 per cent of bank credit, a larger share than that of agricultural loans. Finance for small-scale industries is also provided by various development finance institutions. Many of them are controlled by State governments but receive subsidized refinance from either the RBI or the Small Industries Development Bank (SIDBI), which is itself a subsidiary of the Industrial Development Bank of India (IDBI).

Small industries cover a considerable range of enterprises. On current criteria, the qualification for being 'small' is that investment in plant and machinery should be less than Rs 60 lakhs (or Rs 75 lakhs for ancillary and export-oriented units). If investment does not exceed Rs 500,000, the enterprise qualifies as being 'tiny'. On this basis, small enterprises range from highly sophisticated modern operations to artisans and cottage industries. It is doubtless true that small firms, particularly tiny firms, face an imperfect capital market for the usual well-known reasons. But the following points should be borne in mind.

(i) Small firms, particularly in urban areas, are served by the urban informal market, which is both large and efficient. It is estimated by the RBI that about 40 per cent of credit to small-scale industry comes from the informal sector, 32 per cent from formal credit institutions, and 28 per cent from owned funds. The informal market works by acquiring information about borrowers, establishing relationships which can sustain repeat contracts, and lending with short maturities and movable collateral. The market is competitive: interest rates are high and differentiated as a result of transactions costs and risk, not monopolistic behaviour.

(ii) The small-scale sector contains many modern enterprises, particularly at the larger end of the size distribution, which should be treated on the same commercial footing as medium- and large-scale firms.

(iii) The portfolio quality and financial viability of many State-level development finance institutions has been severely compromised by concessional lending to small firms. The availability of refinance from higher-level institutions has encouraged poor project appraisal.

(iv) It may well be true that there are informational asymmetries which lead to credit rationing of tiny firms. But it is also true that 'there is nothing necessarily wrong with a scenario in which both inexperienced entrepreneurs starting up in a small way and also small established enterprises are unable to get institutional credit. Easy access to such credit for new enterprises can result in adverse selection whether interest rates are high or low, and then there may be too many founders who never succeed. And for established small firms the costs of administering small loans, and of selection (for lending blind is most unlikely to be socially desirable), must always be considered. In short, it is possible to try too hard to serve small firms with institutional credit.'[45]

Speculation apart, the direct evidence of the relative efficiency of small firms is discouraging (see Chapter 5). Not only that, but the share of institutional credit in total borrowing has been found to be negatively correlated with total factor productivity.[46] Thus it may well be that cheap credit had a deleterious effect.

[45] Little, Mazumdar, and Page (1987), ch. 16.
[46] Goldar (1988).

Policy. We now consider the policy implications of our examination of directed credit. We are not in a position to give a blueprint for action but we can outline the main elements that should figure in the strategy that should be pursued.

(i) The case for subsidies on 'market failure' grounds is quite weak. Properly stated, several of the 'market failure' based arguments imply *temporary* subsidies. The Indian reality is that rural institutional credit has been subsidized for 25 if not 45 years, a period long enough to overcome market failures arising from high fixed costs, externalities and lack of competition. This is not to deny that there may still be a valid justification for subsidies in specific cases for institution-building or extending financial services to the few as yet underbanked regions. But, even in these instances, there is no case for interest rate subsidies.

(ii) The equity-based argument for subsidies has also not stood the test of experience. It has proved very difficult to prevent cheap credit being captured by rich farmers. Moreover, there is a strong presumption that provision of credit is an inferior instrument of poverty alleviation compared to other alternatives.[47] The very poor generally do not have any asset backing and therefore lack debt-capacity. Direct transfers and public employment schemes are more suitable for their circumstances. Ironically, cheap credit programmes may be effective as anti-poverty measures only in the case of farmers who, while not rich, have some land. It follows that if credit-based programmes are undertaken, the eligibility criterion should be based on some appropriate asset-size (say two to four acres of land) rather than

---

[47] Erstwhile optimism about credit programmes was based on the possibility of a 'free lunch'. It was thought there were plenty of very high return investments available for the poor to undertake, with the potential for simultaneous increase in output and reduction in poverty. Optimism has been dented both as regards the availability of high-return projects and the debt-capacity of the poor. See Drèze (1990).

on size of loan.[48] Experience also suggests that targeting is possible only if credit programmes are small and highly focused.

(iii) An important question that needs to be addressed is whether there is any merit in directed credit as such, if the concessionality is removed. We take the view that direction is unnecessary in the long run, if interest rates are deregulated as recommended below, and perhaps harmful. But it would be wise to be gradualist in phasing out directed credit. In the short run, it may be necessary to guard against credit to priority sectors drying up due to laziness, excessive risk aversion, or urban and modern-sector bias on the part of financial institutions. Direction, in the sense of having lending institutions with a sectoral focus, will also have to continue, particularly in the case of agriculture, because of the need for specialist and local knowledge in their operations.

(iv) Deregulation of interest rates must be an essential element in reforming priority sector credit. We would advocate the removal of restrictions and subsidies on interest rates for priority sector credit other than those (*a*) that apply economy-wide and (*b*) that are applied to some highly specific poverty alleviation programmes discussed under (ii) above. Regulated interest rates have impeded deposit mobilization by co-operatives. They have distorted the allocation of loanable funds. They have created perverse incentives for rich borrowers to pre-empt credit and for lenders to acquiesce in this because interest rates are too low to cover the risks of lending to poor borrowers. The fear that if interest rates rise to breakeven levels, the poor could not afford to pay them is exaggerated: in the informal credit market in which poor borrowers are mainly to be found, interest rates are between 30–100 per cent per annum. Deregulation of interest rates would improve the access of the poor to credit by reducing

[48] Conceivably, cheap credit programmes could be of help in enabling small, self-sufficient farmers to adjust to liberalization of agricultural trade. This category of farmers stands to lose input subsidies without gaining from higher output prices. (See Chapter 3.)

credit market segmentation and diversion of credit. Recently (1994), the government has deregulated the interest rates of the co-operatives, hoping that they would adopt a structure of rates better geared to making them financially viable. So far, co-operatives have made no response, which is not surprising. First, such a move cannot work without parallel interest rate deregulation of the priority sector credit of commercial banks and RRBs. Co-operatives are in no position to start an interest rate war! Secondly, many co-operatives are controlled by rich farmers who gain from low lending rates. It is unlikely therefore that co-operatives will change their interest rates unless they get a convincing message that their losses will not be subsidized by the state.

(v) Financial institutions dealing with the priority sector must become financially self-sustaining. Too many of them have become mere disbursement windows with sloppy procedures, poor credit evaluation, and complete lack of financial discipline. They must get a credible signal that budget constraints are no longer soft. If some subsidies are kept, they should be transparent. Both liquidation and recapitalization of institutions will have to be part of the strategy, depending on the circumstances. Various issues arise as regards the organization of the new system. Some observers have suggested that the most coherent way to proceed would be to vest responsibility for priority sector lending in identifiable bodies which receive subsidies that taper off over a specified time-period. One suggestion is that (a) a new subsidiary of NABARD should absorb both the rural branches of commercial banks and RRBs, (b) a new apex institution, the National Co-operative Bank, should preside over the network of co-operative banks and (c) all lending to small-scale industries should be handled by SIDBI and the commercial banks should bow out of this activity. Others have suggested that this plan is too centralist and would simply repeat the existing weaknesses on a giant scale. On this line of thinking, it would be better to reform the existing institutions on a stand-alone basis. Yet another suggestion is that RRBs should be merged with their 'sponsor' commercial banks. We cannot pronounce on these issues but note only that they have to be faced as a matter of some urgency.

(vi) Reform of priority sector financial institutions will involve action at the micro-level. Studies of successful rural financial institutions in other developing countries suggest that in addition to appropriately remunerative interest rates the critical common feature is various devices to induce financial discipline among borrowers. These take the form of (*a*) obligatory savings schemes requiring borrowers to contribute to loan insurance, (*b*) intensive loan collection procedures and incentives to repay and (*c*) group-monitoring schemes which make use of peer pressure to secure repayment. In the latter, a loan is made to a group rather than to an individual and no member of the group can receive further credit so long as any member is in default on the loan.[49] In this context, it is also important to note the need for government behaviour to change. In recent years, India has had several programmes to write off rural debt—Maharashtra in 1978, Tamil Nadu in 1979, Andhra Pradesh in 1987, and finally All-India in 1990. These schemes have eroded the moral code of debt repayment. Inadequate loan collection is the most serious shortcoming of India's directed credit schemes.[50]

To summarize, we are in favour of rapid deregulation of interest rates on directed credit and the removal of interest rate subsidies except for a few highly focused purposes and schemes. Credit-based anti-poverty programmes should be phased out and the money saved used for other types of poverty-alleviation measures (see Chapter 6). We also advocate a gradual but decisive move towards making all institutions involved in priority sector credit financially viable. We would keep some

[49] For a good discussion of such schemes, see Hulme and Mosley (1996).
[50] Korea, Malaysia, and Japan are sometimes held up as examples of the successful application of directed credit. It should be noted that their programmes were generally small and characterized by very high repayment of loans (between 90–100 per cent) and the absence of large subsidies.

directed credit targets for commercial banks for the time being (without the concessionality), but phase them out by, say, 2001. As for the scope of activities covered by directed credit, we think the time has come to drop small-scale industry altogether. Directed credit targets for agriculture should continue (on a tapering basis) until 2001 to guard against the possibility of a sudden decline in lending. The reform of directed credit is a complex operation, involving many institutional and sequencing issues and requiring the co-operation of State governments. The government does not have a coherent plan as to how to proceed. It would be desirable to set up a committee to tackle the issue. It should have the prestige of the Narasimham Committee and should be asked to be equally swift in producing its report.[51]

4.2.7. Competition and Ownership

India has a large number of commercial banks. In 1991, there were 27 public sector banks and 26 domestic private scheduled banks with 60,000 branches, 24 foreign banks with 140 branches and some 20 foreign banks with a representative office. The four-bank concentration ratio was 45 per cent, lower than in many countries. Nevertheless, there was in practice very little competition. This was partly because of the detailed stipulations of the RBI with regard to interest rates and consortium require-ments for lending. But in other respects too the public sector banks, which dominated the banking industry in terms of size of assets, acted as a monolith. One expression of this was the Indian Banks Association (IBA) of which all banks were members. This was virtually a cartel and played a major role in fixing wages, prices, and service conditions.

The government has accepted the need to make Indian banking more competitive and more competition has been

---

[51]   The Narasimham Committee did examine directed credit but in a rather cursory manner. It requires closer examination.

introduced by changes in policies such as deregulation of interest rates and dilution of consortium lending requirements. In addition, banking has been opened up to entry by the private sector, albeit with some restrictions. In January 1993, the Reserve Bank announced guidelines for the entry of new banks. These guidelines were intended to ensure that the new entrants were well capitalized (the minimum stipulated capital base is Rs 100 crores) and technologically advanced, and to prevent practices such as cross-holdings with industrial groups. New banks are also expected to meet the 8 per cent capital adequacy norm from their inception.[52] The entry restrictions on capital are sensible, for reasons outlined in Section 4.2.2. Indeed some analysts have gone further and argued that safe banking requires that entry should be restricted sufficiently 'to ensure a high franchise value' in banking.[53] But the Reserve Bank has also pursued a restrictive policy as regards allowing the new banks to open branches. We would advocate allowing new banks (which satisfy the initial entry restrictions) to expand rapidly to increase competition for existing banks. We think also that further measures are required to increase competition: (i) the government must allow more competition between banks and non-bank financial intermediaries;[54] (ii) the cartel-type activities of the IBA

---

[52] The Reserve Bank has issued licences to 12 new private banks of which six have started operation. Approval has also been given to four new foreign banks and 16 new branches of foreign banks.

[53] See Caprio and Summers (1993).

[54] In this context, note that the deposit rates of non-bank financial companies are controlled by the RBI, making it difficult for them to compete (legally) with banks. Potentially, competition for banks could also come from money market mutual funds (MMMFs), which the government has permitted to be set up since 1992. But such funds have not come into existence because they were heavily restricted as regards size and permitted investments. Many of these restrictions were withdrawn in 1995 but not all. The most significant ones that remain are: (*a*) only individuals are permitted to invest in MMMFs, companies are not; and (*b*) deposits with MMMFs have a lock-in period of 46 days, thus effectively preventing them from offering chequing facilities. There is a strong case for removing all these restrictions, in order to integrate wholesale money markets. The main objection is that deregulation would

should be ended. The government still uses the IBA as a front to exercise suasion on all banks and to prevent competition; (iii) there must be a significant move towards bank privatization.

The Narasimham Committee fudged the issue of the relationship between competition, managerial autonomy, and ownership in Indian banking: 'Ensuring integrity and autonomy of functioning of banks and DFIs is in our view by far the more relevant issue than ownership. Issues of competitive efficiency and profitability are in this sense ownership neutral'.[55] In theory, publicly owned banks could compete vigorously with one another and with private banks, and the requirements of competition would bring managerial autonomy in their train. In practice, this is far-fetched. First, existing public sector banks possess significant advantages in terms of branch coverage, customer base, and knowledge of the market.[56] The competitive threat from private banks is thus too distant to outweigh the interests of ministers and bureaucrats in intervening. Secondly, public banks would find it more difficult to be tough in dealing with trade unions than private banks because of their inevitable closeness to the political process. This is important as bank unions in India are powerful, militant, and retrogressive in outlook. Thirdly, the government would find it difficult to accept genuine competition for and between public sector banks. Competition would result in winners and losers among public banks and the government would feel impelled to prop up the losers.[57] Experience in the rest of the world indicates that

weaken monetary base control by the RBI. Nevertheless, the appropriate direction is clear even if the pace has to be modulated by the RBI's ability to institute prudential regulation of non-bank financial intermediaries and to develop indirect but effective instruments of monetary control.

[55] The Committee did, however, recommend abolition of the Finance Ministry's Department of Banking, in order to further bank autonomy. The government rejected this recommendation.

[56] To use the jargon of modern economics, banks do not operate in a 'contestable' market.

[57] It could justifiably be argued that the government would not allow a (large) private bank to fail and for perfectly good reasons. Even so, the

banking is no exception to the general rule that autonomy, competition, and hard budget constraints cannot be achieved without privatization.[58] Efficient nationalized banks in France and Austria are an exception that proves the general rule and it should be noted that France too is now privatizing its banks.

In India, the empirical case for privatization in banking is especially strong as it is clear that public ownership has virtually paralysed the management efficiency of banks due to political and administrative interference in the allocation of credit. Further, the government has often appointed bank boards without regard to professional competence. The same applies to the appointment to the key position of chief executive officer. The tenure of chief executive officers has been highly uncertain and dependent on political and bureaucratic whims.[59] In addition, the managements of public sector banks have had little control over the recruitment process which is in the hands of recruitment boards. As a result, many banks have not developed a competent professional cadre.

The government's response to the above problems has been threefold, broadly in line with its policies concerning other public sector enterprises: (i) it has taken steps to expand private sector equity in banks while maintaining ownership. The relevant Banking Acts were amended in 1994 to allow banks to raise private equity up to 49 per cent of paid-up capital; (ii) it has recapitalized banks out of budgetary funds and World Bank

---

government would find it easier to undertake radical restructuring of a failing private bank than of a failing publicly owned bank.

[58] This is not to say that autonomy and competition can always be achieved *with* privatization. Even with privatization, (*a*) anti-trust legislation may be required to prevent the emergence of future monopolies, particularly in the case of non-tradable outputs, (*b*) in the case of natural monopolies, regulation would obviously be desirable to curb monopoly pricing and behaviour. These issues are discussed in Chapter 5. Note, however, that banking is not a natural monopoly. The case for regulation in banking is a different one and applies whatever the form of ownership (see Section 4.2.2 above).

[59] Sometimes, banks have gone on for months on end without chief executive officers in place.

loans to give them sufficient financial strength to approach the capital market for funds; (iii) it has tried to put in place new rules for the constitution of bank boards to give them a more professional orientation and to allow representation for private shareholders (up to 6 out of 15 members when the private shareholding is 49 per cent). It has also introduced the procedure of 'memoranda of understanding' as for other public sector enterprises.

We believe that these measures do not go far enough. Rather than go through a futile process of attempting to secure autonomy within the framework of government ownership, the government should prepare a plan to privatize several public sector banks. The same conclusion applies as regards institutional strengthening of banks which the government regards as critical.[60] It is difficult to fault the list of desirable changes outlined by the government: formulation of corporate recovery strategies, better management of credit portfolios, strengthening of internal control systems, modernization of information technology, better human resource management, better customer service. Undoubtedly, the RBI has a role to play in cajoling banks to make these changes and in arranging to provide technical help. We think, however, that the government is taking much too sanguine a view of what can be achieved in these respects without privatization, especially as we think that without privatization it would be practically impossible to have genuine competition.

4.3. The Non-Bank Financial Sector

Banks are at the heart of the financial system and reform of the banking system is the most pressing element in financial reform. But an efficient financial sector also needs other financial institutions which offer ultimate borrowers and lenders an array

---

[60]   See Government of India (1993*a*).

of services and products of varying liquidity, risk, and maturity. Some examples will suffice. Savers need protection against major risks, and long-term benefits in retirement. Insurance companies and pension funds answer this need. Savers also want to diversify their risks and have their wealth managed by professionals. Mutual funds can offer such services. Ultimate investors (companies and the government) need long-term funding. This can be provided both by institutions such as insurance companies and by debt and equity markets. (In many third world countries, including India, governments have tried to make up for underdeveloped debt and equity markets by setting up development finance institutions to provide long-term finance.) In order to function effectively, primary capital markets need the support of liquid secondary markets on which securities can be traded. An efficient financial system also has money markets in which liquid funds can be held, and derivatives markets in which risks can be hedged. It also needs agents who do not borrow or lend on their own account but provide ancillary services such as underwriting, brokerage, and credit rating.

India's financial sector has all these facilities to a greater or lesser extent, and since 1991 there has been significant growth in most of them. We concentrate on development finance institutions and capital and insurance markets, both because of their quantitative importance but also because they have raised controversial issues. Due to limitations of space, other segments of the financial sector are ignored.

4.3.1. The Capital Market

India's capital market has experienced rapid growth in recent years as judged by the number of issues, market capitalization, and trading volumes.[61] The authorities were clear from the start of the reform process that liberalization of the capital market has to proceed hand in hand with regulation. It is important, on the one hand, to reduce micro-intervention in the capital market activities of firms and investors. But it is also important, on the other hand, to ensure investor protection. Maintaining the fairness and integrity of securities markets is valuable not only in itself, but because it promotes capital market development by increasing investor confidence.

A regulatory body, the Securities and Exchange Board of India (SEBI), was set up in 1988. It was given statutory powers in January 1992 and these powers were reinforced in 1995. SEBI faced a delicate task. It had to acquire a reputation for strength and independence in the face of opposition from entrenched interests, such as the broking community, but it also had to avoid being hamfisted and hyperactive. It has had a stormy ride but it has made some progress despite inexperience and lack of skilled personnel.

Primary market for equity. Prior to reform, under the Capital Issues (Control) Act, firms were required to obtain approval from the Controller of Capital Issues for raising capital and fixing the premium on the issue price. This Act was repealed in 1992. Statutory control on flotation and pricing of issues has been abolished, subject only to certain disclosure requirements.

SEBI has enacted disclosure rules but events have shown how difficult it is to enforce them. There have been several cases where investors have got their fingers burned. A dramatic example was the M.S. Shoes case in early 1995, when the price of the shares was driven up sharply prior to a new issue by misinformation in the prospectus combined with price rigging. When doubts emerged, SEBI forced the company to return money to subscribers. The share price then collapsed and the

---

[61]   Various issues in reforming India's capital markets are discussed in International Finance Corporation (1993) and Securities and Exchange Board of India (1994).

issue devolved to the underwriters who disclaimed responsibility. The broker who had ramped up the price on behalf of the
promoter defaulted on his payments and the ensuing crisis
resulted in the closure of the Bombay Stock Exchange for three
days. This episode confirmed the existence of several problems:
inadequate criteria for disclosure; lack of broker capital adequacy and of a margin system; a proliferation of merchant
bankers managing poor quality issues; and inadequate regulation
of merchant bankers and underwriters.[62]

Experience has also shown that the process of public
subscription in India has various features which raise the costs
of issue. For example, 60 days have to elapse after subscriptions
are closed before a security can be listed, a period during which
investors are illiquid. Naturally, this is reflected in the price that
investors are willing to pay. It is considerably cheaper to raise
money through global depository receipts (GDRs) than on the
domestic market.[63] (Note in this context that the gap between
subscription and listing in the GDR market is only two days).
Various improvements have been suggested to tackle the high
costs and uncertainty surrounding primary issues, such as
permitting 'bought out deals' in which a new issue could be sold
to underwriters in the first instance who in turn sell it retail.
These suggestions have yet to be acted upon.

Secondary market for equity. It is obviously important to have
orderly, liquid, and transparent secondary markets if the primary
market is to thrive. One of SEBI's principal tasks was to

---

[62] Problems connected with disclosure were recently examined by the
Malegam Committee whose recommendations have been accepted by SEBI
with some modifications. Among the changes to be implemented are the
following: draft prospectuses are to be made public and objections invited; and
financial projections made in prospectuses are to be appraised by financial
institutions. The eligibility criteria for firms being allowed to go public have
also been tightened.

[63] GDRs are equity instruments sold outside the country to non-resident
investors against the shares of the issuing companies held with custodian
domestic banks.

improve the functioning of the Indian stock market which had a well-deserved reputation for being a snake-pit, lacking in fairness and integrity, prone to speculative excess, and showing scant regard for the interests of small investors. It was undoubtedly not a good model for the future and its practices needed urgent reform.

The Bombay Stock Exchange, the premier exchange in the country, was well known for its murky practices. An investor could not be sure he got a fair deal because trading methods were not transparent. Deals were not time-stamped and brokers' contract notes did not clearly separate price, commission, and carry-forward charges. Trades were often executed outside the exchange. Brokers did not distinguish between personal and client accounts. Exchanges were closed down whenever it suited the interests of brokers. There was a significant amount of insider trading. Brokers were undercapitalized. Margins were inadequate and, in any case, not enforced. The 'badla' or carry-forward system made the market prone to speculative instability.

Post-trade settlement procedures were equally deficient. There was a high proportion of failed trades. Various malpractices by brokers delayed settlement, for example, deferral of payments so that they could have use of clients' money. Even after trades were cleared by the stock exchange, registration of stock by companies took several months either due to bad deliveries (caused, for example, by non-matching signatures) or inefficiency or deliberate delay on the part of company registrars. Companies sometimes delayed the whole process in order to create scarcity of floating stock or to prevent a raider from acquiring a large holding.[64]

It has been evident for some time that the above complex of problems, many of which still exist, would be greatly eased by the following innovations: (*a*) a move from 'open outcry' to screen-based trading; (*b*) the immobilization of existing

---

[64] Malpractice by companies in the capital market is quite common. At the end of 1995, there was a sensational scandal (as yet unsettled) over duplicate and fake shares involving one of India's leading companies.

securities in a central depository and their eventual 'dematerial-ization', so that all transfers of shares are made electronically. These changes would make the system more transparent, provide an audit trail, avoid the 'paper crunch' which is rapidly overtaking the system, and speed up settlements.

There has been some progress along these lines, although the pace has been slow. There was initially considerable opposition to screen-based trading from the Bombay Stock Exchange. This was overcome after the establishment, with government encouragement, of the National Stock Exchange (NSE) whose explicit long-term aim was to move rapidly to nation-wide screen-based trading. The NSE began operations in 1994 and has rapidly acquired a reputation for transparency. Competition from the NSE has induced the BSE to adopt screen-based trading and generally to begin reforming itself. Another import-ant recent development (October 1995) is the passing of an ordinance providing for the establishment of one or more depos-itories. Significantly, the ordinance takes away the arbitrary power of company managers to block the transfer of shares. It now looks possible that the first depository will be set up within a year or so.[65] Several delicate issues remain to be decided, for example, whether to have a single or multiple depositories. Even so, this is undoubtedly a major reform, especially for attracting foreign portfolio investment.

A great deal of energy has been spent in battles over the badla or the carry-forward system. Badla is a trading arrange-ment that enables a buyer who does not wish to pay for shares, or a seller who does wish to deliver shares, to carry the contract forward with the help of intermediary financiers who loan the money or the shares on payment of a badla (contango) charge. There is no doubt that badla as actually practised suffered from problems as regards both investor protection and systemic risk. But in banning badla in December 1993, SEBI appeared to be

---

[65] The ordinance has been ratified in the Lok Sabha but not as yet in the Rajya Sabha, where the government lacks a majority. If it is not ratified there before the election of 1996 a significant delay is possible.

chasing the theoretical ideal of a clean separation of cash and futures markets. This attitude ignored market realities. Badla financing provided the market with liquidity, a fact of major importance in a system in which stock lending does not exist, and there are numerous restrictions on bank lending to finance stock market transactions. The appropriate response to the problems of badla, therefore, would be not to ban it altogether but to provide safeguards in the form of screen-based trading, enforcement of adequate margins on badla trades, overall limits on badla transactions as a proportion of brokers' outstanding net positions, capital adequacy requirements for brokers, and audits of broker accounts. Eventually, India should move to a system of derivative markets separate from cash markets, but the change has to be evolutionary. In October 1995, after much to-ing and fro-ing, SEBI relented and agreed to reinstate badla with safeguards from January 1996.

We end this section by emphasizing the importance of stock market reform for corporate control through the take-over mechanism. Discussion of the latter is postponed to Chapter 5. Here, we note only that the mechanism cannot work efficiently in the absence of honest and transparent trading practices.[66]

Debt markets. The volume of outstanding bonds in India is very large but there was until recently little in the way of a debt market. Conditions have not been favourable for the emergence of such a market because most of the debt was issued by the government at administered interest rates, and banks and other

---

[66] Some recent writing has emphasized the shortcomings of the Anglo-Saxon practice (contrasted with German–Japanese practice) of banks providing short-term capital in an arm's length manner and the stock market providing long-term capital. It is claimed that the stock market is short-termist in outlook and that the take-over mechanism is not an efficient device for disciplining corporate managers. But history and tradition matter in making the choice between the Anglo-Saxon and German–Japanese models. India has a long history of an active stock market that has mobilized a substantial volume of funds. It would be foolish to throw away this resource. Reform, not wholesale rejection, is called for.

financial institutions were compelled to hold it. Corporate investment was financed principally by non-securitized instruments, such as bank credit and loans from development finance institutions, rather than by the issue of corporate bonds. Secondary markets for both government and corporate debt were almost non-existent.

Changes such as the deregulation of interest rates and reduction in government pre-emption of funds have revived the debt market to some extent. The creation of a primary auction market for government securities has established a yield curve making it possible for other issuers to offer debt products using government debt as a benchmark. Nevertheless, demand for corporate debt is still constrained by the stringent portfolio restrictions faced by domestic insurance and provident fund institutions as well as by foreign institutional investors.

In the government securities market, the RBI has announced its intention to encourage a system of primary dealers to make the market more active and liquid. Primary dealers would underwrite the sale of government paper and offer firm two-way quotes for government securities. But such a system will take time to evolve. First, primary dealers need adequate finance. But it would defeat the object of the exercise if they had unlimited access to RBI funds. They could borrow from the call market but that would expose them to risks which they could not easily hedge in the absence of a market for derivatives. Secondly, primary dealers can function effectively only if they can trade actively in the secondary market with other financial institutions. One of the factors holding back the secondary market is the propensity of banks to hold government securities to maturity because sale would lead to a capital loss on the balance sheet. Currently, only 40 per cent of their portfolio of government securities has to be marked to market. It is generally agreed that this should in due course be raised to 100 per cent, but that cannot be done overnight.

There are many calls on the government to be pro-active in the creation of debt markets. We think that the main role of the government should be an enabling one. This involves action in three main areas: (i) in the debt market, as in the equity market, it is vital to encourage the development of the appropriate infrastructure, such as electronic trading and depositories; (ii) there are currently too many regulators in the bond market: Ministry of Finance, Department of Company Affairs, RBI and SEBI. Simplification of the regulatory structure is needed; (iii) the government should over time open the market to a larger number of participants and reduce the portfolio restrictions that are still allowed to operate.

4.3.2. *Development Finance Institutions*

Some attention must be given to the development finance institutions (DFIs) which have a prominent position in India's financial structure, with assets in the region of 50 per cent of the assets of commercial banks.   DFIs were set up to plug the perceived gaps in the provision of medium- and long-term finance for investment.   There are 59 DFIs, all but three of which are involved in lending to industry.[67] A further three are 'investment institutions' that provide finance mainly by the purchase of debt instruments and primary equity, viz. Life Insurance Corporation of India (LIC), General Insurance Corporation of India (GIC), and Unit Trust of India (UTI).[68] The rest are All-India and State-level term-lending institutions. The most important All-India institutions are the Industrial Development Bank of India (IDBI) and its subsidiary the Small Industries Development Bank of India (SIDBI), Industrial Credit and Investment Corporation of India (ICICI), and Industrial

---

[67]   The three exceptions are the National Bank for Agricultural and Rural Development (NABARD), National Housing Bank, and EXIM Bank.

[68]   UTI was established as a public sector monopoly for the promotion and management of mutual funds.

Finance Corporation of India.[69] Finally, there are 44 State Financial Corporations and State Industrial Development Corporations. In this section we concentrate on the industrial DFIs, particularly on the term-lending institutions, though much of the discussion is also relevant to the investment institutions. The latter are further discussed in the following two sections.

The DFIs share several features with commercial banks that have resulted in making both themselves and the companies that borrow from them financially weak. We discuss these features below and examine changes that have occurred since the reforms began.

(i) Competition. Until recently, the DFIs did not compete as borrowers or as lenders. Term-lending institutions could borrow cheaply, sharing in the allocation of SLR funds. The investment institutions did get their funds directly from the public, but their monopoly positions made it unnecessary to compete. Much of the lending of the DFIs was done on a consortium basis, leaving their clients little choice. Since 1991, some competition has been introduced. The privileged access to funds of the term-lending institutions has been withdrawn and they now have to raise money in the capital market. It is no help to them that debt markets are still quite shallow and that they still face many restrictions on operating in the money markets. DFIs now also compete with each other and with banks in their lending operations since consortium requirements have been significantly diluted.[70] As a consequence of the above changes, DFIs have faced quite severe pressure on their profit margins.[71] IDBI

---

[69] Of these three, only ICICI is in the private sector in the sense of having a government equity holding of less than 50 per cent. There are five other smaller, more specialized, All-India institutions lending to activities such as shipping, tourism, and development of technology.

[70] The above discussion relates principally to the term-lending institutions. Investment institutions are still insulated from competitive pressures.

[71] Competition between banks and DFIs has had the effect of shortening the maturity structure of DFI loans, raising fears of a re-emergence of a shortage of long-term lending. We think these fears, while largely exaggerated, may have

and ICICI have responded by diversifying strongly. For example, IDBI has entered equipment leasing and merchant banking; ICICI has floated a mutual fund and started a commercial bank. But State-level institutions are finding it hard to withstand competitive forces, since cheap refinance from apex institutions is much harder to secure in the new environment. The resource needs of the All-India term-lending institutions have forced the government's hand in allowing them access to the capital market. The government has also recognized that access would become easier if their status was changed from statutory companies to ones explicitly governed by company law, so that government and other shareholders have parity of treatment. This has now happened in the case of both IDBI and IFCI and their government shareholding has been reduced to 73 per cent and 62 per cent respectively.

(ii)   Autonomy.   Some of the problems of DFIs arise from government ownership. As in the case of banks, the government has taken the dubious line that autonomy requires dilution, but not surrender, of ownership. This view is belied by the arm-twisting that is still known to continue in finding buyers for the government's disinvestment programme. In the case of State-level DFIs, autonomy is a key issue. These institutions still act at the behest of State governments in both appointments and lending decisions.

(iii) Accounting norms and regulation.   The philosophy of development finance combined with soft accounting norms and practices led to expansion of lending without careful appraisal, monitoring, and recovery. The consequence was the creation of many weak, highly leveraged firms on the one hand and a deterioration of DFI portfolio quality on the other hand. Recently, there has been some improvement. In 1994, accounting norms similar to those for banks were imposed on the major term-lending institutions and they were also brought under the

some relevance in the context of the massive investment requirements of the infrastructure sectors.

ambit of the Board of Financial Supervision. There are, however, two outstanding problems. The overhang of bad loans continues to contaminate DFI portfolios and the present practices of the BIFR tend to perpetuate the problem by keeping moribund firms alive with financing packages that involve continuing losses for DFIs (see Chapter 5). Second, accounting norms have not yet been imposed on State-level DFIs. These institutions now face severe difficulties. They suffer from political interference and portfolios of poor quality and, in the new environment of deregulated interest rates, they can no longer get cheap refinance. There is an urgent need to clean up their operations by a combination of liquidation, capital infusion and financial regulation.

(iv) Corporate governance. For a long time, DFIs were so overwhelmingly important in project finance that they came to acquire dominant positions as holders of companies' debt and equity. But as a result of their own soft accounting procedures combined with signals from government that existing promoters should be left undisturbed, they did not perform the corporate governance role that should have been expected of them. They mostly just sat on their holdings of debt and equity and did not use these to monitor promoters or dislodge those among them that were inefficient. (In the theory of corporate governance, concentrated ownership is seen as an answer to the free-rider problem that accompanies dispersed share ownership. But this assumes that concentrated owners are motivated by profit and insulated from political interference.) There has been little change in these respects since 1991. The DFIs did not oppose the preferential allotment scheme which favoured promoters, nor have they used their position to make take-overs of inefficient firms easier.[72] (For a further discussion see Chapter 5.)

---

[72] Our remarks about corporate governance apply to both term-lending and investment institutions.

4.3.3. Insurance and Mutual Funds

The insurance industry in India currently consists of two government-owned monoliths, viz. LIC and GIC and its four subsidiary companies which are pure monopolies in their respective segments. Though they have both mobilized a large volume of savings, they have fallen far short of what can be expected. Premia and tariffs are too high, variety of cover is not adequate, customer service is poor, and there is considerable overstaffing. Part of the problem, as with banks, is low profitability resulting from compulsory pre-emption of insurance funds for the use of government activities. But part is undoubtedly also due to lack of competition and the general inefficiency that afflicts nationalized companies.

The committee appointed by the government to make recommendations on insurance reform reported in January 1994.[73] Its recommendations, while not in our opinion going far enough, were sensible. The principal recommendations were as follows, stripped of detail:

(i) The insurance industry should be opened up to competition by allowing domestic and foreign private sector entry, with suitable restrictions as to minimum paid up capital (Rs 100 crores) and maximum promoters' holding (40 per cent). There should be a level playing field for all insurance companies, government-owned and private.

(ii) LIC and GIC should be restructured with a view to reducing the government's holding to 50 per cent of equity through phased disinvestment.

(iii) Mandated investments in government securities and socially oriented activities should be reduced, thus increasing profitability and permitting cheaper premia and tariffs. In particular, LIC's mandated investments should be reduced from 75 per cent to 50 per cent of its portfolio.

---

[73]   Government of India (1994).

(iv) A strong and effective regulatory agency should be set up, along the lines of SEBI.

We have two objections to these recommendations. First, they do not go far enough in breaking up the entrenched monopoly of LIC and GIC. In our judgement, the committee should have given more attention to the possibility of breaking up LIC into several companies and privatizing some of them fully. Second, the committee should have been bolder in its proposals regarding mandated investments. It is too restrictive to require that 50 per cent of LIC's investments should be in government securities and socially oriented sectors.

With these caveats, the report provides a good starting point. Unfortunately, it has been hanging fire. Considerable private sector interest has been expressed and several foreign tie-ups have been mooted, but the government has taken no action other than announcing the formation of a regulatory body. Regulation is undoubtedly important—for example, to prevent the entry of fly-by-night operators and to ensure an arm's length relationship between insurance companies and other concerns floated by the same promoters. (A common trick in the pre-nationalization era was to insure the assets of group companies with insurance subsidiaries, claim tax exemptions on the premium payments and then get fictitious claims passed.) But so far a regulatory authority has only received cabinet approval thus enabling an interim body to be set up. There is virtually no chance of the legislation necessary to set up an independent, statutory authority being introduced before the general election in 1996. On the current timetable, genuine opening up of the insurance sector still seems quite a distant prospect. The pace of reform in this field has thus been miserably slow, probably because the government does not wish to fight the trade unions which are opposed to change.

We now turn to the mutual fund industry which has played a significant role in mobilizing savings. The largest mutual fund institution is the UTI which was set up in 1964 as a public sector monopoly to promote mutual funds. Its exclusive monopoly was broken in 1987 when the government allowed nationalized banks to form subsidiaries specifically for this activity. In 1992, the industry was opened up to the private sector, domestic and foreign. Currently, there are 14 mutual funds. UTI accounts for 80 per cent of net assets of the industry and private sector mutual funds for 5 per cent.

The industry's potential for growth is substantial. Though UTI is no longer a monopoly, its dominant position remains a major problem and there is a strong case for breaking it up. It has been criticized, justly, for being inefficient in investor servicing, bureaucratic and non-transparent in its operations, and lacking in autonomy in its relationship with the government. We have already alluded above to its failure as a corporate governor.

4.4. Liberalization of Capital Flows

An important issue concerning financial sector liberalization is whether to deregulate international capital flows and, if so, at what pace. The basic rationale of capital account liberalization is to secure the benefits of full integration into the world economy. It is only when the capital account has been fully liberalized that investment and savings can be optimised and full risk diversification achieved. The major problem with capital account liberalization is the risk of volatile inflows and outflows. This can cause difficulties in the real sectors of the economy, as we saw in Chapter 2. Here we concentrate on another difficulty: that volatile capital flows can dislocate the financial sector (ultimately, this could of course dislocate the real economy as well).

The Indian government's attitude to capital account liberalization has been cautious. Outflows by residents are still forbidden or highly controlled. Inflows and outflows by non-residents, have been partially deregulated. We confine ourselves here to portfolio flows since direct investment is discussed in Chapter 5. Portfolio investment in India is allowed but only through foreign institutional investors (FIIs) consisting mainly of broad-based funds such as investment trusts, pension funds, etc. FIIs come under the jurisdiction of SEBI, and some 300 FIIs have been registered to date. They are allowed to invest only in listed securities of which a maximum of 30 per cent can be in bonds, the rest being equity shares in companies. The tax on dividends for offshore FIIs is 10 per cent, the long-term capital gains tax is 10 per cent, and the short-term capital gains tax is 30 per cent.[74] Within bonds, FIIs are not allowed to buy government debt, but only bonds of public and private companies.

Off-shore borrowing by Indian companies is under the jurisdiction of the Ministry of Finance which exercises strict control over it. Since the improvement of the balance of payments position in 1992/93, Indian companies have been allowed to mobilize funds by floating GDRs and Eurobonds (but without government guarantee). There are controls both on the end-use of the loans (priority is given to projects in the oil and infrastructure sectors) and on the maturity of the loan (in February 1995, a minimum seven-year loan maturity was fixed for Eurobonds greater than $15 million in value). There is also currently an overall cap of $3.5 billion on external borrowing.

Foreign deposits in domestic banks are allowed through recognized schemes whose terms have in recent years become considerably less favourable than they used to be. In general, there are strict controls on the foreign asset and liability positions of domestic banks.[75] Foreign portfolio investment by residents is forbidden.

We take the view that selective opening of the capital account is the correct strategy. The attractiveness of the Indian market could be increased considerably, even with the present

---

[74] Many FIIs escape these taxes by locating for tax purposes in Mauritius (and a few other countries) with whom India has a tax agreement providing for capital gains tax exemption.

[75] This statement holds notwithstanding some relaxation in the overnight exposure limits of domestic banks in the foreign exchange market at the end of 1995.

levels of deregulation, simply by improving the trading and settlement system in securities markets. We do not favour full-scale liberalization at this stage of the reform process. The danger of excessive capital inflows is that they can lead directly or indirectly to an excessive expansion of bank balance sheets. Experience in many countries both in Asia and Latin America has shown that in this process two significant dangers arise: (*a*) a deterioration in credit quality as banks increase their risk exposure (this phenomenon is encouraged by the fact that in practice banks can always rely on a governmental safety net); (*b*) maturity mismatch as short-term capital inflows are invested in long-term or illiquid assets resulting in acute difficulties when the funds are pulled out. In India, these potential dangers have to be taken seriously because regulatory systems are in their infancy, banks are inexperienced in managing credit, interest rate and foreign exchange risks, and capital market institutions are as yet not liquid and resilient enough to absorb shocks arising from sudden volatility.

While we espouse the aim of capital market liberalization, we thus agree with those who believe that it should come later in the reform process after trade liberalization, financial regulation, and fiscal consolidation are further advanced.

4.5. Concluding Remarks

An overall assessment of India's financial sector reform must surely be positive. Major changes have taken place in the banking sector. Banks have been recapitalized and are healthier than they were. Compulsory capture of bank deposits by the government has been reduced and there has been a significant amount of interest rate deregulation. Further progress on this front now depends on the success of fiscal consolidation. There has been a move towards greater competition. A beginning has been made with respect to setting up systems for regulation and supervision, though the difficulties in achieving independence, professionalism, and honesty of the regulators have still to be faced. Various other problems remain. Non-performing assets (including loans to 'sick' firms) continue to drag down bank profitability. There has not been much progress in speeding up debt recovery. There has been virtually no reform in the area of directed credit. The time has come to impose hard budget constraints on institutions lending to agriculture and small-scale industry, and to eliminate most concessional credit to these sectors. Concessional credit is not a cost-effective method of poverty alleviation. But the government lacks a coherent plan for phasing out directed credit. Finally, Indian banks continue to have high spreads and are still extremely inefficient by international standards. They are massively overstaffed, but bank unions are holding up rapid computerization. We do not believe that the appropriate changes can be brought about without privatization.

The non-bank financial sector is also undergoing rapid change, as attested by the large increase in the range and variety of products on offer. In the capital market, a regulatory authority has been set up, but it has not yet found its feet. The pace of change has been very slow in improving the trading and settlements system in the stock market, but there have been some important recent advances, such as the introduction of screen-based trading and the acceptance of the principle of setting up depositories. So far, there has been no progress in opening up the insurance sector. There has been some liberalization of international capital movements, but of a justifiably cautious variety.

India has made a good start with financial sector reform. But there is still a long way to go in creating an efficient financial sector suitable for a sophisticated modern economy.

5

Industrial Policy and Factor Markets

5.1. Introduction

The strategy of Indian industrialization did not change much from Independence to 1990. It emphasized heavy industry, public ownership, and import substitution. This went along with contempt for the price mechanism, and a belief that competition was harmful. A licence was needed to start or expand substantially any industrial activity giving employment to more than fifty workers. Big private business, both domestic and foreign, was feared and distrusted. Special obstacles were put in the way of expansion by 'dominant' companies and those with significant foreign ownership. Yet at the same time the political support of private industry was needed. Thus businessmen were protected in many ways from both foreign and domestic competition. Their incumbent workers, like those in the public sector, were doubly protected as it was made illegal to sack anyone without permission, or even to vary the kind of work.

As far as industrial policy went, Indian socialism became both bourgeois and exclusive. Those who promoted these protective policies ignored the fact that they benefited only the relatively well off and excluded large numbers of much poorer people with no jobs in medium- or large-scale factories. The 'permit raj' as the regime came to be called created a high-cost inflexible capital-intensive industry with a preponderance of very large factories in the public sector. In the private sector many small enterprises were encouraged by various concessions that were both capital intensive and far too small to realize possible economies of scale.[1] It was only in the late 1980s that the prejudices and beliefs which had led to this unsuitable industrial development came to be widely questioned.

The stated intention of the reformers is now to foster a competitive dynamic industry which will be highly labour-demanding and competitive in world markets. But the old system has deposited a complex interrelated mass of procedures, laws, and institutions, which is unsuitable for the development of the kind of industry envisaged. Consequently, there is a lot to reform. But this is difficult, for although there has been a remarkable volte face in élitist economic thinking there are still strong currents of antediluvian prejudice, and many politicians and bureaucrats have vested interests in the old system of controls. A wide enough constituency for the new policies is still lacking. No doubt it is for this reason that the present government (that of Narasimha Rao) has hardly begun, after four years, to tackle the legal and institutional road blocks to the reform of the non-financial industrial sector which we shall be discussing in the rest of this chapter.

In the next section we consider those policies that have had, and continue to have, a major bearing on the ownership and size-structure of industry. In Section 5.3 we consider policies that are more closely related to ongoing operations, though these too have, of course, some effect on the structure of industry.

5.2. The Structure of Industry (non-financial)

The most important element in any discussion of the structure of industry is the division between public and private ownership.

5.2.1. *The Public Sector and the Case for Privatization*

Before 1991, a series of industrial policy resolutions beginning in 1948 divided industry into three groups. The first consisted of

---

[1]   See Kumar (1991), quoted in Anant and Goswami (1995).

'commanding height' industries—those related to defence, heavy industry, mining, aircraft, air and rail transport, communications, and power. There was no mandatory nationalization, but all future projects were to be in the public sector. A second in-between category would be open to both public and private initiative. The third category included most consumer good industries, which were to be left to private enterprise. All, however, were subject to the licensing of production and investment. In practice, the public sector has expanded into consumer good areas such as tourism and hotels, and as a result of nationalizing 'sick' private sector units (see below).

The Statement of Industrial Policy 1991 reduced the list of industries reserved for the public sector from 17 to eight, since when a further two areas have been de-reserved, so that only six remain reserved. By the end of 1994, the only areas in manufacturing which continued to be so reserved were those related to defence, strategic concerns, and petroleum. Even here the government may invite the private sector to participate, as it has in the case of oil exploration and refining.

Table 5.1 gives some figures for the share in GDP of the public sector both in total and for various sectors. It shows that the share rose very rapidly in the 1960s and 1970s. It continued to rise in the 1980s, though less fast; and no reversal had occurred by 1992/93. The public sector is dominant in mining, in the public utilities, and also in railway transport, banking and insurance, and communications.

The inefficiency of the public sector has been documented and emphasized by many institutions, committees, and authors.[2] There is a large difference between the petroleum sector, whose gross profit (i.e. after depreciation but before interest) to capital employed has been about 20 per cent in the 1990s, and other sectors.[3] For the non-petroleum public sector the corresponding figure was about 9 per cent. The corresponding figure for the

---

[2] See e.g. Ahluwalia (1985, 1991); Goldar (1986); Government of India (1991b); Centre for Monitoring the Indian Economy (1986); Mohan (1996).
[3] It does not follow that all is well with the petroleum sector (see below).

Table 5.1. Share of Public Sector GDP in total GDP (1980–81 prices)

	1960/61	1970/71	1980/81	1990/91	1992/93
Agriculture	1	2	2	2	2
Forestry	10	10	10	8	13
Mining	19	31	91	100	100
Manufacturing	5	10	13	14	15
Electricity, gas, water	79	92	91	95	95
Construction	6	7	16	20	20
Trade and hotels	1	3	6	3	3
Railways	100	100	100	100	100
Other transport and storage	24	9	31	20	19
Communications	100	100	100	100	100
Banking and insurance	35	69	85	86	83
Public admin. and defence	100	100	100	100	100
Other services	14	26	39	46	44
Total	8	14	20	24	25

Source: Mohan (1996), table 1 and NAS 1995 for 1992/93.

private corporate sector was 15.5 per cent.[4] The returns to investment in public sector manufacturing from 1976/77 to 1986/87 have been estimated as 3–5 per cent compared with 17–23 per cent for private sector manufacturing.[5] The public sector has always absorbed a lot of investment and given little back. Most recently (1993/94) it absorbed 42 per cent of gross fixed capital formation while producing 29 per cent of GDP. This was a big improvement on earlier years. For instance, in 1986/87 it

---

[4] All figures from Mohan (1996) tables 11, 12, and 13.
[5] Joshi and Little (1994), ch. 13.

absorbed 50 per cent of investment while producing 27 per cent of GDP.

A large number of public sector enterprises make losses. In 1992/93, 104 out of a total of 237 central public sector enterprises (CPSEs) made losses (after interest).[6] The losses amounted to Rs 3,951 crores. A good many, but not all, of these loss-makers were technically 'sick', i.e. they have negative net worth. This problem is examined in the next section. We have no similar figures for State public enterprises. These are believed to number about 800, but they are relatively very small; their total assets are probably no more than 20 per cent of those of the central public enterprises. It is certain that many make losses.

It is clear that there is a prima-facie case for privatization on grounds of efficiency. There is also the fact that loss-making enterprises are a drain on the central budget. This is, in a sense, another aspect of the efficiency argument. Public revenue could be better spent than meeting the losses of public enterprises: for this is not a good way of achieving social ends (meaning employment, since most loss-making enterprises have no other special social obligations).

The case for privatization is empirical. All large corporations whether public or private have a potential 'agency' problem, arising from the fact that the interests of managers (agents) differ from those of their owners (principals). Managers whether in the public or private sectors will always intrude their personal interests, to some extent at least. But in the case of private corporations they are given incentives and are constrained in various ways to give a lot of weight to shareholders' interests. A public sector manager's constraints and incentives are usually more confused. The ultimate shareholder is the nation. But the national interest is interpreted by the responsible minister. He too may intrude personal interests. In turn the minister is constrained by the government of which he is part:

---

[6] See Government of India (1991*b*).

but then the government also has political interests. There is a long rusty chain between the public and the public sector manager who is seldom, if ever, given the clear objective of maximizing profits. There are in the world only a few public sector enterprises that are widely acclaimed to be very efficient. This is because of the insoluble problem of reconciling managerial autonomy and public accountability. Some countries have achieved a better compromise than others. India is among the worst.

However, the strength of the case for privatization varies with the type of industry. The most important distinction is between industries producing tradable commodities, and those producing non-tradables. The former comprise almost all manufactures and mining products. The latter include most of the economic infrastructure—power, water, transport, and communication networks. The public industrial production of non-tradables is mainly by central departmental enterprises (railway transport and communications) or by State enterprises (power and water). We consider these later. The CPSEs that we first dealt with produce mostly tradables. Tradable commodities can always be made subject to competition, provided international trade is not restricted. Wherever effective competition can be promoted there is a very strong case for privatization. This is because competition annuls one of the main arguments for public ownership, the prevention of monopolistic exploitation.

The CPSEs and the new industrial policy. CPSEs accounted for 53 per cent of the entire public sector in 1992/93. They do not include departmental enterprises, mainly the railways and post office, which would add another 5 per cent. But they include banking and insurance with which we are not concerned in this chapter. Non-financial CPSEs accounted for 33 per cent of the public sector. They dominate in the utilities (electricity, gas, and water) and in the petroleum industry, which we consider in the following sections. A high proportion—70 per cent or more—of the remaining CPSEs that we consider in this section are in

Table 5.2. Manufacturing—share of central public sector enterprises in total value of production 1990–91

	per cent
Basic metals	35
Chemicals	19
Machinery	25
Transport equipment	15
Textiles	4
Consumer goods	2
Total	14

Source: Mohan (1996), table 6.

manufacturing, producing tradable goods. The CPSE share of total manufacturing output for 1990/91 is shown for various sectors in Table 5.2 The total share of 14 per cent had been significantly reduced since 1987/88 when it was 19 per cent.

By the end of 1994, 53 loss-making manufacturing CPSEs had been referred to the Board for Industrial and Financial Reconstruction (BIFR).[7] Many of these 'sick' companies are fairly small. But they include e.g. Hindustan Fertilizer Corporation, Fertilizer Corporation of India, and the Heavy Engineering Corporation which made pre-tax losses of Rs crores 349, 226, and 127 respectively in 1992/93.[8] They also include many parts of the National Textile Corporation, which together employ upwards of 75,000 persons. Some will presumably be closed. It is undetermined whether any will be privatized. But at least the government has bound itself to consider what to do!

[7] See Mohan (1996), table 14. The BIFR was constituted under the Sick Industrial Companies Act of 1985 (SICA) to decide the fate of sick companies —liquidation or reorganization. The definition of sickness and the operations of the BIFR are discussed in Section 5.4 below.

[8] See Government of India (1991*b*), statement 11.

About another 50 enterprises were making losses in 1992–93—some very large, such as Rashtriya Ispat Nigam, (a Russian designed integrated steel plant) which lost Rs 568 crores in 1992/93. Without some reorganization or other change in their fortunes they were on their way to becoming sick. While the losses, and also the number of enterprises making losses, are very disturbing, yet deeper problems can be anticipated.

The aim of the new liberalization is to make industry more efficient in its use of resources, and thus to contribute more to the welfare of the people. Making it face competition, both domestic and foreign, is instrumental. The domestic private sector is now being allowed to compete in almost all areas: its greater efficiency is not in doubt. Foreign business is now also allowed to compete freely in many areas (but excluding most consumer goods), albeit still often with the handicap of high tariffs.

Unless there is some adjustment, usually involving a reduction of the labour force, it is evident that the profitability of many CPSEs will fall, that some of those now making profits will become losers, and that those making losses will go deeper into the red. The managers of CPSEs are being asked to meet the new competitive conditions with their hands tied behind their backs. The fact that ministerial and parliamentary control of CPSEs reduces the freedom of managers, distorts their incentives and limits their adaptability to changing circumstances, is a problem in all countries with significant public ownership. The belated recognition of this fact has resulted in a world-wide wave of privatization, a wave that has not yet touched India's shores. Yet this typical problem of finding a good compromise between public control and managerial freedom has, in India, been settled more in favour of detailed and often perverse political intervention than anywhere else. The malign effects of such intervention have been widely attested.

The alternative to privatization is a reform of the principles and practice of controlling and managing PSEs that gives far more freedom and security to management, while maintaining reasonable public accountability. The need for such reform has been recognized for thirty years or more, but nothing seems to have been achieved. The problem was again recognized in the new Industrial Policy Statement of 1991 which undertook to give CPSEs greater autonomy by means of an expansion of the system of Memoranda of Understanding (MOUs). No report that we have seen claims that this new (to India) planning instrument has done anything to increase the autonomy of the enterprises. Indeed, MOUs may merely constitute another bureaucratic burden.

The other main policy initiative of 1991 in relation to CPSEs was to begin a partial divestment of the equity. In the three years, 1991–92 to 1993–94 about Rs 7,200 crores were realized from these sales. Thirty-two CPSEs were involved, but over half the receipts came from five companies, two petroleum, one steel, one telephone, one heavy electrical.

The highest proportion of equity sold was 37 per cent.[9] The government announced its intention of not going beyond 49 per cent. In other words, it announced its intention not to privatize. Nor can this be considered in any way an alternative to privatization. If the government owns more than half the equity, the firm is legally a government firm and subject to all the rules, regulations, and procedures connected with public ownership. From a public finance point of view these asset sales may also be criticized. First, so far as aggregate demand and inflation are concerned there is no essential difference between selling one bit of paper and another, and hence no reason for the sale of share certificates to reduce the fiscal deficit, while the sale of bonds does not. The fact that by convention they do reduce the deficit may have resulted in less pressure being put on reducing subsidies or raising revenue from taxes. Admittedly, the government debt is less than otherwise, if revenue and expenditure are unchanged. This has to be set against the possibility that they are adversely affected. This consideration has to be borne in mind even in the case of full privatization. Secondly, the

---

[9] Figures from Mohan (1996), table 15.

question should be asked whether these sales are a good bargain for the government in terms of cash flow—in other words whether any reduction in debt service will more than offset the loss of dividends. We have seen no analysis of this, but there are a priori grounds for suspecting a bad bargain. Why would an investor want to buy a minority equity stake in an enterprise whose dividend policy will be controlled by the government, and whose profitability will be determined by the government both directly and indirectly (and the government may have an interest in reducing its profitability in pursuit of some other aim)? One therefore suspects that these sales will have been made at unfavourable prices. Of course, it is an altogether different matter to sell part of the equity when it is announced policy that more than 50 per cent will be sold in the not too far distant future.

The case of the oil and natural gas industry. The production is dominated by two public sector companies, Oil India Limited (OIL) and Oil and Natural Gas Corporation (ONGC). Even prior to the New Economic Policy of 1991, exploration and development was opened up to private parties (with no results!). Since 1991 there have been further efforts to attract private enterprise into exploration and development; and the entry of private enterprise into both refining and marketing has been allowed. The import of some products, notably LPG, kerosene, and naphtha has been decanalized. But there has been no departure from a rigid system of administered prices. These administered prices are way out of line with landed prices, which has resulted in some costly anomalies, products being imported that could be supplied at lower border cost from domestic refineries. Apart from this, there is nothing to be said for administered prices which not only cause production inefficiencies within the industry, but also tax or subsidize other activities in ways that are often arbitrary, opaque, and without social justification.[10]

In February 1995 the Ministry of Petroleum and Natural Gas issued a comprehensive report on how best to deregulate the industry to function in the more competitive environment envisaged and promised by the New Economic Policy.[11] This report recommended immediate and complete repeal of the administered price system and reliance on market prices.[12] Imports should all be on open general licence. The report also raised the question of privatization. It would seem that privatization is less urgent in the case of this very profitable industry, which should still be viable in a more competitive environment, than it is in the case of a good many other public sector industries. Nevertheless the report considered that the many constraints under which public sector enterprises, including OIL and ONGC, operate, made privatization an issue. The pay structure is one of the most serious impediments. Private sector competition could leave PSUs without any management. To quote, 'If ONGC and OIL are to play a major role in this high tech field towards meeting the demands of the country, they need to have more autonomy and flexibility to operate on commercial lines; privatization of these companies is an option that may be considered for achieving this'.[13]

On the subject of exploration and production, invitations to bid for contracts have had a very sluggish and disappointing response. It appears that foreign companies are put off not only

[10]   Taxation or subsidization of products for fiscal reasons or to benefit certain consumers (kerosene is widely used by poor rural dwellers for cooking) should be explicitly budgeted by the Ministry of Finance.

[11]   Government of India (1995*b*).

[12]   Only some minor restrictions to deal with a few special cases that had arisen under the regulated system were suggested.

[13]   The report makes an interesting suggestion for quasi-privatization. If the government retained 40 per cent of the shares, and sold 11 per cent to public finance institutions such as the UTI, this would amount to public ownership, but the companies would apparently become non-government companies which would give their boards greater freedom and power.

by bad past results, but also by bureaucratic procedures and delays, and the belief that the playing field is slanted in favour of OIL and ONGC. The report makes suggestions to improve the climate.

On the subject of refining, we take issue with the report. Its figures suggest that refineries would be profitable under free trade conditions. It calculates indeed that existing refineries would earn enough to enable them to invest in improving their productivity. But it thinks that new refineries would not be profitable enough to attract enough investment in refining— whatever 'enough' may mean. We suspect that 'enough' means near self-sufficiency. It lists a number of advantages to be had from domestic refining. But none of these advantages are externalities: in other words they would help to make domestic refining profitable.

The report suggests zero import duty on crude, zero on kerosene, and 10–45 per cent on other products. This compares with the current 35 per cent on crude, zero on naphtha and kerosene, and 30 per cent on other products—a tariff set which would give negative protection for refining. The report's suggested tariff would imply an effective rate of protection of refining of nearly 50 per cent. We cannot see that any good reason, strategic or other, has been adduced for giving high protection to a highly capital intensive activity producing tradable commodities. India is very much a capital hungry country, and many non-tradable activities such as power and transport are in dire need of capital, both domestic and foreign. There is no reason to depart from our general recommendation of a 10 per cent uniform tariff which would give 10 per cent effective protection.[14] Nor is there any reason to have duty free imports of kerosene, or a high tariff on motor spirit. Taxes or

---

[14]   The report states (para. 9.8.2) that with zero duties the gross refining margin on a new coastal refinery would be $4.47 per barrel. Our calculation from its table A9-3 is that the gross margin would be $5.02. With 10 per cent duties this would be $5.52. The report claims that a margin of $6.76 would be needed to attract enough investment in refining. (Government of India 1995*b*).

subsidies on final consumption should be made by the appropriate fiscal authority, not indirectly by industry.

Departmental Central Public Sector Enterprises. These CPSEs produce mainly non-traded goods or services. Considerations as to the desirability or otherwise of privatization are much less straightforward than in the case of enterprises producing tradable goods. This is because competition may or may not be possible to arrange or implement. In many non-traded good industries there is an element of natural monopoly—that is, competition is impossible for natural or technical reasons. But this may apply only to part of the industry. The most obvious case is electricity supply, where the distribution network is a natural monopoly but generation can be competitive. There are similar possibilities, of varying degrees of difficulty and complexity, in water and gas supply, in rail transport, and telecommunications. Where monopoly is inevitable, so also is the desirability of regulation. Whether it is easier to produce a good outcome by regulating a private, or overseeing a public, monopoly is debatable. Many monopolies in the industrial countries have been privatized in the past fifteen years, with varying regulatory institutions and formulae. An advantage is that the regulation of a private monopoly can be made more independent of wayward political influence than the responsible minister often is in the case of a public monopoly. But every case is different, and the best solution can be approached only after careful and complex analysis. We have neither the expertise nor the time or space to examine fruitfully all the possibilities in India, and shall therefore content ourselves with a brief review of the scene, and some indications of where the main problems seem to lie, and what steps, if any, have been taken to solve them. We revert to the general problem of public or private ownership and control after considering the State enterprises.

The Centre has a monopoly of the railways and telecommunications. There has been much criticism of the operation of these important and essential parts of the infrastructure. Indian transport, like most of the infrastructure, is inadequate to the point of being a major impediment to the rapid growth of production in both industry and agriculture. Investment in the railways has always enjoyed a high priority in central planning. But, as everywhere, rail has lost out to road, which now accounts for over 60 per cent of freight traffic and over 80 per cent of passenger travel. Both the railways and much of the trunk road system are extremely congested.

Indian railways and its tariff structure is very much a creature of Parliament. As a result passenger traffic is heavily subsidized by freight. India and Sri Lanka have the lowest fares in the world (except possibly in some ex-communist countries) though many passengers evade even these fares, and travel free. Passenger trains crowd out freight trains and so not enough freight is carried. Sufficient funds cannot be mobilized to provide an efficient freight service with this passenger competition and much freight which should be carried by rail goes by road (despite the congestion there). As technological change reduced the need for labour, Indian railways failed to reduce its labour force, and so there is also a huge problem of redundancy. As many as half a million workers are paid to do nothing effective.

The remedies are obvious, and need not be spelled out. The reasons why nothing has been done to impose these remedies are also obvious. Privatization would be difficult, except for ancillary activities such as hotels and the production of rolling stock and other equipment, and indeed seems to be inconceivable.

Expenditure on road construction and maintenance has been inadequate over the years. Many road improvements show very high rates of return. There are two main problems. The first is how to channel a higher proportion of public expenditure into roads. Economists dislike earmarking. If one assumes fully rational decision-making, earmarking some revenue source can only prevent an optimum allocation of expenditures. The allocation of Indian public money is far from rational. There may be a good case for a road fund financed by fuel taxes. More efficient freight transport also requires that some substitute be found for 'octroi', a municipal tax on freight movements. The inadequacy of expenditure on roads has been recognized. The *Economic Survey 1994/95* reports that the National Highways Act has been amended to permit tolls which would allow the private sector to participate on a 'build operate transfer' (BOT) basis. Such participation has been invited for 17 projects on national highways with an investment of Rs 850 crores. Externally aided road projects are also to be encouraged, and the National Highways Authority has been reactivated for this purpose, bypassing State government Public Works Departments.

For trade liberalization to be as successful as possible, good port services are necessary. Charges at Indian ports are relatively high, and delays long. Private participation in the construction and operation of facilities is now being encouraged.

There has thus been since 1991 some recognition of the transport bottleneck, and some steps have been taken to widen it including the liberalization of domestic air services. But these steps are quite minor. The glaring problem of the politicization of railways tariffs and services has not been tackled at all. As long as tariffs bear no relation to costs, an economic transport system, with efficient co-ordination between road, rail, and air is impossible.

Telecommunications have been a less intractable part of the infrastructure for reform. A new telecommunications policy was announced in May 1994. The main feature was the licensing of private competition for both basic and 'value added' services to the erstwhile public monopoly of the Department of Telecommunications (DOT). Foreign ownership of competing licencees is permitted up to 49 per cent. A new regulatory Telecom Regulatory Authority of India (TRAI) was set up to regulate and ensure compliance with the licensing conditions. There has been much criticism of the sale of licences which appears to have been mishandled.

State enterprises. State-owned enterprises produce some traded goods. These are not very important. A few have been privatized and many more could be. Far more important are State public sector enterprises producing non-traded goods and services. These are notoriously large loss-makers, partly through inefficiency and partly because they are not allowed to charge economic prices. Some, such as road transport services, are potentially competitive and could be privatized—though bus fares, which would rise, are a highly politicized issue. But the biggest problems lie with the supply of irrigation and power. The State Electricity Boards (SEBs) make huge losses. This is largely as a result of charging absurdly low prices, especially to farmers, (in some States, e.g. Tamil Nadu, electricity is given free to farmers); but also because of extraordinary transmission losses, resulting presumably from theft. There is also the usual excess employment. The shortage of power in India has long been a brake on production which threatens to become far worse. The behaviour of the SEBs (or rather of the politicians who control them) is an important factor. The excessive use of power which they encourage by low tariffs is part of the problem, but probably not the major part. It has become very difficult to finance new generating capacity. The authorities have had to call upon the private sector, both domestic and foreign.[15] But the SEBs are not trusted to pay their bills. India is in a weak bargaining position, and foreign investors have demanded high guaranteed rates of return.[16] But State government guarantees are not always enough, and the Centre has been called upon to provide counter-guarantees. It agreed to do so for some of the first proposals, but has since reversed this policy.[17]

[15]   The SEBs are responsible for a high proportion of generating capacity as well as transmission. The Centre has some generating capacity—nuclear power and some hydroelectric.
[16]   This recalls the nineteenth century, when British railway enterprises demanded and obtained guaranteed rates of return.
[17]   The World Bank is developing a programme for the use of World Bank guarantees, to be given if the States undertake agreed reforms. See World Bank (1995*s*), para. 3.53. The World Bank is also promoting and supporting a

Negotiations have been under way for three years or more. At the time of writing no agreement has been finalized with any State. Agreement had been reached in 1994 for the Enron project at Dabhol in Maharashtra. But the new State government in 1995 reopened the matter and later repudiated the agreement. The terms had been much criticized. India had certainly negotiated a questionable bargain. A major criticism is that tenders were not invited. It is also doubtful whether the terms of the agreement gave the right incentives to Enron to achieve the agreed rate of return in the most favourable manner for India. The agreed rate of return may also have been too high. We cannot go fully into these rather intricate matters: but it is clear that the Ministry of Power and the Central Electricity Authority's guidelines for attracting foreign capital into power generation need rethinking.[18] This, however, does not imply that it was wise of the Government of Maharashtra to repudiate an agreement made by its predecessor. Many other infrastructural projects involving foreign investment are in process of negotiation. The foreign investor's perceived risk will have been increased, to India's disadvantage.

In the case not only of power but also other infrastructure, the need to look to foreign investment and financing arises from using the industry as a politicians' welfare state instrument to secure middle class votes. Obviously, power, transport, and communications enterprises should be profitable enough to generate their own funds for investment, or be able to borrow on their own account without government guarantees or other involvement. The subsidized public operation of these essential services not only reduces national savings, but also makes more

---

programme for reform in Orissa involving the privatization of generation (ibid. box 2).

[18] On all this, see especially Kirit Parikh (1994*a*) and (1994*b*). See also World Bank (ibid., ch. 3C). It is good news that Professor Parikh is reported to be a member of a small expert committee that will try to negotiate a new agreement with Enron.

difficult the appropriation of savings for investment in their future provision.

Irrigation is another case in point. Charges cover only a small fraction of operating expenses and maintenance (OM). The subsidy involved has been estimated at almost 0.6 per cent of GDP, over Rs 4,000 crores in 1993/94.[19] At the same time, maintenance is neglected and systems are falling into disrepair. In 1992 an expert committee (the Vaidyanathan Committee) recommended a six-fold increase in water charge collections, which would do little more than cover OM. Institutional changes with the role of the State Irrigation Departments limited to wholesale supply, and farmers' groups given a retailing function was also recommended.[20] In only a few States has there been any progress.

Privatization and regulation. We have already indicated that there is often an element of natural monopoly in industries producing non-traded goods. These are the industries usually referred to as the utilities. In all countries, these utilities have until recently existed mainly as vertically integrated monopolies, public or private, even when only part of the structure, that is the network of cables, pipes, or track, was a natural monopoly. Until recently in the UK, as in India, electricity was monopolized from top to toe: and this was also true of telecommunications, gas, water, and rail travel. But now innovations in technology and better understanding of the problems have made it feasible for many competitors to provide services using the same network.

---

[19]   The estimate was Rs 2,600 crores in 1989–90, 'using the historical cost valuation method'. World Bank (1995), para 2.80. A far higher figure would result if a reasonable return on replacement cost were assumed. Thus Hanumantha Rao (1994) gives an estimate of Rs 18,900 crores for 1989/90 (table 13.1).

[20]   As reported in Pursell and Gulati (1993). The Vaidyanathan report has not been published, but its main conclusions are summarized in Vaidyanathan (1993).

This feasibility obviously depends on legal obligations and constraints, and on the structure of the industry. The network owner, the essential monopolist, should be legally separated from the potentially competitive elements that may include both production and final supply to the consumer. Indeed, there should usually be a ring-fence around the naturally monopolistic activities, with the monopolist denied the opportunity of operating in the competitive areas. Where sufficient competition can be engineered, regulation can be dispensed with (or be concerned only with such matters as safety or the environment). Thus a new structure for the industry, maximizing the amount of competition, should generally be part of the privatization project. (It may sometimes be advisable to retain the naturally monopolistic part in the public sector).

In its hurry to privatize, for political reasons, the Thatcher government in the UK seriously neglected opportunities for promoting competition, with the result that more reliance had subsequently to be placed on regulation (which in turn failed to prevent excessive rewards for both management and shareholders). To quote an authoritative account and critique of the British experience, 'It is far better to achieve structural reforms to promote competition before an integrated monopoly is privatized'.[21] Despite the errors made in the great British privatization drive, the outcome seems on balance to have been favourable. Certainly there have been big efficiency gains and the quality of service has improved.

However much competition can be engineered, the need for regulation will remain. This is true even if the core monopoly activities are not privatized—as, for instance, when rail tracks or a national grid remains in the public sector. Regulation is now the subject of a large literature, much of it impenetrable to those who lack deep mathematical training. We can give only a few indications as to where some consensus seems to have emerged. Each industry should have a separate regulator, as their problems

---

[21] Armstrong, Cowan, and Vickers (1994).

and the expertise needed to deal with them vary greatly. The regulator must be independent of government, although decisions on some matters must ultimately be with government or the legislature. On this we quote the same authors writing of British experience

Independent regulation, together with privatization, has limited the ability of ministers and politicians to intervene in the industries concerned. Comparison with the era of nationalization suggests that this more arm's-length relationship between government and industry is a good thing—indeed it is an important part of the case for privatization—and on general grounds explicit interventions are preferable to hidden ones.[22]

The regulator and his staff must also be independent of the industry. The chief safeguard against 'capture' would seem to be openness. The industry's accounts and performance figures must be made public in prescribed forms. Similarly the regulator's reports and recommendations need to be open and fully argued.

The regulator's primary business is to see that the industry acts in accordance with the conditions of its licences, and to control prices so as to allow an adequate but not excessive return to investment. There seems now to be a wide agreement that the British system of capping prices is better than the USA's direct control of rates of return to capital. But there may often be opportunities for the regulator to suggest changes which would promote competition in the industry, and so lighten his regulatory task. He is therefore in the business of promoting competition. Since there are, or should be, other institutions with similar mandates (in the UK these are the Office of Fair Trading and the Monopolies and Mergers Commission), the mutual relationships and responsibilities of these need careful definition. For instance, in the UK, both the regulator and industry may refer disputes to the Monopolies and Mergers Commission.

[22]   Ibid. 360.

At present, India seems to lack a positive competition policy. The old Monopoly and Restrictive Trade Practices (MRTP) Committee with its pre-1991 mandate was as much in the business of restricting competition as promoting it. It needs to be given, or find, a new role, and this will become more urgent as privatization proceeds and as the public enterprises that remain are faced with increase competition.

It seems to us that India is not institutionally prepared for restructuring the public sector, a restructuring that must include the privatization of some PSEs, and designing the conditions of entry of private competition into areas previously reserved for the public sector. The mess which appears to have been made of private entry into both power and telecommunications is evidence of this.

For a start, there are far too many ministries. Every broadly defined industry has its own ministry. Together they lack the incentives, imagination, and professional skills to help promote the major public sector reforms that are needed. The problems are intricate, and transcend the knowledge and interests of particular ministries. What should be sold? How should it be sold, and how fast? How best to balance cash returns with the optimum long-run structure of the industry? Should those parts that are to be sold be restructured or refinanced before sale? The problems of regulation of privatized industries, discussed above, also have to be faced. And where the industry remains largely public, the conditions and controls over private entry and competition (if any) have to be settled. One could carry on with such awkward questions almost indefinitely.

There is by now a great wealth of experience of these matters to be derived from the UK; from Chile, Argentina, and Mexico; and from Poland, Hungary, and the Czech Republic; and no doubt others. But we have found no extensive study of these problems in India: nothing so far as we know to compare with the NIPFP's studies of taxation. Surely this needs to be urgently remedied.

At a more operational level, the Economic Adviser to the Ministry of Industry (which has a broader outlook and responsibilities than the administrative ministries) has made a strong plea for a new 'high-powered and expert institution for public sector restructuring'. He argues that most countries undertaking public sector reform have created special high level bodies reporting directly to the Finance Minister or Prime Minister. But others may be wary of the constitution of any such high level body in India. Dr Mohan ends his important paper on a sad note: 'It is argued that, within the Indian governmental structure as it exists today, there is little likelihood of a well thought out systematic, orderly, and strategic approach that has been argued in this paper'.[23]

Redundancy. Very large numbers of workers in the public sector are redundant. The 56 sick CPSEs that have been referred to the BIFR employ about 400,000.[24] We do not know how many of these enterprises will be closed down, but there is little doubt that many should be. Many other loss-making, even profitable, public enterprises will need to shed labour.

A major reason for excessive employment in the public sector is that Indian industry has been far too capital intensive, for many well known reasons—import-substitutes being preferred to exports, excessive investment in heavy industry, labour laws that discourage employment, and low interest rates, among others. With disappointingly little productive employment being generated, governments have felt unable to resist encouraging unproductive employment in the public sector at relatively high wages. This has been a general phenomenon in developing countries, avoided only by those far Eastern 'miracle' countries whose private industrial development was highly labour demanding.

---

[23]   Mohan (1996).
[24]   Ibid. (1995).

The government naturally fears making large numbers redundant. This is probably the main factor blocking privatization. Paying (indirectly) large numbers of workers relatively high wages to do nothing useful, prevents the government from promoting schemes (including employment guarantee schemes at low wages) which target the very poor. Yet it is true that the loss of a job, involving both reduced circumstances, even absolute poverty, and loss of status, is worse than just being poor. The government's concern is thus not merely political, but also humanitarian.

The solution to this daunting problem is easier than it might seem at first sight. Consider the case of a fully redundant man in a public industrial enterprise. He is producing nothing: indeed he may well have negative productivity for he takes up space, absorbs some administrative time, and may well cause trouble. The enterprise pays him directly, but the government (ultimately, the tax-payer) pays him indirectly—obviously so if the government has to cover the losses of the enterprise, but also even if the enterprise makes a profit, for the profit which belongs to the government is thereby reduced. In the case of negative productivity, which may not be all that extreme, it would actually improve the public finances if the government paid full wages until retirement age on condition that the excess labour walked away. We do not, of course, suggest anything so extreme. As a flier one might suggest the *lower* of either (*a*) a lump sum equal to the present value of half-pay until retirement age (discounted at the deposit rate of interest) or (*b*) a lump sum equal to three months' pay for every year of service.[25] Any existing pension rights would, of course, be protected. These suggestions can be juggled with and negotiated. The point we want to make is that it is surely possible to arrive at a scheme which would make the shedding of surplus labour advantageous to all parties. We suggest such good terms only for existing

---

[25] It is reported that two months' wages for every year of service is common in voluntary retirement schemes in the public sector. Private sector schemes are often more generous. See Singh (1995).

public sector employees with expectations of permanent employment. They would be too generous for new contracts, whether public or private, since redundancy payment liabilities discourage employment. Redundancy payments are discussed again below in Section 4 on sick companies, bankruptcy, and exit policy.

There is a problem as to whether surplus labour should be shed before privatization, or left to the new owners. In general, the new management should be in a better position to decide how much labour to retain. But the government could sell the enterprise with a guarantee to underwrite redundancy payments for some limited period.

Most of those made redundant would find some new employment. The more efficient, dynamic, and labour-intensive is future industrialization, the more likely is this to be true. From a macroeconomic point of view it should be noted that these proposed copper-handshakes might be largely saved. This would mean that privatization with generous redundancy payments could be pushed ahead quite fast without much fear of inflation.

The problem of redundancy has been recognized with the establishment in 1992 of the National Renewal Fund. It is supposed to provide for compensation and retraining of workers affected by industrial restructuring, in both the public and private sectors. The Fund is being provisioned in the central budget, at the rate of about Rs 700 crores a year, and has also received contributions from IDA. In practice it is being used mainly to support public sector voluntary retirement schemes. 75,000 workers, mostly in the textile sector, had thus been retired by March 1994.[26] There may be as many as two million redundant workers in the public sector. So there is a long way to go. Even if one allows a ten-year horizon, the release of redundant labour needs to be accelerated.

---

[26]   Government of India, *Economic Survey 1994–95*, 10, para. 22.

5.2.2. *The Extent and Treatment of Foreign Investment*

Since Independence, in line with development establishment thinking, new foreign investment has been rigidly controlled. Existing foreign-controlled enterprises were discriminated against, and compelled or persuaded to exit or relinquish control. New investments were mostly restricted to industries where it was felt that the acquisition of foreign technology was important, or where the promise of exports was convincing. The Foreign Exchange Regulation Act of 1973 (FERA) was a landmark. In most industries, foreign shareholdings in rupee companies had to be reduced to 40 per cent and operations by subsidiary branches of foreign registered companies were largely eliminated. Companies with a foreign shareholding of 40 per cent or less were supposed to be treated equally with other companies. Larger shareholdings in some industries deemed to be of national importance, and where foreign technology was needed, might be permitted. Such companies were called FERA companies and their activities were strictly controlled. The relative importance of foreign ownership in the private corporate sector fell significantly in the next decade.[27] IBM and Coca Cola notably withdrew.

The attitude towards foreign investment began to change in 1985, as part of Rajiv Gandhi's drive for advanced technology. But major changes awaited the reforms of 1991/92. The limit of 40 per cent was raised to 51 per cent for a wide range of industries, deemed to be of national importance, and where high technology was thought to be needed. In these industries approval of foreign investment was 'automatic'. Proposals of up to 100 per cent ownership would be considered by a Foreign Investment Promotion Board which was intended also to be a forum for quick decision-making. Restrictions such as the tying

---

[27] The share of total private corporate sales of foreign branches and foreign controlled rupee companies fell from about 30 per cent to about 20 per cent. See Chandra (1994). The share of total sales of manufactures is far smaller when the public sector and unincorporated enterprises are taken into account.

of remittances to exports have been removed. There has been some response. Foreign direct investment rose from $150 million in 1991/92 to $756 million in 1994/95.[28] But the latter figure is still very small compared, for instance, with China, Indonesia, Thailand, Mexico, and Brazil, where the inflow is measured in several billions of dollars.[29] While the change in the climate for foreign investment has been remarkable, even dramatic, foreign investors still find that the so-called automaticity of approval has a hollow ring. There are in practice numerous hurdles to jump, erected by the State governments, if not by the Centre.

The general restriction to a 51 per cent interest without special approval, and to a limited set of industries where foreign technology is thought important, also suggests (rightly) to the foreign investor that there is still a good deal of mistrust, which could lead to some reversal of the liberalization policies.[30] The situation is indeed contradictory. While this mistrust remains a fact, India is almost desperately trying to attract foreign capital into power supply and other parts of its very seriously inadequate infrastructure, with as yet little success (see above for a brief account of the power supply situation).

All countries restrict or control foreign investment in a few industries of clear strategic or political importance. Beyond this, as long as the import of products is uncontrolled and not overly protected, there is no good reason to treat foreign owned enterprises any differently from domestically owned enterprises. Mergers and take-overs over a certain size should be subject to approval on the advice of the MRTP as part of competitive

---

[28]   Government of India, *Economic Survey, 1994/95*, table 5.3.
[29]   See World Bank (1994*b*), table 21.
[30]   The figure of 51 per cent seems to lack rhyme or reason. Furthermore a minority local holding in a TNC controlled company gives rise to a perverse incentive to make profits accrue abroad by transfer pricing or other means.

policy, but this should apply as much to take-overs by domestic as by foreign controlled companies.[31]

The proviso 'so long as the import of products is uncontrolled and not overly protected' is of some importance. Notoriously in the 1960s, many independent motorcar assembly plants, each producing at high cost too few cars to realize economies of scale, were licensed in developing countries to exploit a highly protected secure market. There seems to be a risk that this may again happen in this and other industries, especially consumer goods where import restrictions remain and protracted high effective protection may be anticipated. Strictly speaking, this is no reason for treating foreign investments any differently from domestic ones. It is rather an argument for retaining investment controls in a few industries where increasing returns are known to be important, until such time as effective protection has been reduced to its long-run desirable level.

5.2.3. The Size Structure and Small-Scale Industry Protection

A high proportion of Indian manufacturing employment, perhaps about 75 per cent is in the 'unorganized' or non-factory sector, where a factory is defined as having ten or more workers with power, or twenty or more without power.[32]

Within the factory sector there is a high proportion of employment in very large units. In 1976/77 some 48 per cent of employment and 65 per cent of capital was in units with more than 1,000 workers.[33] Internationally, India stood out as having an exceptionally high proportion of employment, output, and

---

[31] There has been some doubt as to the rights and powers of the MRTP in the case of Hindustan Lever's (recently again a foreign controlled company) take-over of the Tata Oils Mills (see *Economic Times*, 2 October 1994).

[32] There are no up-to-date estimates of household and workshop employment, so one can only be vague about employment percentages.

[33] Little *et al.* (1987), table 6.9.

capital in such very large units, compared not only with other developing countries but also with the USA and Japan.[34] There is thus some indication that India's industrialization policies have led to a relative deficiency of medium-sized enterprises, while there is also some evidence world-wide that medium-sized firms tend to be relatively efficient.

We have emphasized that India's industrialization policies since independence biased development towards capital intensity and against employment. The exception, at least in intention, has been a package of programmes and measures favouring small industrial enterprises. These programmes were never given large public resources, but a wide range of incentives have been enacted, the most important of which have been tax exemption and product reservation. As we shall see, it is questionable whether the bias against employment has been significantly offset by these measures or even offset at all.

A distinction must be drawn between traditional and village industries on the one hand, and modern small-scale enterprises on the other. The former are unquestionably labour intensive and were protected and fostered from the early 1950s by a number of boards. A little later the Small Scale Industries Board (SSIB) was set up to encourage small modern enterprises.

Of traditional industries, handloom weaving is by far the most important. Indian textile policy severely handicapped mill production, the idea being to expand handloom production. It did expand slowly. But the main result was a very rapid unplanned rise in (non-mill) powerloom production. While weaving is more labour intensive than it would have been, it is very doubtful whether India's textile policies as a whole favoured employment. India's share of the world textile market halved in the 1960s and 1970s: and India missed out altogether on the great world boom in the very labour-intensive sector of garment exports. Despite recent quite rapid growth her garment exports remain a small fraction of those of East and South-East

---

[34]   Ibid. (1987), figs. 6.4–6.7.

Asia. While these failures have wider causes than textile policy as such, there is no doubt that the favouring of small scale in both cloth and garment production is a contributory cause.[35]

Turning to modern small-scale manufacturing enterprises, the evidence both from India and other countries is that within particular industries small firms (as measured by employment) are not reliably more labour intensive than larger firms, especially medium-sized firms.[36] The relative size of different industries is far more important than the relative size of firms within an industry in determining the overall demand for industrial workers.[37]

In India 'small' was originally defined as 50 workers or less *and* fixed assets (original cost) of no more than Rs 5 lakhs. The employment part of the definition has been dropped and the capital limit frequently raised: it is now Rs 60 lakhs original value of plant and machinery.[38] Many such small enterprises extend well into the medium range in terms of employment. When size is defined by the cost of fixed assets, rather than employment, there is some evidence that small firms are more labour intensive. One cannot, however, ignore output. Policy-makers should, above all, be interested in the efficiency of the use of resources, combining both labour and capital productivity.

Goldar (1988) examined 12,000 small firms in different industries comparing them with large firms.[39] The former had higher capital productivity and lower labour productivity as expected, but also lower total factor productivity almost across

---

[35] On the above see Little *et al.* (1987), esp. chs. 3 and 4. There has recently been some relaxation permitting exports from larger firms.

[36] By small, we here mean less than 50; medium, 50–499; and large, over 500 workers.

[37] See Little *et al.* (1987), chs. 7 and 16.

[38] It has been recently reported that the Ministry of Industry favours raising the figure to Rs 1 crore (about £200,000).

[39] The evidence dates from 1977. The comparison more precisely was between small enterprises assisted by commercial banks, and the census sector of the Annual Survey of Industry, consisting of factories with 50 or more workers.

the board. The implication is that employment was promoted at the expense of output. Moreover, in industries in which small firms have low capital-labour ratios, with an advantage in terms of employment creation, they are relatively inefficient; and in industries in which they are more or less as efficient as larger firms, they have little or no advantage in employment creation. Thus small-scale industries cannot be relied on to generate a large amount of employment efficiently.[40]

In 1987/88 a second survey of modern small industry was made, and reported in 1993. (The first was in 1972). We have seen no new comparison of small and large using this basis. But some comparisons with 1972 have been made.[41] The average size of a small enterprise fell, whether measured in terms of employment, capital, or value added. Capital intensity has increased. Fixed investment per employee (at constant prices) has risen by 66 per cent, with labour productivity rising far more than capital productivity (by about 5.9 per cent p.a. against 2.3 per cent p.a.). As the author remarks, this suggests that 'as a purveyor of employment, modern small industry will play only a modest role in future'.

Small enterprises have been favoured in numerous ways, including subsidized loans (see Chapter 4) and preferment in public procurement. But the two most important ways have been (*a*) the reservation of an increasing number of products (in recent years 800–900) for exclusive production by small scale enterprises (SSEs), and (*b*) tax exemptions.

Product reservations have been widely attacked, and we have seen no good defence of them.[42] This is not surprising. It was inevitable that such a ham-handed interference with the structure of production would result in inefficiency. More than half the reserved products fell within the light engineering sector,[43]

[40] Ibid. 117.
[41] Sandesara (1993).
[42] Notable and strong denunciations of reservations and other SSI policies have been made by Desai (1993), 233–6.
[43] See Little, *et al.* (1987), table 3.3.

which has hindered the emergence of the production pattern that is typical of other countries, large firms producing the final product using many components bought in from other smaller firms. Product reservation results in small firms producing quite complex products instead of specializing in components. The reduction of competition, both between large and small and among the small, has also resulted in the production of low quality components, which larger producers cannot then rely on.[44]

At the same time the growth of efficient producers is effectively prevented. Product reservation is also a barrier to exports. Small firms are at a disadvantage in exporting, which often requires some marketing overhead and an ability to cope with large orders. They typically export a lower proportion of their output than medium and large firms. It is a mistake to think that large firms cannot lead in the export of labour-intensive products. Often the technique in a large firm is the same as in a small firm: but the large firm saves capital by lower building costs and smaller inventories per unit of output. There are many examples of this in China and South Korea.[45] One cannot prove it, but it is probable that product reservation reduces the demand for labour.

SSEs receive many other favours by way of credit subsidies, price preferences in public procurement, sales, and excise tax concessions.[46] Excise tax exemption or reduction is often the most important. It is based on turnover not on the definition of

---

[44]   Ibid. (1987) 43–8.

[45]   A recent leader (15 December 1994) in the *Economic Times*, pleads powerfully for the abolition of product reservations on the grounds that exports are hindered or prevented. It is reported that the Confederation of Indian Industry considers that 53 items should immediately be de-reserved on these grounds. The leader rightly remarks that 'large-scale plants exporting billions of dollars will add to employment not reduce it.' It cites China as exporting $20 billion of plastic toys and other products. It may be noted that the size restriction for ready-made garments has been raised to Rs 3 crores of investment, subject to an export obligation.

[46]   For an analysis of the situation in 1980 see Little *et al.* (1987), table 3.1.

'small'. In the 1995/96 budget speech it was announced that the turnover limit beyond which there would be no concessions was to be raised to Rs 3 crores.

These concessions act in a peculiar way. Luxury goods, and other 'demerit' goods, are naturally subject to the highest excise taxes. So SSEs producing those goods receive the most valuable preferences. For instance, on social grounds, cosmetics are subject to very high excise duties. This does not mean that most consumers pay high prices. They buy from small excise-tax-exempt producers. This much reduces the point of high taxation of luxury goods.

Very small producers are always exempt from indirect taxes because it costs too much to collect revenue from them. For the proposed VAT the NIPFP has suggested a turnover exemption limit of 3 lakhs. We think that is rather low and propose 5 lakhs. This is of a different low order of magnitude to the present limits for excise tax concessions. We see no economic or adminis-trative reason for the present concessions. The limit keeps on being raised because it inhibits firms from growing. But wherever the line is drawn, it discourages growth. The logical end of this process is to give concessions to all firms i.e. abolish excise duties, or to none (except for the very small because of the costs of collection). Obviously the first is fiscally impossible, so the second should be adopted. Since it is reckoned that SSIs produce about 40 per cent of manufacturing turnover[47] the loss of revenue from these excise tax concessions must be considerable. This is not a good use of public money. The Finance Minister should reduce the limits, not raise them— or at least let inflation reduce their real level.

The concessions to small enterprises have created a strong small-enterprise lobby, which makes it politically difficult to remove them. Also, investment has been undertaken in the expectation that concessions would remain. So they cannot be removed overnight without creating confusion and waste. But it

---

[47]   Figure from Government of India, *Economic Survey 1994–95*.

should be part of the Finance Ministry's medium term plan to eliminate them, bearing in mind the need to integrate with the development of the VAT system.

In a recent article[48] Mr L. C. Jain, a former member of the Planning Commission, who has made a life-long study of small and decentralized industries, complained that the government had completely failed to live up to its promise of removing small enterprises from the burden of receiving an army of inspectors, keeping the records and making out the returns demanded, and complying with a large number of Acts and laws (it is well known that such interference costs small enterprises relatively much more than it does their larger competitors). Mr Jain implies that interference costs more than the value of concessions and other benefits received. To quote:

The foremost step however is to abolish inspector raj, which will be a least cost but highly productive measure. That step will bring the Indian economy closer to a competitive climate and give the small enterprises a chance to die or live. It would not matter thereafter even if the government were to wind up its small scale development establishment and the so-called subsidies or concessions.

It is often maintained that small enterprises suffer relative disadvantages other than those directly imposed by the government. Some of these relate to controls which have been largely removed—e.g. difficulty in obtaining imported goods as a result of India's 'own use' import policies. Freer competition generally will make for a more level playing field. A widely canvassed disadvantage is access to credit. This the government has sought to overcome by including SSI in the priority lending targets for commercial banks, by setting up the Small Industries Development Bank of India (SIDBI) and specialized branches of public sector banks. Complaints that small enterprises get little credit—especially from formal institutions—are universal, but such lending is both costly and risky, and it has contributed to the very poor quality of the portfolios of Indian banks (see

---

[48]   Jain (1994).

Chapter 4). Some examples exist in the world of successful small-scale lending; if these can be emulated that would be great. But we do not believe that a case has been made for subsidizing small loans, and this subsidized priority lending by the commercial banks should be discontinued.[49]

There are, in principle, possibilities of institutions which seek to internalize for SSEs economies which they cannot realize by themselves—notably in R and D, the acquisition of knowledge, and marketing. There are many such institutions in India, as elsewhere, and we do not have an opinion as to whether some or all of them are doing a worthwhile job.

5.3. Corporate Governance in the Private Sector

5.3.1. Introduction

We are here concerned with the influences and restrictions on managerial behaviour arising from the obligation of management to serve shareholders' interests subject to the operation of laws or customs which protect the interests of other claimants on a company's assets—creditors, employees, and pensioners. We are also concerned with what determines the ownership and management of the corporation; that is, with the market for corporate governance, or lack of it.

There are some continuing restrictions which may be hopefully described as the 'fag end' of the regime of the permit raj. These are mostly on trade and have been described elsewhere, as has the reservation of products for small-scale industry. But it should be noticed that there is widespread complaint that administration and procedures have still not caught up with the liberal spirit of the reforms.[50] Pointless

[49]   See Little *et al.*, (1987), ch. 15.
[50]   Four years after the trade reforms, copies of the *Economic Times* arrived in England with a label reading 'exempted from PP Form procedure by the

institutions and procedures remain, such as those under FERA, which should be replaced. The few remaining restrictions on foreign exchange transactions could be handled by the RBI. There are other restrictions that are desirable in any industrial society. The presence of excessive pollution is an obvious example. Here the main point to be made is that there is often a choice between requiring a licence or permit for a potentially offensive activity, and defining standards of behaviour with penalties for misbehaviour. India has tended to adopt the former line. For instance, investment projects require environmental clearance, and it is alleged that this often furthers corruption more than it prevents pollution or otherwise protects the environment. In contrast, the MRTP Commission may require businesses to desist from restrictive or unfair business practices.[51] For the future, the amount of specific regulation of private corporations will depend on the extent to which certain natural monopolies are privatized.

In the rest of this section we consider those restrictions on corporate behaviour which are quite general and apply to any corporation in any branch of industry. They relate to the ownership and use of the three traditional factors of production, capital, labour, and land, and are embodied in company law, laws governing employment and the purchase and sale of land.

5.3.2. Company Law

The Indian Companies Act of 1956 is a highly repressive piece of legislation which, in principle, gives government control over a host of decisions which are the normal preserve of the owners or the management. These include the name of the company, the issue of shares and debentures, the appointment and pay of

Reserve Bank of India Exporters Code No BB 000033 of 12/10/66 permit no EC By RSR 1436 1500-3 of 10/3/53'.
[51] The role of the commission in relation to take-overs and mergers needs clarification.

directors, management, and auditors, and so on, through a long catalogue of requirements and returns, neglect of which could involve the management in criminal proceedings. It is recognized that the Act needs reform. A new Bill was introduced in 1993 which made limited amendments, but it was withdrawn following strong criticism from private business and the press.

We consider first only those aspects which have a bearing on ownership and control, that is on what has come to be called the market for corporate governance. The structure of ownership of most large Indian private companies is unusual. Most are still controlled by a small group of shareholders, often belonging to the same family, that owns a minority of the shares, often as few as 10 per cent. These controlling groups are known as 'promoters': no doubt often in the distant past, they did promote the companies. A large block of shares, some 40–50 per cent is held by public financial institutions, the UTI, GIC, LIC, IFCI, IDBI, and ICICI. They also hold most or all of the long-term debt. The institutions seldom sell their shares and rarely challenge the promoters.

This structure has its roots in the pre-independence managing agency system, in the manner in which the government abolished that system through the Companies Act of 1956, and in the government's subsequent discouragement of any active market in shares or bonds. The Companies Act restricts transfers of shares in various ways. In particular the government can refuse transfers if it is satisfied that they would create 'a change in the controlling interest of the company ... and that such a change would be prejudicial to the interests of the company or to the public interest'.[52] This, together with the fact that the courts appear to be prejudiced in favour of existing 'promoters', makes hostile take-overs almost impossible.[53]

---

[52] Section 108D of the Companies Act quoted in Goswami (1996).
[53] Even those sanctioned by the BIFR (see Section 5.4 below).

The highly restrictive control of capital issues was abolished in 1992, with some favourable effect on corporate investment.[54] The Securities and Exchange Board of India (SEBI) which was created in 1988 was given statutory powers in 1992, enabling it to become an effective regulator of capital markets. There is no doubt that the capital market was extremely inefficient and corrupt. Investors were always ill-served and sometimes swindled, and companies could raise little capital by share issues. The SEBI has tried to improve liquidity, increase investors' protection, encourage share ownership, and companies' resort to the market.

But its mode of operation and the details of its regulations have been severely criticized.[55] In particular it seems to have introduced regulations which strengthened the serious imperfections in the market for corporate governance. It first endorsed the issue of shares at a discounted price to incumbent 'promoters', a highly inequitable practice nevertheless permitted by the Companies Act if authorized by a general meeting and sanctioned by the Company Law Board. It later banned the practice, but decreed a five-year lock-in for such discounted shares. Both the endorsement and the ban were thus barriers to take-over. Worse was the extraordinary new take-over code announced in November 1994. No one may raise her or his shareholding above 10 per cent without making a prior public announcement of intention and a public offer to purchase at the average market price of the previous six months (or higher), and thus acquire at least a 30 per cent holding.[56] There is no doubt that this strange provision will discourage take-overs, and, since no other rationale is discernible, that was presumably the intention.

One of the most important ways in which the management of a corporation may be monitored is by the threat of take-over. It

---

[54]   Desai (1993), 74, n. 8.
[55]   Ibid. (1993), ch. 10.
[56]   It is not clear what happens if a public offer is made at the permitted price, but less than 30 per cent is acquired.

permits shareholders, whose collective voice is hard to mobilize, some control by exercising their right of exit. It appears that the SEBI is unaware of one of the functions of the efficient capital market that it is supposed to help create. More generally, the purchase and sale of both going concerns and productive assets should be facilitated. These are discouraged not only by SEBI regulations but also by the Income Tax Act which does not freely permit losses to be traded against profits, and by heavy stamp duties.

It is clear that the idea of the beneficial social role of competition, and of the need to foster it (and only rarely moderate it) has not spread far outside the North Block in New Delhi.

Another mode of monitoring would be for the six public finance institutions mentioned above, which together have large shares in many big companies, to flex their muscles rather than implicitly protecting management. They could also encourage wider public equity participation by selling shares. They have both voice and exit.

5.3.3. Labour Laws

The Industrial Disputes Act (IDA) requires any firm with 100 employees or more to issue a 'notice of change' to any employee with a year's service who is likely to be affected by changes in employment conditions. This is so general that any change in pursuit of productivity is sure to be covered. An affected worker may appeal to government conciliation where the case is likely to linger for years. Thus employers find it very difficult to dismiss workers, even in clear cases of misbehaviour. This results in a bias in favour of temporary workers and employment contractors. The IDA over-protects the workers, *in large companies only*. There is furthermore a clear need for institutional reform to expedite the resolution of disputes.

The IDA also requires the company to seek the permission of government (usually the State government) to retrench workers.

For political reasons, this is seldom given. In practice, illegal retrenchment is often avoided by the use of voluntary retirement schemes with the agreement of workers or their unions.[57] Nevertheless, the introduction of the government into labour management in medium and large firms is an egregious absurdity which reduces the flexibility of the labour market and can only be to the detriment of the whole workforce which outnumbers those protected by 20 times or more.

The closure of a company, amounting to retrenchment of the whole labour force, is even more difficult. This is dealt with in Section 5.4 below.

5.3.4. Land Use and Sales

There are restrictions on the acquisition and use of land for industrial purposes in all countries, for environmental and regional and town planning reasons. Although there is some evidence that such controls are not well formulated or wisely operated in India,[58] we discuss only one Act, whose provisions are unique to India, and whose consequences are pernicious. This is the Urban Land (Ceiling and Regulation) Act (ULCRA). It was one of Mrs Gandhi's ill-thought-out populist measures, enacted in 1976. The declared objectives were, of course, admirable. In India there have long been ceilings on holdings of agricultural land. Surely people should not be allowed to profit by large holdings of urban land either. The Act was passed 'with a view to preventing the concentration of urban land in the hands of a few persons and speculation and profiteering therein and ... to bringing about an equitable distribution of lands in urban agglomerations to subserve the common good'.[59] It was ill-designed to further these fine sounding ill-defined objectives.

---

[57]   Some examples of this, as well as the growing use of contract labour are given in Singh (1995).
[58]   See Goswami (1994).
[59]   Quoted by Goswami (1996).

ULCRA bans private holdings of *vacant* land above certain low limits (500 m^2 in the great cities). Anyone with excess land must declare it. The State may then buy it for a song. Part of any land thus purchased was supposed to be used for low-cost housing. But the state can exempt the land from acquisition if there is a proposal to use it in a manner useful to the public interest, or if acquisition would cause hardship to a firm that owns it.

One does not have to be very sophisticated to understand that ULCRA was a charter for corruption. Extremely little land has been acquired by the State, and still less used for low-cost housing. Exemption from State purchase did not imply that the owner could sell to anyone else. Either for this reason, or because excess land was not declared, the Act has seriously reduced the supply of land and raised urban land values. ULCRA, together with rent control and other municipal regulations, has resulted in Bombay, a city with millions of people with virtually nowhere to live, having the highest land values in the world.

The special relevance of this to industrial policy is that many 'sick' firms have extensive surplus land, even in the heart of Bombay, which they cannot sell. Much very valuable land suffers from this legal blight. The same applies to sick cotton mills in Ahmedabad, jute mills in Calcutta, and engineering firms in many towns. We draw attention to this waste when considering the problem of sick firms and closure in Section 5.4 below. Proceeds from the sale of such land could either go to revive the sick mills, or satisfy claimants on the firm, including the workers.

One cannot wholly prevent private capital gains arising from land sales, and the attempt to do so prevents development, while such gains are in any case taxable. It has encouraged the profiteering it was supposed to prevent. It has promoted corruption, and done nothing for the poor. It is a major impediment to the rational use of urban land.[60]

5.4. Sick Companies, Bankruptcy, and Exit Policy

India is unique in having a very large number of sick companies.[61] Indeed, the very concept is almost unique to India.[62] A large stock of sick companies implies that many companies make losses, and are not liquidated. Of course, in all countries many firms go bankrupt, failing to pay their debts on time. The number thus becoming bankrupt may be relatively very large in India, as a result of bad industrial policies.[63] But in India bankrupt companies do not disappear. In most, if not all, other countries it is illegal to trade when bankrupt, or when insolvency can be clearly foreseen.[64] In India, the reverse is true. As we have seen, the Industrial Disputes Act makes it

---

[60] This has been recognized by the Ministry of Finance. See Government of India (1993*c*), para. 73.

[61] In 1990, sick firms were reckoned to number over 2,000 large and medium scale, and over 200,000 in total. See Goswami (1996), table 2.4.

[62] The Sick Industrial Companies Act (SICA) of 1985, amended in 1994, requires the sick company to have been registered for five years and to have negative net worth (accumulated losses exceeding equity plus reserves).

[63] For instance, textile mills form a high proportion of the medium and large sick companies. This is a direct result of government policies that favoured the powerloom and handloom industries, while also preventing investment in the mills that would have helped them to adapt. Again, in the 1970s and early 1980s, the government subsidized many small engineering plants that were too small to survive in a competitive market. In the public sector, the government invested in industries where India had a comparative disadvantage. Finally both the Centre and State governments have failed to provide reliable infrastructural services, especially power: power failures have been a frequent cause of loss.

[64] A firm may be bankrupted by its creditors because it cannot pay its debts as they become due. But it may be solvent, that is, its assets will be sufficient to pay off the debt in due course. In a perfect capital market a solvent firm should always be able to reschedule its debt to avoid bankruptcy: but capital markets are not perfect.

illegal to close down without State government permission which is almost never given. For this and other reasons it has also been almost impossible for creditors to enforce liquidation. There is no way the law can make a firm pay its workers if it has no money. Inability to close, and illegal closure, has often meant the disappearance of all assets other than land which the firm is prevented from selling by ULCRA. Consequently, the workers are deprived of arrears of pay, and any redundancy benefits they might have received. Faced with this situation the government nationalized many sick firms and continued to run them at a loss. The nationalized banks were also encouraged to continue to lend to loss-making—even bankrupt—companies with the result that non-performing loans had reached crisis proportions by 1991.[65] The waste of productive resources tied up in these loss-making activities was mounting all the time. Whatever the benefit to the workers in those firms, this can only have been at the expense of the growth of productive employment in the economy as a whole.

The Sick Industrial Companies Act (SICA) was passed in 1985 in an attempt to solve the sick company problem. Excessive emphasis was put on rehabilitation, with the interests both of the company promoters and the workers to the fore.

Under the Act the Board for Industrial and Financial Reconstruction (BIFR) was set up. It should be recognized that some institution which can mediate between the claims of creditors and those with an interest in preserving the company as a going concern is needed: otherwise the creditors of a bankrupt but not insolvent company may dismantle what could have been a viable enterprise. Since creditors can get no more than their pound of flesh, they do not mind killing the victim to get it.[66] But the provisions of SICA, the BIFR's own strong preference for reconstruction, and the legal procedures which continue to make liquidation by the courts almost impossible, together

---

[65] See Chapter 4.
[66] See William Shakespeare, *The Merchant of Venice*, I. ii.

ensure that many thousands of moribund or loss-making companies continue to be a drag on rapid industrial growth.

Sick companies have to register with BIFR, but the definition of sickness is such that they are mostly moribund.[67] But a decision to recommend liquidation is not taken quickly—the mean delay is more than two years.[68] The BIFR can sell the assets and forward the proceeds to the High Court for division among the claimants. But apparently it seldom does this.[69] When otherwise it recommends liquidation, the case passes to the Courts, and is governed by the Companies Act. This, however, is not great news for the creditors. Only 41 per cent of cases have been finalized within ten years. It would not take ten years for almost all the assets except land to disappear one way or another. This obviously makes creditors more likely to agree a rehabilitation package which involves concessions on their part. By 1973 no BIFR recommended liquidation had been finalized.[70]

The moribund state of the sick companies has not discouraged attempts at rehabilitation in most cases. In some, the company, often before its BIFR registration, has itself succeeded in securing agreement to a reorganization package that did not involve any large sacrifices or new commitment of subsidized funds. BIFR sanction (Section 17(2) of SICA) then permits the parties concerned to overcome other legal obstacles, such as the IDA. Where no such agreement is forthcoming the BIFR will, if it considers that rehabilitation is in the public interest, appoint an operating agency (usually a financial

---

[67] Goswami (1996).

[68] They are mostly highly insolvent, judged by book values. On average, as of December 1994, accumulated losses were over three times net worth (ibid). A few of them may be solvent if they could realize the market value of their assets. Land is the main asset whose market value exceeds book value. But companies are usually prevented by ULCRA from selling surplus land. SICA over rides IDA but not ULCRA.

[69] Possibly because SICA does not over ride ULCRA, and so BIFR cannot sell land.

[70] Goswami (1996).

institution) to recommend liquidation or submit a rehabilitation scheme which if sanctioned by the BIFR is known as a 18(4) scheme. As of July 1992, 911 BIFR cases admitted from 1987–1991 had been dealt with or were pending in the following proportions: 17(2) 14 per cent; 18(4) 29 per cent; liquidation 19 per cent; pending 38 per cent.[71]

Like liquidation, the finalization of a BIFR 18(4) scheme takes several years. In the meantime, the incumbent management remains in charge (unlike the UK where an independent administrator is appointed to run the company). This gives it an important advantage. Examination of a number of 18(4) cases showed that in about half existing equity, which should be worthless, was scheduled to gain, while secured creditors made sacrifices.[72] These sacrifices, made by the development finance institutions and nationalized banks, stemmed from the governmental philosophy in favour of rehabilitation.

The bias for rehabilitation is also shown by the excessively optimistic sales and cost projections that were often made in the reconstruction proposals. This excessive optimism shows up in *ex post* data. To quote, 'In 1991 BIFR published follow-up data on 164 rehabilitation schemes: 62 continued making losses; for another 39 the schemes failed and had to be re-opened. Thus 62 per cent of the rehabilitation schemes failed one way or the other. More recent data show no improvement.'[73] Leaning over too far in favour of rehabilitation not only wastes resources by keeping losing companies alive, but also gives promoters faulty incentives. Reducing or eliminating the cost of failure encourages bad management and the taking of undue risks. The BIFR has had some successes, but it falls far short of resolving the sick industry problem in an economically acceptable manner.

As with company law and labour law, the SICA/BIFR system seeks to protect incumbent promoters and management and, above all, the workers. Since the promoters may be favoured

---

[71]   Government of India (1993*c*), table 3.3.
[72]   Goswami (1996).
[73]   Ibid.

largely because of the employment they give, we shall concentrate on the latter.

In loss-making companies workers are not usually worth what they are being paid (or what they are owed if wages are in arrears). These workers are being subsidized by funds which could be used to create similar jobs in profitable ventures where they *would* be worth their wages. As we saw earlier when discussing public sector redundancy, it cannot be in the public interest to employ people in ways which reduce output below its potential. But there can be, and is, a public interest in reducing or eliminating the human costs of redeploying resources. Redundant workers must be made redundant, but should be given enough severance pay to compensate them for the need to find other work. In assessing the public interest in rehabilitation, the BIFR should do a social cost benefit analysis (inevitably rough, but with proper discounting) of every proposal that comes up, which reflects this cost of change. There is no evidence that it uses any such yardstick. Every cost benefit analysis requires a counterfactual for comparison. The counterfactual to rehabilitation is liquidation. The simple way to allow for social costs is to subtract a shadow redundancy cost from the proceeds of liquidation. A further and possibly desirable step would be to make the shadow redundancy cost a reality, by making a suitable redundancy payment a legal requirement, while also giving workers secured creditor rights for arrears of wages and redundancy payments due.[74]

Having made it clear that present policies and institutions are not on track towards creating a good system of bankruptcy law and procedures we need to outline the most important elements in a reform programme.

The most essential step is to facilitate liquidation and closure. Subject to appeal to the BIFR or similar body, creditors should

---

[74] At present a retrenched worker in an enterprise with 100 workers or more is entitled to 15 days' pay for each year of service. It has been suggested that this be raised to 30 days' pay (by the Bajaj Committee): see Government of India (1992*a*).

be able to enforce liquidation on non-payment of dues for a certain period, say 180 days. Obstacles such as those erected by ULCRA and IDA should be removed. Labour's rights should be protected by making dues owed to them most senior debt. But none of this will be of much avail if the liquidator is not given very strong powers to enforce time-bound compliance and if there are long court delays. The authors are no experts in how to streamline legal procedures and increase the capacity of the legal system, but the urgent need to do so is clear. Other countries also experience long delays, but not on the Indian scale.

We have already stated that some defence is needed against creditors, where (*a*) the firm is solvent but cannot itself arrange the debt rescheduling that is indicated, or (*b*) the debt is greater than the expected present value (excluding the debt) as a going or rehabilitated concern, and where this present value is greater than the liquidation value. In these circumstances the company may register as sick (but not moribund), but this should not be mandatory. If the company can sort itself out without the BIFR or similar institution, that is all to the good.

When the company is registered as sick, it should be managed by an administrator who will try to find a solution (which may of course include new investment financed by new loans and equity) that satisfies all parties (with liquidation as a threat). The administrator should be able to rebuff any seizure of assets by any class of creditors.

In case (*b*) above it is desirable that the company continues as a going concern but some debt write-off is required. In this case existing equity is technically valueless. But if the existing management is to continue after the administrator retires, some sop may be needed. The administrator may, in such a case, try to obtain agreement between equity holders and creditors through debt-equity swaps. If there is an impediment in Indian law to such swaps it should be removed.

The above is a sketch of what we believe to be a good system: it closely follows British practice.[75] We repeat that minimum rather generous redundancy payments should be enacted in the event of liquidation or reorganization, and that these, if unpaid, should rank as most senior debt. In this way the main hurdle to industrial reorganization should be overcome.

[75] Of course, it lacks detail. The reader should also consult Goswami (1996). He discusses a very elegant and equitable system, proposed in Aghion, Hart, and Moore (1992), 8. 3. 523–96.

6

The Social Sectors, Poverty, and Reform

6.1. Introduction

India lags behind many other poor countries in general educational standards and achievement, and also in health and health improvement. This has been stressed by Drèze and Sen (1995) who make a powerful plea for social reform.[1] We support their views. These are sectors where government has an important beneficial role to play. They have been relatively neglected in India, most especially primary education and health care, while government has focused attention on regulating activities that were better left alone. More expenditure is needed, but not only that. Existing priorities are wrong. For instance, higher education is heavily subsidized, benefiting the well off, while the quality of State primary education is lamentable. Unfortunately, to examine the details of desirable reform in these sectors would take us beyond the scope of this book.

However, the major reforms we have applauded or advocated may have seriously differing effects on different social and economic classes. These, especially the effects on the poor, cannot be ignored. Indeed the objective of any reform must be to benefit society, and this surely precludes reforms which harm many poor people belonging to that society.

There are only two ways of assisting the poor. One is to transfer wealth to them. This may include the transfer of income, or assets such as land, or the enhancement of their

---

[1] See also World Bank (1995c) for a comprehensive review of primary health care in India.

principal asset, that is themselves.   Income transfers are considered in Section 6.4 below.   The enhancement of their principal asset, themselves, calls for the increased public attention to and expenditure on health and education that we have endorsed above.   A case can still be made for substantial land reform, but it has proved to be politically impossible, and we do not discuss it.

The other way to help the poor is to increase the demand for their services.   This either gives them more employment and hence income, or it results in an increase in real wage rates. With sufficiently increased demand the results can be dramatic, as witness the rises in industrial employment and real wages in the East Asian 'tigers' in the 1960s and 1970s.   We are confident that the reforms so far undertaken, and the further reforms we advocate, will increase the demand for unskilled labour—and most of the poor in India are unskilled workers, or dependent on them.

India should trade with the rest of the world according to her comparative advantage, and not in pursuit of autarky.   There is no doubt that exports are and will be more labour intensive than import substitutes.   A higher proportion of India's manufacturing output will be devoted to clothing, cotton textiles, processed food, and thousands of light engineering products.   These are both directly and indirectly relatively labour intensive (indirectly because less steel and power is used in their manufacture).   Thus the product mix will be more labour demanding.   But within industries there is also room for more labour intensive methods of manufacture.   The use of capital has for forty years been encouraged by interest subsidies; and the use of labour has been discouraged, especially in the organized sector, by relatively high wages and by over-protective labour legislation.   These distortions need to be removed.   Much the same is true of agriculture.   The search for self-sufficiency has twisted agricultural production in favour of edible oils and sugar which are relatively capital intensive; and capital intensive methods, such as the use of harvesters, have been encouraged by cheap loans.   Almost all governmental interventions have reduced the demand for unskilled labour. By the same token, the comprehensive removal and reform of these interventions will increase the demand for labour.

Growth itself, of course, increases the demand for unskilled labour. But if growth is not very labour demanding, there will be a tendency to increased inequality: while some are employed productively at relatively high wages, others are left scratching a living somehow. If growth is more labour demanding the benefits are more widely spread. Then growth really trickles down.

The structural reforms underway since 1991, albeit still very incomplete, favour the poor by beginning to remove the pervasive bias that exists against the employment of unskilled labour. But we recognize that shifts in the pattern and modes of production are certain to make some people redundant. We return to this problem below, although it must be emphasized that very few of those made redundant will be poor or likely to become poor. However, it remains true that they increase the supply of labour. There will therefore remain a case for public employment programmes for a good many years, though hopefully not for ever.[2]

6.2. Dealing with the Short-Term Effects of Stabilization

Given the labour-demanding nature of the reforms adumbrated in July 1991, why is it that there has been so much protesting that the government's reforms favoured the rich and hurt the poor? Partly, as we shall see, the protests confused stabilization and reform. Stabilization was unavoidable and has nowhere, not even in India, been achieved without hurting poor people to some extent. But the primary reason for protesting has been that the accusation of not caring for the poor is a political stick with

---

[2] Kakwani and Subbarao (1993).

which to beat the government. It was easy to present the removal of much of the 'permit raj' restrictions as good for industry, and then to identify industry's interest with that of the rich.

The protests began long before there could be any facts linking the reforms with the plight of the poor. Later as some relevant facts came to light, mainly from the National Sample Survey (NSS) of calendar year 1992, the accusations could be maintained by continuing to confuse the effects of stabilization measures with those of structural reform. By stabilization measures we mean those taken to deal with the crisis of 1991 which were carefully described and analysed in Chapter 2. We saw there that India's stabilization was extraordinarily successful when compared with most other countries which were forced to effect a large and rapid reduction in their current external account deficits. However, despite the success of the devaluation, some cuts in public expenditure were needed to induce, directly and indirectly, a sufficient compression of imports, and some of these cuts were in the social services (SS), and in expenditure on rural development (RD). In 1991/92, the crisis year, central nominal expenditure on these items (SSRD) rose by 1.5 per cent, and in 1992/93 by 17.5 per cent. The real change depends on the price index used. However, by any measure, there was a sharp fall in 1991/92 of over 10 per cent. The recovery in 1992/93 still left real expenditure below 1990/91 (by 4 per cent using the Consumer Price Index (CPI) for industrial workers, and 8 per cent using the CPI for agricultural labourers). Moreover, the States which account for about 80 per cent of SSRD were squeezed by a fall in transfers from the Centre. Nevertheless, they did better than the Centre with nominal SSRD expenditure rising by 12.7 per cent and 11.9 per cent in the two years. Consolidating Centre and States there was a nominal rise of 10.8 per cent in 1991/92 and 12.0 per cent in 1992/93. This left 1992/93 real expenditure the same as 1990/91 using the industrial workers' CPI, and 4 per cent lower using the agricultural labourers' CPI.

Not all expenditure under the SSRD headings is related to poverty relief. Dr Guhan has separated out those items in the central budget which can be construed as relating to poverty, about two-thirds of the total SSRD.[3] Nominal central expenditure on these items rose by 6.4 per cent and 15 per cent in 1991/92 and 1992/93. In 1991/92 Jawahar Rozgar Yojana (JRY) expenditures fell by 8.8 per cent, other items rising by 21.3 per cent. Unfortunately the same categorization has not been carried out for the States (it would be a major research project).

The general picture is clear. There was a sharp fall in poverty-related real expenditures in the crisis year, with nearly full recovery in 1992/93. But can anything be said about what actually happened to poverty? The NSS rounds of 1991 and 1992 show a considerable rise in rural poverty in 1991 and 1992, and a slight rise in urban poverty in 1992: this followed a period of falling poverty in the 1980s. The causes of this rise in rural poverty have been carefully analysed by S. D. Tendulkar and L. R. Jain.[4]

Rural poverty depends on farm employment and hence agricultural output, on real wages and hence the price of cereals; and on the extent of anti-poverty employment programmes. The monsoon in 1991/92 was below normal. The all-commodity output index fell by 2 per cent, and that of cereals by 4.2 per cent. There was a very large rise in foodgrain prices. The Wholesale Price Index (WPI) rose by 13.7 per cent, but the price of foodgrains rose by 20.8 per cent, and the CPI for agricultural workers by 19.3 per cent. Real rural wages fell by about 6 per cent (but recovered to 1990/91 levels in 1992/93).[5] The demand for labour was not supported by public employment programmes. With no fall in the demand for labour, rural wages

---

[3] This and the previous paragraph rely mainly on Guhan (1995).

[4] Tendulkar and Jain (1995).

[5] Aiyar (1995). It should be noticed that the wage data are gathered from only ten states: Andhra Pradesh, Gujarat, Kerala, Madhya Pradesh, Maharashtra, Orissa, Rajasthan, Haryana, Tamil Nadu, and Uttar Pradesh.

might have risen as fast as the cost of living in 1991/92.[6] The monsoon was not bad enough for 1991/92 to be declared a drought year, and no special relief works were called into play. The employment provided by the JRY fell from 875 million persondays in 1990/91 to 809 million persondays in 1991/92. The government should have protected expenditure on rural employment, and found its budget cuts elsewhere.

The above fully accounts for the rise in rural poverty, caused by the poor harvest and the rise in cereal prices. Whether there is any connection between the rise in cereal prices and stabilization is debatable. Obviously the stabilization measures would have moderated the general inflation of prices: but cereal prices rose more than the WPI. This was to be expected given the fall in output, unless food stocks and the Public Distribution System (PDS) were used to moderate the price rise. Foodgrain stocks were somewhat below target during the year, and there seems to have been little or no net release (offtake less procurement) which would have required lower issue prices.[7] There was a very large rise in procurement prices in 1991/92 and again in 1992/93 (rice: 12.2 per cent and 17.4 per cent; wheat: 22.2 per cent and 20.0 per cent). But in order to limit the rise in food subsidies the issue price of rice was raised by 30.0 per cent in December 1991, and that of wheat by 21.0 per cent—despite which the food subsidy rose from Rs 2,450 crores in 1990/91 to Rs 2,850 crores in 1991/92. The large rise in procurement prices was partly made to compensate farmers for a reduction in fertilizer subsidies. But the fertilizer subsidies were soon restored![8] It could even be argued that the operation of the PDS and the supposed system of food security contributed both to

[6] Dev (1995); it is reported that *usual status* regular agricultural employment fell by 1.6 millions between 1989/90 and 1992, while *usual status* casual employment rose by 4.4 millions. But this may be consistent with a fall in actual person days of employment in 1992; for it is hard to imagine that a reduction of 2 per cent in output, including a 4.2 per cent fall in cereals, would not cause some fall in employment in harvesting, winnowing, and transport.

[7] Government of India, *Economic Survey 1992/93*, tables 4-13, and 4-14.

[8] Fertilizer subsidies rose in both 1991/92 and 1992/93 by 18 per cent.

inflation and to the rise in rural poverty on this occasion. Procurement prices were raised too much, followed by issue prices to limit the food subsidies. The basic error was the rise in procurement prices which cannot be classified as a stabilization measure. The only clear connection between stabilization and the rise in rural poverty was the fall in JRY employment, and the unfortunate dynamics of a politically frustrated effort to reduce the fertilizer subsidies.

One might have expected stabilization to have had a most deflationary effect on industry, and hence to result in some increase in urban poverty. There was indeed some increase, but it was small, from 32.02 per cent to 33.87 per cent by the standard Planning Commission head-count method—probably within the measurement error. The unemployment of males who account for the overwhelming share of urban employment, actually fell. If the figures are to be believed, the burden fell on women.

The verdict remains that India came through the 1991 balance of payments crisis with remarkably little suffering, and that the 1991/92 rise in rural poverty was mainly caused by a fall in agricultural output, and was only weakly connected with the stabilization measures. This is not to maintain that the government's measures were faultless.

We have said that the accusations that the reforms hurt the poor were based on a confusion of stabilization and structural reform. We have seen that stabilization was part of the cause of the rise in rural poverty. But it is hard to think of any connection at all between the rise in rural poverty in 1991/92 and the structural reforms initiated in July 1991, few of which had got very far by the end of 1991/92. The main achievement had been the delicensing of domestic industrial activities, a very limited decontrol of imports, and some friendly moves towards foreign investors. The reform of tariffs, domestic taxation, and the banking and monetary systems were still to come. The only (weak) link may have been the rise in fertilizer prices in July

1991 which might be considered to be a structural reform, though the motive was stabilization.[9]

6.2.1. Poverty-Alleviating Measures after 1991/92

We have already seen that there was a slight recovery of SSRD expenditure in 1992/93. Since then the central budgets have put a great deal of emphasis on increasing such expenditures. In 1993/94 they rose by 29 per cent and in 1994/95 (RE) by 27.5 per cent. In 1995–96 the Finance Minister budgeted for a further increase of 13 per cent, besides arranging for some non-budgetary subventions.[10] The more narrowly defined poverty-related expenditures rose by 48.8 per cent, 28.0 per cent, and 16.1 per cent.[11] Given that inflation has been running at about 10 per cent, these figures indicate remarkable real increases.[12]

The States' SSRD expenditure rose by 14.2 per cent and 14.6 per cent in 1993/94 and 1994/95 (revised and budget estimates), more than keeping up with inflation. Consolidated Centre and States SSRD expenditure rose by 16.6 per cent and 21 per cent in these two years. In 1993/94 they were 7.2 per cent of GDP compared with 7.3 per cent in 1990/91.[13]

Output and employment have also recovered. Agricultural output rose by 5.3 per cent in 1992/93 and 2.9 per cent in

---

[9] Dev (1995) attributes much of the rise in rural poverty in 1992 to what he calls the reforms. But he makes no distinction between stabilization and reform—a distinction that we regard as essential. It is highly misleading to include most of the expenditure cuts as reform, especially when they were restored the following year. The only exception is the abortive cut in the fertilizer subsidy, which could be regarded as an attempt at reform although also certainly part of the stabilization measures. As explained in the text, this contributed in part to the rise in procurement prices, and hence to the rise in issue prices.

[10] See Chapter 3.

[11] See Guhan (1995), table 4.

[12] The acceleration of inflation in early 1995 is, however, worrying.

[13] There seems to be an error in Guhan (1995) table 3, which gives 6.9 per cent of GDP for 1993/94.

1993/94, and GDP   by 4.3 per cent in both years.   Real agricultural wages after rising by 6 per cent in 1992/93, rose again by 2.5 per cent in 1993/94. The *Economic Survey 1994/95* estimates increases in employment of 6.4 million and 5.6 million. Estimates of unemployment and poverty after 1991/92 still await (in August 1995) the 1993/94 NSS round. The dollar value of manufactured exports rose 20 per cent in 1993/94 and 16 per cent in the first half of 1994/95. This was encouraging, especially as many of the measures which should encourage exports were incomplete and not long in place. Taking all this into account it will be very surprising indeed if the increases in poverty of 1991/92 have not been reversed.[14]

6.3. Poverty and Reform in the Longer Run

Reforms which may have serious distributional effects have hardly begun. These are:

(i)   All those reforms in both the public and private sectors which will result in the shedding of labour.   These include privatization, and changes in company laws, labour legislation, and bankruptcy laws.   One might include here the increased competition resulting from domestic decontrol and trade liberalization. This is the problem of redundancy which we have already considered in Chapter 5, but to which we again revert.

(ii) Changes in prices which may adversely effect the poor. We refer mainly to those arising from the major reform of agri-cultural incentives and trade that is proposed, but not started, or even accepted.

---

[14] Since writing the above paragraph in August 1995, the *Business Standard* of 21 December 1995 reported a sharp drop in the Planning Commission's estimates of the percentage of people below the poverty line in 1993/94.

6.3.1. Redundancy Again, and Job Security

In Chapter 5 we considered redundancy mainly from the point of view of achieving a large once-and-for-all shedding of labour from public sector enterprises, and also from those sick private companies under the BIFR umbrella.

Our main proposal was for a fairly generous programme of 'copper handshakes'. However, the rules which may be applied to the existing public workforce, with their expectations of secure employment, need not apply to new contracts. Any legislation governing new contracts should apply without distinction to public and private enterprises.

We saw in Chapter 5 that the legislation under the Industrial Disputes Act (IDA) which sought to provide job security by making it difficult to fire workers and which made closure illegal, not only contributed seriously to industrial inefficiency in India, but also failed to ensure job security and to secure workers' rights in cases of *de facto* closure. The relevant sections of the IDA should be repealed. We suggested however that redundancy payments might continue to be a legal requirement.[15] There is in principle a trade off between higher wages and more job security, since shouldering the risk of redundancy payments is a cost to the employer. It might therefore be suggested that the workers should have some choice in the amount of job security provided, recognizing that more job security would imply lower wages. This could be left to the market, with employers competing for labour on the basis of both wages and job security. Or, where the work force is unionized, the package of wages and redundancy pay could be subject to collective bargaining. Even so, we think that a legal minimum might be desirable especially as it could be presented as compensation for repeal of the relevant clauses of the IDA. It could, of course, apply only to firms above a certain size. It

---

[15]	At present a worker is entitled to 15 days' pay for each completed year of service.

should also be kept fairly low in order not to encourage casual employment as the IDA has done.

Before considering price changes and poverty, we again emphasize that concern for redundancy in the public sector and organized industry is not primarily a concern for the poor. The great majority of those made redundant will either have enough to retire on, or will quickly find other employment. However, this puts pressure on the unorganized sectors; and persons losing their jobs there may well be poor. The seriousness of this will, however, be limited by the increased demand for labour which we expect to be generated by the general reforms we advocate, and by the public employment schemes and other poverty alleviation measures that we discuss below.

6.3.2. *Agricultural Liberalization, Poverty, and the Price of Food*

Agricultural liberalization should have been in the front line of the reforms initiated in 1991. Agriculture is the largest industry, however measured: and it has suffered as much from distortionary interventions as any other industry. But virtually nothing has been done, and no programme of reform has been adumbrated, let alone adopted.

There are many agriculture-related areas, such as research, extension, and investment in infrastructure, where reforms and increased investment are surely desirable. But two major reforms stand out—the removal of input subsidies and the freeing of international trade.

The strong fiscal reasons for reducing or abolishing agricultural input subsidies have been emphasized in Chapter 3. Some may remember that the conventional wisdom of the development establishment of the 1950s and 1960s was that agriculture should be encouraged by subsidizing inputs. This was preferred to higher output prices which did nothing to encourage the new methods that were needed to raise yields.

Peasants were obdurate, moreover, and needed big shoves to get them to move. Whatever the merits, if any, of this argument at the time, input subsidies are now clearly counter-productive. Subsidized electricity causes overpumping of tube-wells. Cheap water, generally, results in its excessive use and unduly encourages water-demanding crops. Cheap loans encourage tractors and harvesters. The fertilizer subsidies have resulted in excessive use of nitrogen relative to phosphates and potash, while also discouraging organic fertilizers. All of these results of input subsidization work in the direction of capital intensity, and help to explain the fall in the employment elasticity of output which has occurred; they therefore tend to be poverty-creating, given the level of output.

In considering the effect on farmers themselves, one must link the removal of subsidies with the higher output prices that would result from trade liberalization. An estimate for 1992/93 suggested that output prices might rise by 15–20 per cent,[16] which would be more than enough to compensate for the loss of subsidies, which may be about 11 per cent of agricultural GDP.[17] We do not have a more up-to-date estimate, but nominal protection rates estimated by the National Council of Applied Economic Research for 1994/95 do not differ much from those for 1992/93 in the case of cereals and cotton. Thus the estimate of 15–20 per cent may still be of the right order of magnitude. Of course, the effects would be uneven regionally, and time for crop adjustment should certainly be allowed. Free trade in agriculture would thus need to be approached slowly. But there is no likelihood that subsidies would be very quickly removed, however dramatic the change of heart among policy-makers. There is possibly no harm in feeling one's way as long as the final objective is understood. Nevertheless one should consider the relative effect on large and small farmers as an approach to market prices is made. It is obviously true that large

----

[16]   Pursell and Gulati (1993).

[17]   11 per cent of agricultural GDP in 1993/94 was about Rs 23,000 crores. The total of subsidies may be approaching this figure.

farmers get most of the subsidies in absolute terms. It is also quite probable that large farmers get relatively more—that is the subsidized inputs account for a higher proportion of costs than is the case with small farmers, though we have seen no figures on this. For these reasons, input subsidization is not itself an equalizing or poverty-alleviating measure. However, the compensation for reduced subsidies is higher output prices, and these are little or no compensation for the subsistence farmer. For this reason some subsidies might be retained for the very small farmer. This is a case where targeting, by the size of ownership and operational holdings, may be relatively easy.[18]

A more serious effect would seem to be the rise in food prices. In the long run one would not expect food prices to be an important determinant of the distribution of income, or the extent of poverty. Certainly food expenditure will form a larger part of the budget of the poor, even in a very rich society. But it is also true that a relative rise in food prices will cause a rise in money wages. In other words, real wages may not fall—or not much—when food prices rise, if there is no concurrent fall in the demand for labour.[19] In a rich country one might expect the incomes of non-workers also to be at least partly compensated for a change in relative prices, whether by familial or public

---

[18] In 1991 small farmers were sheltered from the reduction in the fertilizer subsidy—so presumably this targeting was feasible even if imperfect. Of course, this subsidy would create an undesirable poverty trap. One hopes that eventually development will make it unnecessary to preserve subsistence or near-subsistence farmers.

[19] History is not very helpful here. Not only are real wage figures very unreliable, but also a bad harvest with reduced demand for labour normally accompanies a big rise in food prices. However 1980/81 was an exception. Food prices *and* output rose with a fall in real agricultural wages (but a negligible fall in manufacturing wages). See Joshi and Little (1994), 154–5. But we would still not expect a change in food prices alone to have a lasting effect on either agricultural or urban real wages, even in the absence of any indexation. We have seen that agricultural real wages recovered very quickly after the fall in 1991/92. However, Ravallion (1990) inclines to the view that higher food prices will not be fully compensated by a rise in wages, even in the long run.

transfers.   But in India with no public welfare system this certainly cannot be relied on.   The upshot is that one might expect the old and the incapacitated to be most affected by a relative rise in food prices.

Food subsidies reduce or prevent a rise in the retail price of food when farm-gate prices rise. If, as seems likely, this largely prevents a compensating rise in money wages, then the subsidy does not go mainly to the workers. This suggests that it would be better to target the poor and make direct transfers to them. Those who advocate the kind of reform of agricultural incentives we have described above recognize that some offset to higher food prices would be needed. They also recognize that general food subsidies are a fiscally inept way of attacking poverty. Therefore they call for a reform of the PDS to target the food subsidies towards the poor.   However, the PDS is one of a number of poverty-alleviation schemes which have been in existence for more than twenty years, and therefore are not to be regarded as measures to deal only with a large rise in food prices resulting from drought or a change of agricultural policies, but rather as part of the anti-poverty programme year in year out. We now turn to these schemes.

6.4. Poverty-Alleviation Schemes

There are many such schemes, and several promoted by the Centre on an All India basis. We shall focus on the two main ones, the Public Distribution System (PDS) and the Jawahar Rozgar Yojana public employment scheme (JRY). Discussion of these enables one to address all the difficult issues involved in poverty alleviation.

6.4.1. The Public Distribution System

It has been convincingly shown that the PDS is a grossly inefficient instrument for reaching the poor.[20] Some highlights are:

(i) In seven larger Northern States, comprising over half the rural population of India, more than 90 per cent of the rural population bought nothing from the PDS. Only in the four large Southern States did more than half the population make some purchase. Even in these States the average monthly per caput cereal subsidy came to only 5.1 rupees. With a few amendments much the same is true of the urban population. The urban per caput subsidy in the Southern States was only a little higher, 5.9 rupees.

(ii) Taking only the poorest 20 per cent of all households, rural and urban, as the population, it is still true with one exception that 85 per cent or more made no purchase from the PDS in the seven Northern States.[21] The monthly rural per caput cereal subsidy in the Southern States was Rs 3.9 and Rs 5.3 for the urban poor.

(iii) The above implies that most of the total cereal subsidy goes to the not-so-poor. Indeed with the one exception of Goa, Daman and Diu, in no State does as much as 22 per cent of the cereal subsidy reach the poorest 20 per cent of households.

In 1992 the PDS was revamped. Additional quantities of cereals were made available at a reduced issue price for 1,775 blocks in backward areas. We doubt that this will be the best way of reaching poor households in these areas, especially given the inefficiency and corruption of the Food Corporation of India

---

[20] Parikh (1993). This article was based on the results of the 42nd round of the NSS. An earlier study using a general equilibrium model was Parikh and Srinivasan, in Lipton and van der Gaag (1993).
[21] Urban Madhya Pradesh was the exception with 50 per cent making no purchase.

(FCI) and the food departments of State governments. To quote: 'At least 15 per cent of the foodgrains procured by FCI disappears without trace ... These losses are passed off as wastage, but are actually siphoned off by the staff and sold. The proportion is far higher in the State Food Departments.'[22]

Various suggestions have been made for better targeting of the PDS, while at the same time reducing the fiscal burden. One is to eliminate sugar and edible oils which are relatively little consumed by the poor. Doing this while increasing the subsidy on cereals would both target the poor a little better, and shift consumption away from commodities in whose production India has a comparative disadvantage. Another suggestion is to refuse ration cards to those with visible signs of relative affluence, e.g. owning a car, a telephone, or a substantial landholding or house. But such administrative targeting might be quite expensive for the savings it could make, and would provide yet another avenue of corruption.

Another more exciting idea is to abolish the corrupt PDS, while retaining some food subsidy. This can be done by the use of food stamps, an idea commended by Bhagwati and Srinivasan (1993).[23] Food stamps can do everything the PDS, or a reformed PDS can do, and do it more flexibly and cheaply. The value of the stamps issued can be varied to take care of variations in the price of commodities. Their permissible use can cover a wide basket of commodities, or be limited to a few, for example to cereals only. There would be no need for public distribution and government shops. Government buffer stocks could still be operated, purchases and sales being made through

---

[22]   Desai (1993), 290.

[23]   Food stamps are essentially a second currency doled out to the needy that can be spent only on certain food items. The licensed food retailer is reimbursed in cash by the issuing agency, or he may pass on the stamps to a wholesaler who claims reimbursement. One could not fully ensure that retailers sold only food in exchange for stamps: but neither this leakage nor the fact that stamps could be sold for cash would matter. The recipient of the stamps still gains: and there would be some increase in the demand for food to help reduce the excessive stocks now held.

normal commercial channels. The problem of targeting would however remain.[24]

6.4.2. The Jawahar Rozgar Yojana (JRY) and Other Public Employment Schemes

The post-independence prototype for JRY and its All India cousins is the Maharashtra Employment Guarantee Scheme (MEGS) which was created to counter the very severe droughts in rural Maharashtra in the years 1970–73.[25] The scheme was extremely successful. Conditions which would otherwise have caused widespread misery, starvation, and death, left virtually no adverse trace. At the peak of employment, daily attendance reached nearly five million (from a total rural population of 35 million). In badly affected areas, the relief constituted a high proportion of earnings. It was a genuine guarantee scheme. All were employed who turned up, and were paid very low wages in cash.[26] The essential point of very low wages is not only that the government could finance unrestricted relief, but also that only the very poor turned up. In other words, the scheme was self-targeting. The PDS played almost no part; the bulk of grain purchases was made on the open market. Relief was the essential objective; whether or not the assets created were useful was of secondary importance.

---

[24] When Sri Lanka introduced food stamps in 1979 they were mainly targeted at families with incomes of less than Rs 300 a month. We do not know how income levels were ascertained or estimated. Nearly half the population was disqualified. For an account see Anand and Kanbur, in Drèze and Sen (eds.), 1991. The value of the food stamps was not indexed. Food subsidies were thus rapidly reduced. Not only was the better off half of the population excluded, but also the benefit to the targeted poor was greatly reduced. This is not a feature we have in mind for India.

[25] For a general assessment see Drèze (1990).

[26] Certainly no more than the going agricultural wage—but of course this would itself be affected by the MEGS.

The scheme continued after the drought, providing an average of about 170 million persondays of employment per annum from 1975/76 to 1985/86, at a wage roughly equal to the going agricultural wage. In May 1988, the piece rates paid were doubled in line with a doubling in the State's statutory minimum wage, since a court decision made paying less than the minimum wage illegal. Expenditure fell! Although the authorities deny it, the evidence is that employment has since then been rationed. It is also very likely that the self-targeting nature of the scheme will have suffered—more not-so-poor people will have been employed (statutory minimum wages cannot be enforced, so the MEGS rate may have become higher than actual rates paid by farmers).[27] By 1990/91 persondays of employment had fallen to about 90 million.

All-India public employment generation schemes do not have such a simple objective as the MEGS originally had—a guarantee against starvation or destitution (those who could not work, and with no one to care for them, were directly assisted). By far the biggest is the JRY, carrying a budget estimate of Rs 3,862 ~~6,222~~ crores for 1995/96. It was launched in April 1989, merging two previous ongoing programmes. It is fragmented into several 'streams', each with further earmarkings. Thus there are targets, not only for the employment of scheduled castes and tribes (SC/ST), but for the creation of assets for them (wells and houses). Forestry also has a target. Part of the JRY is confined to backward districts. The smaller Employment Assurance Scheme (EAS), started in 1993/94, has a budget estimate of Rs 1,570 crores. It is confined to 1,752 backward blocks (about a third of all blocks in the country) with earmarked targets for various kinds of rural infrastructure. There is also the MP scheme under which every member of both houses of parliament (790 of them) gets Rs 1 crore per annum to spend on a scheme of his or her choice. Taken together, these

---

[27] This paragraph draws on Ravallion, Dutt, and Chaudhuri (1993). See also Dev (1992).

50

three schemes account for almost 60 per cent of central government rural development and social services expenditure. We have seen no evaluation of the latter two schemes, and concentrate on the JRY.

The primary aim of the JRY was the creation of additional employment for the unemployed or underemployed living below the poverty line in rural areas. The secondary aim was the creation of rural assets, especially such as would benefit the SCs and STs. Various operating conditions were imposed: 60 per cent of expenditure was to be on wages; contractors were banned; at least minimum legal wages must be paid; men and women should be paid the same; and preference given to SCs and STs.

The first concurrent evaluation of JRY took place throughout the calendar year 1992. The field work was carried out by independent research organizations, but the research was planned and the questionnaires designed by the Ministry of Rural Development in consultation with the Planning Commission.[28]

The operational conditions referred to were moderately well satisfied. The All-India wage component was 53 per cent as against the stipulated minimum of 60 per cent with variation from 21 per cent (Punjab) to 83 per cent (Assam). There was some, but very little, reported use of the forbidden contractors.[29] Most States report wage rates close to (a few, suspiciously, exactly equal to) the statutory minimum. Most States report female wages exactly equal to male wages, again suspiciously. More interesting is the relation of the wage paid to the local wage rates. Slightly more States report paying less than the going wage than paying more (for men). But many of those States are small employers. The large States giving employment of more than five persondays per household in the previous 30 days, were Assam, Kerala, Orissa, and Tamil Nadu. Of these Assam and Orissa apparently paid more than the going wage,

---

[28]   We rely on the report of this evaluation by Neelakantan (1994).
[29]   This low use is disbelieved by others. See Chathukulam and Kerien (1995).

and Kerala and Tamil Nadu less. One cannot make much of this.

Fulfilment or non-fulfilment of the operational conditions tells one little or nothing about the social value of the programme. The Assessment does, however, report some other relevant facts. First, the average level of provision of employment was about five persondays per month per family, but the level was well below this in the very poor states of Bihar, Uttar Pradesh, West Bengal and Madhya Pradesh. More seriously, JRY was very badly targeted family-wise. Fifty seven per cent of participants were from families above the family poverty line of Rs 533 a month in 1992. Only 18 per cent fell into the categories of very poor or worse (below Rs 400 per month).[30]

The net transfer to the poor has been estimated by S. Guhan at 14.3 per cent of expenditure. This is shown in Table 6.1 which takes account of the fact that other work is reduced. Five persondays probably represent only three additional persondays of work (see note c to the table).

It is by now obvious that the JRY is very different from the original MEGS. The latter's dominant objective was the relief of destitution. Because of the drought the work provided was almost entirely additional. Because of the low wages, and also possibly because of some community solidarity in the face of near disaster, the employment was well targeted. MEGS was thus very well targeted on poverty. It would clearly have been highly desirable even if no assets were created. In contrast, JRY is poorly targeted. One cannot possibly applaud JRY as a cost effective scheme for poverty alleviation alone. How then does one judge schemes or projects whose value may be partly in poverty relief and partly in asset creation; and how does one compare them with direct transfers to poor families, or with work-related transfers like MEGS where asset creation is of little or no importance?

---

[30] It is scarcely credible that both the IRDP and the JRY use family poverty lines that take no account of the size of the family. For an assessment of IRDP, a credit-based poverty-alleviation programme, see chapter 4.

Table 6.1.   Net Transfer Efficiency of the JRY

1.	Gross expenditure	100.0
2.	Wage component[a]	53.0
3.	Leakage[b]	5.3
4.	Gross wage transfer $(1-2-3)$	47.7
5.	Participation cost[c] (income foregone)	19.1
6.	Net benefit $(4-5)$	28.6
7.	Coverage of poor[d] (targeting efficiency)	0.5
8.	Transfer to poor (6×7) (transfer efficiency)	14.3

[a] As estimated in Government of India Concurrent Evaluation of JRY (January–December 1992), July 1994.
[b] Underpayment of wages at 10 per cent of wage payment (assumed).
[c] 40 per cent of wage payment (47.7) representing foregone incomes based on estimate in Ravallion (1990).
[d] Government of India concurrent evaluation of JRY (January–December 1992), July 1994 estimates this ratio at 0.43. We have improved it to 0.5

The answers to the above questions must lie in the application of a method of cost-benefit analysis which recognizes that equal increments of consumption have different social values depending on the level of consumption or income of the recipient. Ignoring complications, the basis of the method is for the government to settle on a level of consumption so that it regards a rupee of extra consumption at that level, resulting from employment, to have the same social value as an uncommitted rupee in its own hands. Call this level *b*. If a person has a consumption level less than *b*, more money in his or her hands is worth more than public money—if the consumption level is higher it is worth less. This leads toward the estimation of a shadow wage rate, that is the social cost of employing someone.

If there was no reduction of output elsewhere, the shadow wage for someone at the consumption level *b* would be zero. It would be positive at a higher level, and negative at a lower level.[31]

Since the government undertakes programmes primarily to benefit the poor, defined as those below the official poverty line, with only secondary concern for the creation of assets which are themselves supported mainly to benefit the poor later, it would seem that additional consumption at the poverty borderline (average family income level of Rs 533 a month in 1992) may be a fair approximation of *b*. It can thus be argued that the government regards the poverty borderline as that level of income (or consumption) at which extra consumption from earned income has the same value as uncommitted public income.

It follows that there is a real social cost in employing people if they fall above the poverty line, even if there is no reduction of work and loss of output elsewhere. More than half the employment on JRY programmes is from families with consumption greater than *b*. Moreover, there is a significant reduction in other work.[32] There are also non-wage costs of over 40 per cent of the total. There is thus no doubt that JRY employment incurs a social cost. It follows that if JRY is to be justifiable the assets created must be valuable.

In the Evaluation referred to above the quality of the assets created was judged to be good or satisfactory in 74 per cent of cases, *in the judgement of the field agency*. It is unfortunate that this tells us nothing about the social value of the assets. Questions put to the workers should reveal a little more. Ninety seven per cent said they were useful for poor people, and 82 per cent that they met the felt needs of the community.

---

[31] How to calculate the shadow wage when there is some loss of output elsewhere, and some non-wage cost of increased employment, is fully explained in Little and Mirrlees (1974) especially chs. 13 and 14. The method can also be studied in Squire and van der Tak (1975) where *b* is termed 'the critical consumption level'.

[32] Furthermore, the appraisal was made in 1992, a year of reduced agricultural output, and increased poverty.

Unfortunately, such a favourable response can only make one suspicious. Some of the workers were perhaps simply signalling that they wanted more JRY. Some observers have criticized the concentration on roads which account for about 45 per cent of total expenditure and half the employment. Some prescribed areas of activity were very neglected, e.g. forestry, land development, flood protection, and water conservation. S. Guhan has written:

There is enough evidence to show that in practice the thin spread of the JRY, without being underpinned by local level planning or consultation, results in a variety of distortions: non-durable rather than more permanent works are chosen; in many cases works are abandoned incomplete and new ones started elsewhere; and maintenance is sorely neglected.' (Guhan, 1995, 1100.)

It seems that further research is needed using a carefully evaluated shadow wage rate which would in effect quantify the contribution of the works to poverty relief. At present one knows only that there is probably some small contribution, and that the value of the assets created is uncertain. It would admittedly be very difficult to value these assets, but an informed guess is better than nothing. Some indication of the relative value of different kinds of assets, roads, trees, wells, ditches, communal buildings, etc. in different regions, might be forthcoming.

By way of improving the quality of assets, it seems advisable to recognize explicitly that JRY expenditure is primarily for material infrastructural development, and only secondarily for the immediate relief of poverty. Expenditure may then be more efficiently planned and budgeted under different development headings.[33] At the same time, the relief of poverty need not be forgotten (and would be brought out by social cost benefit analysis). More emphasis could be given to backward areas and poor States. And wages should be kept low to improve the poor targeting (thus reducing the shadow wage rate). Finally it has to

[33] This closely follows suggestions in Guhan (1995).

be remembered that a serious drought could change the priorities. For this reason it would seem prudent always to keep some programmes going in drought-prone regions, which could be rapidly enlarged in case of need.

6.4.3. Direct Transfers to the Poor

Since the JRY, EAS, and MP schemes have other rationales besides poverty relief, they are not competitive as a whole with more direct approaches. The 1995/96 budget assumed for the Centre for the first time with the National Social Assistance Scheme a role in helping the States provide such direct transfers. Pensions for the disabled, for the old, and for widows, and allowances for sickness and maternity benefit, are likely to be better targeted to poverty than existing public employment schemes., At the margin, therefore, employment schemes do compete with such transfers. School meals in State schools are another strong contender for the contents of the public purse. We do not have enough knowledge to be able to suggest priorities. But we note that Tamil Nadu has used such transfers since 1989/90.[34] Its experience should be further studied.

6.5. Education and Health

We have said that we cannot consider the details of reforms in these sectors. But increased expenditure on them competes with the poverty-related programmes discussed above. However, expenditure on primary education and health care, and public health, will contribute to the success of the many reforms which favour a more labour-demanding development. There is no clear evidence of a high return to primary education in the absence of a high demand for workers with a little education. But labour-

---

[34]   Guhan (1990).

intensive development will be retarded if much of the workforce is illiterate, innumerate, and of poor physique. In the longer run, expenditure on primary education and primary health care may be more poverty-reducing than other more immediate measures —provided always that the economic, social, and legal systems are not biased against employment. There is no doubt that these sectors should be given high priority.

6.6. Conclusions

We were led into a discussion of poverty and its alleviation because of the need to consider the distributional aspects of the reforms we applaud and advocate. We found that the temporary rise in poverty in 1991/92 had nothing to do with the reform programme that was initiated in July 1991. The most serious threat to the poor might come from the sweeping agricultural reforms we and others advocate, but which are as yet not even part of the reform programme. These reforms could cause a significant rise in the cost of food. The far from certain expectation is that the price of cereals would rise, and those of edible oils and sugar fall, with the former effect outweighing the latter. Anyway, whatever the probabilities, the threat needs examining. But it should not be exaggerated. First, the early 1990s saw rises in the price of cereals probably as large (even relative to other prices) as any likely to result from the reform of agricultural incentives; and the initial rise in poverty was probably reversed even before new central poverty alleviation measures were effective. Secondly, we do not expect agricultural reform to come at all swiftly. This implies that poverty-alleviation measures need not be considered so much as short-term complements to the coming reforms as for their own long-run merits.

A knee-jerk reaction to a possible rise in food prices has been to look to the PDS. Our opinion is that one should quickly look away again. It has been shown to be extremely poorly targeted on poverty, and is believed to be a hotbed of inefficiency and corruption. Food stamps, even if untargeted, would be better. But if either the PDS is maintained, or food stamps substituted, some attempt to limit access should be made. It is important to note that neither the PDS nor food subsidies in any form are required for the operation of a foodgrain buffer stock. Sales as well as purchases can be made on the open market. We believe that the government can and should prevent large temporary rises in foodgrain prices, both by buffer stock sales and by operating in forward markets.

Public employment schemes should be improved both in respect of the quality of assets created, and in respect of employing a higher proportion of poor people. Much research is needed to further these objectives. These schemes compete with many other possible uses of public money. Some of these can be more closely related to poverty in the short run: direct income transfers to the destitute and extremely poor, who can be reasonably well identified administratively. Others may well have greater long-run impact on poverty, for instance primary education. We realize that these are mainly State matters and that the Centre has difficulty in achieving any change of emphasis. We suspect that central public employment schemes may have been pushed too far, and therefore welcome the 1995/96 budget initiative of the National Social Assistance Scheme, which assists the States in providing a social safety net.

In this chapter we have been considering sectors where the State has a major role to play. First the State must assume responsibility for the relief of extreme poverty. This cannot be left to civil society and private charity. While this has not been denied in India, actions in pursuit have been haphazard, intermittent, and the distribution uneven. This is to some extent unavoidable since much of the needed policy implementation lies with the States. However, the Centre could play a larger co-ordinating role. Secondly, the poor cannot buy the levels of elementary education and minimal health care which are widely accepted as rights in society. Such levels are not impossible to achieve in a country even as poor as India. Increased expenditure is needed, but also reforms to improve the cost effectiveness of that expenditure.

Despite the above, the failure of government in India has been more commission than omission. Huge expenditures, and detailed regulation and control, in areas where government has no defensible role, have created poverty. Almost all government interventions in productive activity have increased capital intensity and so reduced the demand for labour. At the same time, almost all controls have channelled the benefits of growth, through corruption, rent-seeking, and the creation of monopoly, to a minority of the population.

7

Summary and Afterthoughts

In Chapter 1 we proposed in rough outline the model of an open, largely market-oriented, and relatively unregulated private economy, albeit one where the state played an essential and benevolent role. We claimed that such a model would produce not merely a relatively high growth rate but one that would embrace the poorest people. By 'relatively' we mean compared with the economic model India adopted from 1947–91.

There is, we believe, very widespread agreement that the old highly protectionist, highly controlled and restrictive India Model failed to achieve the primary objective of a rapid growth in real income that was widely shared by the mass of the people. The elimination of poverty has been repeatedly declared by political leaders to be a primary aim. Many of the detailed regulations that stifled Indian enterprise were justified as having the aim of protecting the poor. More often than not they had the opposite effect as they protected mainly those already relatively privileged. Very little indeed was done, at least until recently, to help the extremely poor, whether by stimulating employment or by direct transfers. At the same time very large subsidies to power, irrigation, fertilizers, and food have been paid, but these accrued mainly to the middle classes. The old India Model may be justly described as one of exclusive bourgeois socialism. It has left behind a dense tangled undergrowth of institutions, laws, and policies that are inappropriate to a competitive, progressive, and open society in which all would share the benefits of growth. We believe that almost everything in the economic sphere in India needed drastic reform in 1991. Although much has been done, much also remains to be done if India is to emulate the success of the Asian 'tigers'.

But widespread agreement that the old must be discarded, and that there can be no going back on reform, does not imply that all the features of the model we have sketched are widely accepted: indeed, in some policy areas there is little or no indication on the part of policy-makers that change is needed.

7.1. Review of Progress

Progress is judged by how far the reforms have brought the economic system into conformity with our model. Lack of progress towards particular features of the model may stem either from disagreement as to its merits, or from the political judgement that the merits are not yet sufficiently recognized for reform to be vote-winning, or from lack of resources and skills needed to design the details of reform, or from inertia, or even simply from exhaustion on the part of the chief proponents of reform. After a brief review of the various areas of reform, indicating the progress made, we shall try to indicate what seem to be the impediments.

7.1.1. Macroeconomic Balance

We start with the problem of macroeconomic balance. Here there can be no serious disagreement as to what is desirable. One can argue about the precise permissible level of government or public sector deficits. But very few will disagree with the judgement that the recent fiscal deficits are unsustainably large. India is heading for another major crisis. Dr Manmohan Singh knows this. Responsible opposition leaders must know it too. Yet in four and a half years, Dr Singh, a naturally prudent person, has been able to make very little progress in reducing deficits. The problem is internal. External liabilities are large, but not dangerously so. Recent levels of current account deficits are manageable; and in the longer run, with proper fiscal discipline and careful management of a flexible exchange rate, they will look after themselves.

It is obviously only the nature of the political system and its balance of forces that prevents India from regaining its erstwhile fiscal discipline. We do not know by what combination of political forces this deadlock is to be broken. It may need another crisis. The future of reform in any of the other dimensions that we now turn to examine will be endangered, or indeed brought to nought, by continuing failure to face up to the macroeconomic disequilibrium that prevails.

7.1.2. Trade and Taxation

Most progress has been made with the trade and tax regimes. Trade controls have been quite largely eliminated, but they remain on most consumer goods and agricultural products. That domestic consumer good industries should be especially protected through import controls (or the highest tariff rate) is a strange anomaly, which can persist only for historical xenophobic reasons. It defies any economic logic and runs counter to the whole idea of an open internationally competitive economy. If Mahalanobis had not been a Hindu he would be turning in his grave knowing that soft drinks are more protected than heavy machinery.

The primary reason why exports of agricultural products, especially cotton, are still restricted is protection of domestic industry, especially hand-loom weaving. Yet it is universally accepted, at least among economists, that the optimum way of subsidizing a particular activity is directly, and not by means which damage other activities (cotton exporting in this particular case). Subsidies should be overt, though no doubt politicians may sometimes find reasons to prefer them to be covert. However, these residual controls probably survive because they conform to some deep-seated prejudices. The hope is that such prejudices will die away as people get used to a more open economy. The government could also do a great deal by way of educative propaganda for its policies—something that it has singularly failed to do.

Once it is accepted that any domestic activity that deserves protection should receive that protection by subsidy, then the trade regime becomes an adjunct of the tax regime. Imported goods should in general be taxed no differently from domestically produced goods. An exception occurs in the case of the output of very small enterprises which cannot be efficiently taxed for administrative reasons. In India small enterprises receive further fiscal favours, as well as the reservation of many commodities for their exclusive production. But in general small enterprises are not efficient employers, and their highly favourable treatment should be discontinued, especially product reservation. However, there is still an employment case for the direct subsidization of a few traditional labour-intensive activities.

This brings us to the subject of tariffs. Tariff reduction is certainly one of the most important achievements since 1991. But unfortunately the final target fixed for the end of the reform period is faulty. Too many rates (seven) are proposed, and the levels are far too high. India would emerge after ten years of reform as one of the most highly protected countries in the world. We make a strong plea for a low uniform tariff. Uniformity eliminates lobbying, 'boundary' disputes, and constant opportunities for corruption. Any change in a system with multiple rates results in changes everywhere in effective protection. The Finance Minister and officials in the Finance Ministry must have spent hundreds of hours in the past four years listening to evidence of anomalies, and making complex calculations to prevent them arising (unsuccessfully!).

Before leaving the subject of trade we must revert briefly to agriculture. While, as we shall see, there are the elements of a new official conception of how industry should work, the same cannot be said of agriculture. Although there has been some excellent work on the subject, especially at the National Council of Applied Economic Research, there is no hint of any official policy. There are several reasons. Uncontrolled trade with the low uniform tariff that we advocate cannot be extended to agriculture without consideration of its profitability and the effects on poor people of the consequential price rises. This would in turn require reform of the present system of giving huge subsidies to agricultural inputs, and of the role of the public distribution of subsidized food, together with other approaches to the relief of poverty.

A further complication is that agriculture is a State subject (and so are the social services) and that a large part of the agricultural subsidies for power and irrigation come from State budgets. Thus, planning for reform should ideally involve, with the assistance of the States, simultaneous reform of the extensive nexus involving agricultural trade, subsidies, the price of food, and poverty relief. This is too much to hope for. But one may continue to hope that policy reforms in one segment of economic activity will permit and lead to complementary reforms in other areas. However, after four and a half years there is little to report, only some very cautious trade liberalization. The main political reason is, no doubt, fear of the farming lobby. It may be very difficult to convince farmers that free trade in farm products would more than compensate them for loss of subsidies.

Customs duties constitute a minor part of the total indirect taxation in India. The major parts are central excises and State sales taxes which together account for almost half of the total tax revenue. Both are levied on essentially the same base—the first point of sale of industrial products. There is no disagreement that these taxes are highly distortionary and their incidence opaque and irrational. The same has been true of the manner in which central taxes are redirected to the States. Excellent work has been done on planning a rational reform of the system, involving the best way in which a value-added tax can be introduced into a federal political system. We have no quarrel with the targets suggested by the National Institute of Public Finance and Policy (NIPFP), except that we would prefer a single VAT rate to the three suggested by the NIPFP. Significant progress has been made with the simplification and reform of central excise duties. Getting agreement of the States to substitute VATs (with extra-State sales zero rated) for sales taxes will inevitably be slow. Considerable education and retraining of staff will also be required. But we are not aware of any fundamental conflicts of interest. Since all the States can be expected to benefit in the end from a more rational system, the seeming lack of political pressure from the Centre is to be regretted. Several other large federal countries in Latin America and Asia have managed to introduce a VAT.

The share of direct taxation in total revenue, and as a proportion of GDP, is very low, even as compared with many other poor countries. It is well known that this is largely due to poor administration, the soft treatment of evaders, and official corruption. There has been some recent improvement. We hope that this will continue.

7.1.3. *The Financial System*

There can be no disagreement about the need for banks and other financial institutions which (*a*) well serve the transactions needs of the community and (*b*) efficiently channel savings into socially productive investments. But after the bank national-ization of 1969, the banks had so degenerated by 1991 that they served neither purpose. They were forced to lend to the govern-ment and to certain priority sectors at low controlled interest rates. By 1991 many were so ridden with bad debts that they were effectively bankrupt. A traditional and essential bankers' skill—how to make good loans—had perforce been forgotten. Last, even if least, trade unions had become powerful, and continued to hamper the development of an efficient transactions service for the public at large.

The banks have now been rescued by an infusion of public capital, and the government has for the moment agreed to pay market rates of interest. The direction of credit to 'priority' sectors remains, but has been somewhat reduced. Although interest rates have largely been decontrolled this is not true of priority sector loans which continue to be heavily subsidized. Useful reforms concerning the prudential regulation of banks and other financial instructions have been made, but there needs to be a further reduction in priority lending and subsidization. Further stock market reforms are also needed if portfolio investment is not to be discouraged.

Agricultural credit is a special problem. Most agricultural credit institutions are insolvent. A high proportion of the subsidized loans go to medium and large farmers. The servicing and repayment record is abysmal. Indeed, debtors have been encouraged not to repay by a series of governmental debt write-offs. Small farmers continue to rely mainly on family savings and money lenders. There is no good case for interest rate subsidization or periodic forgiveness: and effective directed credit requires subsidization. However, there is a case for banks or other institutions specializing in agricultural lending or commercial lines to take the place of the existing maze of insolvent institutions. We cannot here formulate a reform plan, but one is certainly needed.

Perhaps the most serious concern is whether there is sufficient guarantee against the recurrence of short-term exploitation of the banks by the government, and the use of concealed credit subsidies on a damaging scale—that is, a reversion to the policies of the 1970s and 1980s. Such misuse of the financial system is very easy when the banks are predominantly public and fiscal deficits are large. Indeed, it was announced in the 1995/96 budget speech that the banks would be required to subscribe to a new Rural Infrastructural Development Fund.

We consider that privatization of the banks, or most of them (and other financial institutions, including the insurance companies) is needed for the development of an independent and efficient financial system. But there is no sign that privatization is on the government's agenda. Nor does there seem to be any strong private pressure for reversing Mrs Gandhi's radical reform of 1969. Privatization is also not in sight for the industrial sector, to which we now turn.

7.1.4. Industrial Policy

The public sector is dominant in the non-financial infrastructure, that is the provision of non-trade services, transport, telecommunications, power, and water. India's infrastructure is in poor shape. Rail freight services are inadequate and many main roads are highly congested. Ports are also congested and delays endemic. Telephones are scarce and connections erratic. Parts of the irrigation system are said to be falling into disrepair. But power shortages are probably the most threatening for economic growth. All this results from a sorry history of under-charging and underinvestment. The undercharging comes from political control of pricing, and the fact that politicians in both the Centre and the States are unable to resist the short-term popularity of subsidizing rail and bus travel, and giving farmers subsidized, even free, electricity and irrigation water. Looking after the really poor takes second or third place.

The undercharging implies that the extent of underinvestment is difficult to estimate; but there is little doubt that even with economic prices that cover long-term marginal costs massive investment is needed, now far beyond the possibility of public sector finance. The underinvestment in infrastructure stems in turn from the waste of public revenue on subsidies, and on investment in manufacturing projects with very low returns.

The urgent need to intrude private investment, both domestic and foreign, into infrastructural projects on a large scale seems to be accepted in principle. In practice the modalities for doing so, thus permitting competition with the public sector, do not seem to have been fully researched, let alone settled. The same is true of the problem of regulating natural monopolies where adequate competition cannot be ensured.

The public sector is also very important, if not dominant, in heavy industry, including steel and other metals, the oil industry, heavy machinery, and fertilizers. These traded good sectors will be facing competition not only from new private investors, as in the case of the infrastructure, but also from imports. The public sector is very inefficient, and there is little hope of its becoming more efficient. Managers are impeded by ministerial interference, by confusion of objectives, by lack of incentives for efficiency, and by regulations on pay, and hiring and firing, which prevent the creation of an efficient managerial structure. All this has been known for thirty years, but nothing effective has been done. With increasing competition, these public enterprises will need increasing subsidies. But this cannot be allowed, and 'hard' budgeting is promised. Long-drawn-out decay, involving a serious waste of resources, is a real possibility. Privatization is an urgent need. But it is not on the agenda, not even being seriously studied. The sale of minority shares in public enterprises is not, of course, privatization: and there is little to be said in its favour.

Privatization, and introducing private competition into infrastructural services, are, or should be, the most burning issues in industrial policy. But there are also a good many legal impediments to the efficient use of productive resources. Indian businessmen have long been harassed by restrictive regulations, but also protected from competition. These features have been reduced, but not eliminated. Company Law, Labour Laws, and Urban Land Laws have combined to create the Indian phenomenon of sick industries—firms that are bankrupt but cannot be closed down. Creditors cannot sell the assets and labour is unpaid. The waste of assets that should be redeployed is considerable. These laws were presumably enacted with good intentions, but no understanding of economics. Civil servants and legislators seldom understand that protection of incumbent workers in larger firms reduces their demand for labour, and thus by exclusion harms the poor outsiders, nor that company laws which protect incumbent management often preserve an inefficient use of assets.

A thorough revision of all the legislation that affects the ownership and use of industrial assets is needed. Labour legislation that favours only a tiny minority of the workforce must be looked at askance. The scope for appeal to the law needs also to be reduced. The courts are too overburdened, and delays too long, for justice to be dispensed. More generally, some critics have maintained that the once proud Indian legal system has degenerated to the point that it can no longer fulfil its essential commercial role of impartially administering property laws and enforcing contracts.

7.1.5. *The Social Sectors*

We consider the social sectors insofar as stabilization policies and the structural changes we advocate might have worrying distributional consequences. The only major consequence that one can predict is a rise in the price of cereals, if and when Indian farm prices are linked to world prices.[1] This would certainly hurt the poor, but it does not follow that the best counter would be to increase food subsidies via the present Public Distribution System (PDS). There is too much evidence that the PDS mainly benefits those who are relatively well off; furthermore increased food subsidies would moderate a rise in agricultural wages that would otherwise at least partly compensate farm labourers. The rise in farm output prices would compensate the farming community as a whole for the reduction

---

[1]   At the time of writing (December 1995) world wheat prices are exceptionally high. However, over the years world prices have usually been higher than domestic prices.

in subsidies which would be an essential and highly desirable accompaniment of the liberalization of prices: but it would not compensate the poorest farmers who have little or nothing to sell, and some way of helping them would need to be found.

If food subsidies are not increased, whether by food stamps or a reformed PDS, then further reliance needs to be placed on public employment schemes and on direct welfare benefits for those who cannot or should not work. Despite a good many enquiries, there is still considerable ignorance and disagreement about how well targeted and cost effective the various schemes are, and how they can be improved. More objective research is certainly needed. But such evidence as there is seems to favour these modes of poverty alleviation to food subsidies. Higher spending on primary education and primary health care is also a high priority, as has been emphasized by Drèze and Sen (1995). When cuts in expenditure are essential for stabilization reasons, the social sectors should be protected as far as possible.

7.2. Reasons for Success and Causes of Failure

The macroeconomic crisis of 1991 was the occasion for reform. But while adjustment, in the sense of a large reduction in the domestic absorption of resources, was forced by the crisis, this was not true of the accompanying programme of structural reform. A realization that a major change of economic system was needed had been slowly gaining ground in policy-making circles over the previous decade. The crisis permitted the new Prime Minister to take full advantage of this change of outlook and initiate a wide-ranging programme of reform with devastating speed.

It is amazing how much has been achieved given the tiny base from which the reforms have sprung. There were in the beginning, to all intents and purposes, only two politically active reformers, the Prime Minister and his Finance Minister, Dr Manmohan Singh. They were supported by a small select band of like-minded economic advisers, nearly all in the Ministry of Finance. Dr. C. Rangarajan, the Governor of the Reserve Bank, has also played a strong supportive role.

In the past year, Mr P. Chidambaram, the Minister of Commerce, has also shown himself to be an enthusiastic reformer. But unfortunately the Prime Minister seems to have decided after the State electoral set backs for the Congress Party at the end of 1994, that any change would lose votes in the forthcoming national election. Moreover, the Congress Party is not a party of reform, and many ministers were probably quite reluctant to agree to many of the changes they promoted. The Finance Minister has continued to argue strongly for reform, but his wings have clearly been clipped. Almost nothing was achieved in 1995, although the economy was booming. The momentum of reform has been lost.

Given the base of the reforms it is not surprising that most was achieved in areas that were the direct responsibility of the Prime Minister or the Minister of Finance. The Prime Minister held the Ministry of Industry portfolio from which sprang the decontrol of industrial investment and production. The other major achievements are almost all in the purview of the Finance Ministry: the reduction of protection; the reforms of the domestic indirect tax system; and the reforms of the financial system including exchange controls, though here the Reserve Bank also had a large role to play. The encouragement of foreign investment was presumably promoted by both the Prime Minister and the Finance Minister.

Despite his very remarkable achievements, far more than any other Finance Minister since independence, our plaudits for Dr Singh are not unqualified. The principal failure lies with expenditure control. Most important are the fertilizer and food subsidies (export subsidies went out quite easily with devaluation), but pay and employment in the public sector have also not been adequately curbed. The loss of revenue from favours to small scale industries (excise tax reductions and interest rate subsidies) is also not negligible. Explanation of failure in all cases lies with the reluctance to confront a powerful interest group—the farmers, the bureaucracy, public sector trade unions, and the small-scale industry lobby. We suspect that the Finance Ministry has lacked support from the Prime Minister and the Cabinet (not to speak of the particular ministers involved).

The two main areas of darkness are public sector reform and agriculture. Public sector reform cries out for privatization, of banking and other financial institutions, and of many industrial enterprises. While private competition in most sectors has been welcomed, if only because sufficient investment by the public sector has become impossible, the authorities have balked at privatization. It seems unlikely that the electorate at large would be concerned, and so the political barriers to privatization must again be the bureaucracy and the public sector unions. It has also been suggested that the issues involved in privatization and public enterprise reform are too complex to be solved within the present institutional framework of highly disseminated adminis-trative responsibility and lack of expertise in the modalities of industrial restructuring. A kind of super-ministry for reform might be needed which could perhaps also promote reform in company law and other matters affecting corporate governance. However, it is also possible that the reformers themselves have not been convinced of the necessity for privatization. Lastly, one should note that the States have in this respect been more reformist than the Centre. Even the Marxist government of West Bengal has been actively courting the multinationals. Several have embarked on a programme of privatization.

We have indicated that agricultural reform is very complex, necessarily involving reforms in other policies and the co-operation of the States. But it is not clear that there should be any long-run insuperable opposition, since the opening of trade would very probably more than compensate most farmers for loss of subsidies, and the poor could be compensated in various ways for a rise in cereal prices. Nevertheless very careful phasing and co-ordination involving several different ministries as well as the States would be desirable. However, there is no over-arching institution to steer the process of reform. We have mentioned the same lack in connection with industrial restructuring and privatization. It is ironical that reforms leading to an unplanned economy seem to need planning: and one must bear in mind the danger that institutions which should quickly make themselves redundant would actually survive.

7.3. Reform Priorities

Although almost everything needs reforming, some things are more urgent than others. The most urgent are reforms needed to ensure fairly rapid growth of GDP—say 6 per cent—in the next few years. Given that, many difficulties in the way of further reform, poverty alleviation, and growth will be eased.

7.3.1. Government Deficits

One must first single out the central government fiscal and current deficits. We have shown that present levels are unsustainable. Unsustainability of deficits might be thought of only as a problem for the long term. But this is not so. Present fiscal deficits will very soon bring debt to levels that threaten stability and a loss of credit-worthiness. Not only that, they are currently threatening growth. In order to contain inflation, the government is borrowing heavily on the market rather than 'printing money'. This forces up interest rates to levels which must reduce investment. There is too much monetary restraint because there is not enough fiscal constraint.

There is no doubt that government expenditure on infra-structure investment should rise. The small curtailing of the fiscal deficit has been achieved by restricting public investment, not current expenditure. There is little or no possibility of rapidly raising revenue (as a percentage of GDP). This all means that it is the current revenue deficit that is the villain of the piece, and that this deficit must be reduced (in other words government savings must be increased from the present negative level) by reducing current expenditure (as a percentage of GDP). This in turn implies reducing the subsidies, reducing public employment, restraining public pay levels, and reducing public enterprise losses. Expenditure on poverty alleviation, and those social services which relate primarily to the poor should remain sacrosanct. The States also run deficits. In theory the Centre can control these deficits. In practice it is far from easy, and the States must play their part in fiscal adjustment, especially through greater cost recovery.

7.3.2. The Infrastructure

Shortages of power and transport services are even now holding back industrial production. Power is the most serious. The roots of the problem are in the State Electricity Boards (SEBs). They heavily subsidize—even give away—this vital scarce resource: and are otherwise mismanaged and corrupt. Consequently they are insolvent, and cannot be trusted to pay for electricity bought in from independent generators.

To satisfy the present rate of increase of demand projected over the next decade, would require an investment over the next five to six years that is far beyond not only the means of the public sector, but of the Indian private sector as well. Massive foreign investment is required. This has been recognized since 1992. The new Maharashtra government elected in 1994 repudiated its predecessor's agreement with Enron to build the very large Dabhol power project. This was the first of a number of 'fast-track' foreign-backed power projects to be agreed. After protracted renegotiation it is reported (January 1996) that agreement has again been reached. The Maharashtra government may have secured some cost reduction, but at a huge cost to India. The xenophobic politicization of the issues will cause other States to seek to renegotiate and will have made foreign investors even more wary than they already were.

The way forward can come only via an urgent and drastic reform of the State Electricity Boards (SEBs) that requires them to adopt commercial standards and practices in general, and in particular to charge economic tariffs to all customers. Power supply has to be primarily a State responsibility. The Centre should give expert technical assistance in negotiations with foreign suppliers and on the tariffs and conditions of purchase of power from any source by SEBs that will best economize in both capacity and fuel: it should do the same for sales. Unfortunately the guidelines laid down by the Ministry of Power (advised by the Central Electricity Authority) in 1992 for 'Widening the scope for private participation' do not inspire confidence that the economic expertise available to the Ministry was adequate. It seems that these guidelines may have contributed to the Dabhol debacle. Finally the Centre must never provide 'counter guarantees' of payment by SEBs unless and until they have been fully reformed. As in other areas, privatization may be an essential part of the reform. It is reported that Orissa has grasped the nettle of privatizing the SEB and installing independent regulators to see that economic non-political tariffs are set. Other States must be encouraged to follow suit.

Transport is the other part of the infrastructure where the need for improvement is both difficult and urgent. The railways should play a larger part in freight transport, which requires not only investment but also, like power, a reform of the tariff structure which has been heavily politicized. More investment in both ports and roads is needed. Both the urgency of the problems and the means of solving them are fully appreciated by the central government and its bureaucracy. Unfortunately, in India it does not seem to follow that anything much is done.

7.4. The Future of Reform, 1996–2001

Even in the unlikely event that the Congress Party can form a majority government, or a very strong minority government, after the national elections of 1996, it cannot be presumed that there would be rapid progress towards the model of the economy that we have espoused. The Congress is not a party of liberal reform, and some features of the model cannot be assumed to be fully and widely accepted. Examples are full freedom for foreign corporate ownership; extensive privatization; a low uniform tariff and no import controls even on consumer goods; virtual free trade in agricultural products; and the reform of company and labour laws. Moreover, the momentum of reform has been lost.

However, progress on certain fronts would probably continue, for example, tax and tariff reform and simplification; and further liberalization in the financial sector, such as insurance. Gradual improvement of the public finances might also be expected, together with stronger efforts to improve the infrastructure. These latter may almost be forced by economic circumstances. But we have seen that the government has balked at tackling the more politically difficult reforms, such as privatization and agricultural trade: and there is no obvious reason to hope for greater resolve on the part of a new Congress-led government. If the reforms are stalled, there will remain enough inconsistencies and impediments in the Indian economy to prevent it achieving the very high rates of growth which we believe to be possible.

What happens if some other party or a coalition forms a government? This is especially difficult to predict because parties in India do not proclaim economic programmes, and do not stand for any clear model of society. Thus elections are not mainly about economic issues. All parties, however, claim that they are in favour of economic reform, and almost all observers agree that there will be no going back on reform. However, we take this to mean that there will be no going back to the 'permit raj' or 'licence raj' that is so widely discredited. In other words, comprehensive controls over domestic production and investment will not be resorted to. But we are not confident that import restrictions would not be reimposed in the event of balance of payments difficulties that might arise from populist policies. This has happened in many other developing countries. Exchange controls could also be tightened, and foreign investment restricted to sectors where the government believes the need is manifest. In short, the conviction of the benefits of a very open competitive economy may not be sufficiently deep in India to prevent resort to such policies. There is still enough xenophobic sentiment to confer some popularity on measures to restrict foreign trade and capital inflows. Even if there is no backsliding, there seem to be no very good grounds for hoping that a BJP or United Front-led government would pursue reform with greater resolve than a Congress-led government, though this is a possibility.

Some observers believe that there will be an increase in the power of the States whatever the result of the national elections. A few States have shown themselves to be more aggressive in reform than the Centre, especially in privatization and inviting foreign investment: other States may copy them. But the States cannot do a great deal independently of the Centre.

India is beset by an extraordinary diversity of economic, regional, communal, and caste interests. The Congress party effectively managed a wide range of conflict for a long time, but it was not a party of reform. Its dominance has now been overtaken by the rise of many parties with narrower interests which are quite weak at the national level. This, and the continuing growth of pervasive corruption, casts some doubt on the ability of the Indian political system to deliver governments which are strong and cohesive enough to avoid fiscal excesses and promote difficult reforms.

We end therefore on a mildly pessimistic note. The achievements of the past four and a half years are impressive, and will lead to higher growth for the Indian economy. But we do not think that the many further reforms we believe to be highly desirable will be made at all quickly. India is not likely to achieve its full potential this century.

Bibliography

Acharya, Shankar (1995) 'The Economic Consequences of Economic Reforms', Sir Purushottamdas Thakurdas Memorial Lecture. Indian Institute of Bankers, Bombay.

Aghion, P. O., O. Hart and J. Moore (1992), 'The Economics of Bankruptcy Reform', *Journal of Law, Economics and Organization*, 8. 3. 523–96.

Ahluwalia, I. J. (1985), *Industrial Growth in India* (New Delhi: Oxford University Press).

—— (1991), *Productivity and Growth in Indian Manufacturing* (New Delhi: Oxford University Press).

Ahluwalia, Montek S. (1994), 'Structural Adjustment and Reform in Developing Countries', *International Monetary and Financial Issues for the 1990s*, vol. iv, Special Issue: Proceedings of a Conference sponsored by the G-24 on the occasion of the 50th Anniversary of Bretton Woods (New York: UNCTAD).

Ahmad, E. and N. H. Stern (1991), *The Theory and Practice of Taxation in Developing Countries* (New Delhi: Cambridge University Press).

Aiyar, Swaminathan A. (1995), 'Stuck in the one per cent groove', *Economic Times*, 24 Feb.

Anand, S. and S. M. Ravi Kanbur (1991), 'Public Policy and Basic Needs Provision: Intervention and Achievement in Sri Lanka', in Jean Drèze and Amartya Sen (eds.), *The Political Economy of Hunger* (Oxford: Clarendon Press), vol. iii.

Anant, J. C. A. and Omkar Goswami (1995), 'Getting Everything Wrong: India's Policies Regarding "Sick" Firms', in D. Mookherjee (ed.) *Indian Industry—Policies and Performance* (New Delhi: Oxford University Press).

Armstrong, M., S. Cowan, and J. Vickers (1994), *Regulatory Reform—Economic Analysis and British Experience* (Cambridge, Mass.: MIT Press).

Ashok, G. (1993), 'Development Cost of Irrigation in India', International Food Policy Research Institute and National Council of Applied Economic Research.

Athukorala, P. and K. Sen (1995), 'Economic Reforms and the Rate of Saving in India', *Economic and Political Weekly*, vol. xxx, no. 35.

Bagchi, A. (1995), 'VAT and States: Misconceived Fears', *Economic Times*, 8 Feb.

Bardhan, Pranab (1984), *The Political Economy of Development in India* (Oxford: Basil Blackwell).

Bery, Suman K. (1992), 'India: Reform of the Financial Sector', mimeo, Reserve Bank of India, Bombay.

—— (1993), 'The Financial Rehabilitation of Public Sector Commercial Banks: Some Conceptual and Policy Aspects', Reserve Bank of India Staff Studies, Bombay.

Bhagwati, Jagdish and T. N. Srinivasan (1993), *India's Economic Reforms* (New Delhi: Government of India, Ministry of Finance).

Bhattacharya, B. B. and S. Kathuria (1995), 'Dynamics of Inflation in India', paper read at the 31st Annual Conference of the Indian Econometric Society.

Binswanger, Hans and S. R. Khandker (1992), 'The Impact of Formal Finance on the Rural Economy of India', World Bank Policy Research Working Paper No. 949, Washington DC.

Buiter, Willem and Urjit Patel (1996), 'Solvency and Fiscal Correction in India: an analytical discussion' in S. Mundle (ed.) *Fiscal Policy in India* (New Delhi: Oxford University Press).

Burgess, R., S. Howes, and N. Stern (1993), 'The Reform of Indirect Taxes in India', Suntory-Toyota International Centre for Economics and Related Disciplines, EF No. 7, Nov.

—— —— —— (1994), 'Reform of Domestic Trade Taxes in India—Issues and Options' (New Delhi: National Institute of Public Finance and Policy).

Calomiris, Charles and C. Himmelberg (1993), 'Directed Credit Programmes for Agriculture and Industry' in *Proceedings of the World Bank Annual Conference in Development Economics* (Washington DC: World Bank).

Caprio, Gerard and Lawrence Summers (1993), 'Finance and its Reform: Beyond Laissez-Faire', World Bank Research Working Papers No. 1171, Washington DC.

—— Izak Atiyas and James Hanson (1994) (eds.), *Financial Reform: Theory and Experience* (Cambridge: Cambridge University Press).

Cassen, Robert and Vijay Joshi (1995), *India—The Future of Economic Reform* (New Delhi: Oxford University Press).

―― ―― and Michael Lipton (1992), 'Stabilization, Structural Reform and IDA Assistance to India' (New Delhi: Ministry of Finance, Government of India).

Centre for Monitoring the Indian Economy (1986), *Public Sector in the Indian Economy*, Bombay.

―― (1995), *Monthly Review of the Indian Economy*, Bombay.

Chandra, N. K. (1994), 'Planning and Foreign Investment in Indian Manufacturing' in T. I. Byers (ed.), *The State and Development Planning in India* (New Delhi: Oxford University Press).

Chathukulam, J. and V. K. Kerien (1995), 'Jawahar Rozgar Yojana: An Assessment', *Economic and Political Weekly*, vol. xxx, no. 6, 11 Feb.

Cho, Yoon-Je and Deena Khatkhate (1989), 'Lessons of Financial Liberalization in Asia', World Bank Discussion Paper No. 50, Washington DC.

Copestake, James (1996), 'The Integrated Rural Development Programme Revisited' in D. Hulme and P. Mosley (1996).

Chopra, Ajai, Charles Collyns, Richard Hemming, and Karen Parker (1995), 'India: Economic Reform and Growth', Occasional Paper 134. International Monetary Fund, Washington DC.

Dandekar, V. M. (1993), 'Limits of Credit, Not Credit Limits', *Economic and Political Weekly*, 28. 39. A74–A85.

Deaton, A. (1987), 'Econometric Issues of Tax Design in Developing Countries' in D. Newbery and N. Stern (eds.), *The Theory of Taxation for Developing Countries* (New York: Oxford University Press).

DeMeza, David and David Webb (1987), 'Too Much Investment: A Problem of Asymmetric Information', *Quarterly Journal of Economics*, 102. 281–92.

Desai, Ashok, V. (1993), *My Economic Affair* (New Delhi: Wiley Eastern).

Dev, S. Mahendra (1992), 'Poverty Alleviation Programmes: A Case Study of Maharashtra with Emphasis on Employment Guarantee Scheme', Indira Gandhi Institute of Development Research, Bombay.

―― (1995), 'Economic Reforms and the Rural Poor', *Economic and Political Weekly*, 19 Aug.

Drèze, Jean (1990), 'Poverty in India and the IRDP delusion', *Economic and Political Weekly*, 25. 39. A95–A104.

Drèze, Jean (1990), 'Famine Prevention in India', in Jean Drèze and Amartya Sen (eds.), *The Political Economy of Hunger. Famine Prevention* (Oxford: Clarendon Press) vol. ii.

— and Amartya Sen (1995), *India, Economic Development and Social Opportunity* (Oxford: Clarendon Press; New Delhi: Oxford University Press).

Ettori, F. M. (1992), 'Measure and Interpretation of Effective Protection in the Presence of High Capital Costs—Evidence from India', World Bank Policy Research Working Paper No. 873, Washington DC.

Feldstein, Martin and C. Horioka (1980), 'Domestic Saving and International Capital Flows', *Economic Journal*.

GATT (1993), *Trade Policy Review: India*.

Goldar, B. N. (1986) *Productivity Growth in Indian Industry* (New Delhi: Allied Publishers).

—— (1988), 'Relative Efficiency of Modern Small-Scale Industries in India', in K. B. Suri (1988).

Goswami, Omkar (1994), 'Fencing in Growth Prospects', *The Economic Times*, 10 Oct.

—— (1996), 'India, Legal and Institutional Impediments to Corporate Growth', OECD Development Centre Conference Volume.

Government of India (various years), *Economic Survey* (New Delhi: Ministry of Finance).

—— (various years) *National Accounts Statistics* (New Delhi: C.S.O).

—— (various years) *Indian Public Finance Statistics* (New Delhi: Ministry of Finance).

—— (1991*a*), *Report of the Committee on the Financial System* (Chairman, M. Narasimham), (New Delhi: Ministry of Finance).

—— (1991*b*), 'The Performance Status of Central Public Enterprises', *Public Enterprises Survey 1992/93*, monograph, Department of Public Enterprises, Ministry of Industry, New Delhi.

—— (1992*a*), *Report of the Inter-Ministerial Working Group on Industrial Restructuring* (Bajaj Committee), New Delhi.

—— (1992*b*), *Final Report of the Tax Reforms Committee* (New Delhi: Ministry of Finance).

—— (1993*a*), *Public Sector Commercial Banks and Financial Sector Reform: Rebuilding for a Better Future* (New Delhi: Ministry of Finance).

—— (1993*b*), *Economic Reforms—Two Years After and the Task Ahead* (New Delhi: Ministry of Finance).

—— (1993*c*), *Report of the Committee on Industrial Sickness and Corporate Restructuring*, (New Delhi: Ministry of Finance).

—— (1994), *Report of the Committee on Reforms in the Insurance Sector* (Chairman, R. N. Malhotra), (New Delhi: Ministry of Finance).

—— (1995*a*), *Export and Import Policy* (New Delhi: Ministry of Commerce).

—— (1995*b*), *Hydrocarbon Perspectives: 2010* (New Delhi: Ministry of Petroleum and Natural Gas).

—— (1996), *Budget at a Glance 1996/97* (New Delhi: Ministry of Finance).

Greenwald, Bruce and Joseph Stiglitz (1986), 'Externalities in Economies with Imperfect Information and Incomplete Markets', *Quarterly Journal of Economics*, 101. 229–64.

Guhan, S. (1990), 'Social Security Initiatives in Tamil Nadu 1989', Madras Institute of Development Studies.

—— (1995), 'Social Expenditures in the Union Budget 1991–96', *Economic and Political Weekly*, vol. xxx, nos. 18–19, May.

Hanumantha Rao, C. H. (1994), *Agricultural Growth, Rural Poverty and Environmental Degradation in India* (New Delhi: Oxford University Press).

Hulme, D. and P. Mosley (1996), *Finance against Poverty*, (London: Routledge) vols. i, ii.

Indian Banks Association (various years), *Public Sector Banks: Performance Highlights* (Bombay: IBA).

International Finance Corporation (1993), *India: Capital Markets Review*, Washington DC.

Jain, L. C. (1994), 'Reforms: Inspector Raj Must Go', *Economic Times*, 22 Oct.

Joshi, Vijay (1994), 'Macroeconomic Policy and Economic Reform', Exim Bank Annual Lecture, Bombay. Reprinted in K. Banerji and T. Vakil (1995), *India: Joining the World Economy* (New Delhi: Tata McGraw Hill Publishing Company).

—— (1995), 'Democracy and Development in India', *Round Table*, 333, 73–79.

—— and I. M. D. Little (1993), 'Future Trade and Exchange Rate Policy for India', *Economic and Policy Weekly*, vol. 28, no. 31, reprinted in Cassen and Joshi (1995).

Joshi, Vijay and I. M. D. Little (1994), *India: Macroeconomics and Political Economy, 1964–1991* (Washington DC and New Delhi: World Bank and Oxford University Press).

—— —— (1996), 'Macroeconomic Management in India, 1964–1994', in V. Balasubramaniam and D. Greenaway, Trade and Development: Essays in honour of J. N. Bhagwati (London: Macmillan).

Kakwani, N. and K. Subbarao (1993), 'Rural Poverty in India, 1973–87', in M. Lipton and J. van der Gaag (1993).

Khatkhate, Deena (1993), 'Indian Banking System: Restitution and Sequencing', mimeo, Washington DC.

Kumar, L. M. (1991), *Industrial Licensing: Policies and Procedures* (New Delhi)

Lal, D. (1975), *Appraising Foreign Investment in Developing Countries*, (London: Heinemann).

Lipton, Michael and Jacques van der Gaag (1993), *Including the Poor* (Washington DC: World Bank).

Little, I. M. D. (1982), *Economic Development—Theory, Policy and International Relations* (New York: Basic Books).

—— (1994), 'Trade and Industrialization Revisited' in *The Pakistan Development Review*, vol. xxxiii, no. 4.

—— D. Mazumdar, and J. M. Page (1987), *Small Manufacturing Enterprises—A Comparative Analysis of India and Other Economies* (New York: World Bank and Oxford University Press).

—— and Mirrlees (1974), *Project Appraisal and Planning for Developing Countries* (London: Heinemann)

Mckinnon, R. I. (1973), *Money and Capital in Economic Development* (Washington DC: Brookings Institute).

—— (1989), 'Macroeconomic Instability and Moral Hazard in Banking in a Liberalising Economy', in P. Brock, M. Connolly and C. Gonzalez-Vega (eds.), *Latin American Debt and Adjustment* (New York: Praeger).

—— (1991), *The Order of Economic Liberalisation: Financial Control in the Transition to a Market Economy* (Baltimore: Johns Hopkins University Press).

Mani, Sunil (1995), 'Economic Liberalisation and the Industrial Sector', *Economic and Political Weekly*, May 27.

Manor, James (1995), 'The Political Sustainability of Economic Liberalization in India', in R. Cassen and V. Joshi (1995).

Mistry, Percy S. (1995), 'Financial Sector Reform in India: Hesitant Pursuit of an Incomplete Agenda' in R. Cassen and V. Joshi (1995).

Mohan, Rakesh (1996), 'Public Sector Reform and Issues in Privatization', OECD Development Centre Conference Volume.

Mudgil, K. and Y. Thorat (1996), 'The Regional Rural Banks Experience in India', in D. Hulme and R. Mosley (1996).

Mulji, Sudhir (1995) 'Monetary Policy and Inflation', *Business Standard*, 3 May, New Delhi.

Mundle, S. and M. Govinda Rao (1991), 'Volume and Composition of Government Subsidies in India, 1987–88', *Economic and Political Weekly*, vol. xxvi, No.18, 1157–72.

National Bank for Agriculture and Rural Development (1993), 'Institutional Arrangement for Agricultural Credit', mimeo, Bombay.

—— (1994), 'Viability of Rural Credit Institutions', mimeo, Bombay.

National Institute of Public Finance and Policy (1994), *Reform of Domestic Trade Taxes in India: Issues and Options*.

Nayak, P. Jayendra (1993), 'Financial Sector Development in Asia: The Reform of India's Financial System', mimeo, Asian Development Bank.

Neelakantan, M. (1994), 'Jawahar Rozgar Yojana, an Assessment through Concurrent Evaluation', *Economic and Political Weekly*, vol. xxix, no. 49. 3 December.

Parikh, K. S. (1993), 'Who Gets How Much From PDS—How Effectively Does It Reach the Poor?' (Bombay: Indira Gandhi Institute of Development Research).

—— (1994*a)*, 'Encouraging Private Power', *Business Standard*, 23 May.

—— (1994*b*), 'Power Sector Needs Competitive Bidding and Two-Part Tariff', *The Hindu*, 11 July.

Pulley, R. V. (1989), 'Making the Poor Creditworthy: A Case Study of the Integrated Rural Development Programme in India', World Bank Discussion Paper No. 58, Washington DC.

Pursell, Garry and Ashok Gulati (1993), 'Liberalizing Indian Agriculture—An Agenda for Reform', World Bank Working Papers WPS 1172, reprinted in R. Cassen and V. Joshi (1995).

Rajaraman, Indira (1995), 'Presumptive Direct Taxation: Lessons from Developing Countries', *Economic and Political Weekly*, vol. xxx, No.18, 1103–24.

Rangarajan, C. (1993), 'Autonomy of Central Banks.' Tenth Kutty Memorial Lecture delivered at Calcutta. Reserve Bank of India, Bombay.

Rangarajan, C. (1994*a*), 'Developing the Money and Securities Markets in India'. Paper presented at the Sixth Seminar on Central Banking, mimeo. IMF, Washington DC.

—— (1994*b*), 'The Reform of the Financial Sector: Choices and Lessons', *RBI Bulletin*, Bombay.

Rao, C. H. H. (1994), 'Policy Issues Relating to Irrigation and Rural Credit in India', in G. S. Bhalla (ed.) *Economic Liberalisation and Indian Agriculture*, (New Delhi: Institute for Studies in Industrial Development).

Rao, M. Govinda and T. K. Sen (1993), 'Public Finance and Economic Development: Lessons from India', National Institute of Public Finance and Policy, Occasional Paper no. 3.

Ravallion, M. (1990), 'Market Responses to the Anti-hunger Policies: Effects on Wages, Prices and Employment', in J. Drèze and A. Sen (eds.) *The Political Economy of Hunger* (Oxford: Clarendon Press) vol. ii.

—— (1990), 'Reaching the Poor through Rural Public Employment: a Survey of Theory and Evidence', World Bank Discussion Paper No. 94. World Bank, Washington DC.

—— M. G. Dutt and S. Chaudhuri (1993), 'Does Maharashtra's Employment Guarantee Scheme Guarantee Employment? Effects of the 1988 Wage Increase', *Economic Development and Cultural Change*, vol. xli.

Reserve Bank of India (various years), *Annual Report*, Bombay.

—— (various years), *Report on Trend and Progress of Banking*, Bombay.

—— (1985), *Report of the Committee to Review the Working of the Monetary System* (Chairman, S. Chakravarty), Bombay.

—— (1989), *Report of the Agricultural Credit Review Committee: A Review of the Agricultural Credit System in India*, Bombay.

Sandesara, J. C. (1993), 'Modern Small Industry 1972 and 1987–88', *Economic and Political Weekly*, vol. xxviii, no. 6, Feb.

Sargent, Thomas and Neil Wallace (1981), 'Some Unpleasant Monetarist Arithmetic', Federal Reserve Bank of Minneapolis, *Quarterly Review*.

Seabright, Paul (1992) 'Quality of Livestock Assets under Selective Credit Schemes', *Journal of Development Economics*, 37. 327–50.

Securities and Exchange Board of India (1994), 'Indian Securities Markets: Agenda for Development and Reform—A Discussion Paper', Bombay.

Sengupta, Arjun (1994), 'The Financial Sector and Economic Reforms in India'. Sir Purushottamdas Thakurdas Memorial Lecture, Indian Institute of Bankers, Bombay.

Shaw, E. S. (1973), *Financial Deepening in Economic Development*, (New York: Oxford University Press).

Sheng, Andrew (1991), 'The Art of Bank Restructuring: Issues and Techniques', EDI Working Paper, World Bank, Washington DC.

Singh, Gurbir (1995), 'Who Needs an Exit Policy Anyway?', *Economic and Political Weekly*, vol. xxx, no. 23, June.

Squire, Lyn and H. G. Van der Tak (1975), *Economic Analysis of Projects* (Baltimore: Johns Hopkins University Press).

Stiglitz, Joseph (1993), 'The Role of the State in Financial Markets', in *Proceedings of the World Bank Annual Conference on Development Economics* (Washington DC: World Bank).

—— and Andrew Weiss (1981), 'Credit Rationing in Markets with Imperfect Information', *American Economic Review*, 71. 393–419.

Suri, K. B. (1988) (ed.) *Small Scale Enterprises in Industrial Development—The Indian Experience* (New Delhi: Sage Publications).

Tarapore, S. S. (1993), 'Issues in Commercial Banking Reform', *RBI Bulletin*, Bombay.

—— (1994), 'Rural Banking at the Crossroads', *RBI Bulletin*, Bombay.

—— (1995), 'Banks' Response to Reforms', *RBI Bulletin*, Bombay.

Tendulkar, Suresh and L. R. Jain (1995), 'Economic Reforms and Poverty', *Economic and Political Weekly*, vol. xxx, no. 23, June.

Vaidyanathan, A. (1993), 'Agricultural Policy', *Business India*, Apr.

World Bank (various years), *World Debt Tables*, Washington DC.

—— (1993), *The East Asian Miracle* (Oxford: Oxford University Press).

—— (1994*a*), *India—Issues in Trade Reform*, Washington DC, June.

—— (1994*b*), *World Development Report* (Oxford: Oxford University Press).

—— (1995*a*), *India: Country Economic Memorandum*, Washington DC.

—— (1995*b*) 'India: Financial Sector Development Project—Staff Appraisal' Report No. 13740–IN, IBRD, Washington DC.

—— (1995*c*), *India, Policy and Finance Strategies for Strengthening Primary Health Care Services*, Report No. 13042–IN, IBRD, Washington DC.

Yaron, Jacob (1994), 'What Makes Rural Finance Institutions Successful', World Bank Research Observer 9. 1.

Index

of GDP 15, 16–18
of manufacturing 16–18

health care 242–3
primary 219, 257
Heavy Engineering Corporation 177
Hindustan Fertilizer Corporation 177
Hindustan Lever 197n.

IBM 195
Income Tax Act 208
imports
competition, role of 68–70
canalization 63, 66–7, 69, 85, 180
controls 63–4, 67–70
Indian Banks Association 114, 148
Indian Companies Act 205
Industrial Credit and Investment Corporation of India 160–2
Industrial Development Bank of India 142, 160–2
Industrial Dispute Act 208
Industrial Finance Corporation of India 142, 161
industrial policy 8, 65–6, 171–217
history of 171–2
roadblocks to reform 172
industrial structure
central (non-departmental) public sector enterprises 175, 176–85, 192; divestment of equity 179–80; loss-making and 'sick' companies 177–8; managerial constraints 178–9; share in GDP 176–7; the oil and natural gas industry 180–83
departmental central enterprises 183–5; natural monopoly and

the case for privatization 183–4; port services 185, 254; railways 183–4, 254; road transport 184–5; telecommunications 185, 254
private sector 204–11
public sector; case for privatization 172–6, 188–92, 255, 259; inefficiency of 173–5; power shortages 186–8, 254; share in GDP 173–4
small scale industry 197–204; access to credit 142–3, 203–4; bureaucratic burden on 203; efficiency of 199–200; modern 199–200; product reservation 200–1; tax favours 201–3; traditional and village industries 198–9
state enterprises; irrigation 188, 254; State Electricity Boards 186–7, 261–2
inflation 3, 16–17, 19, 20–1, 44–9
inflation tax 20, 25, 26
infrastructure (*see also* industrial structure) 254, 261–2
insurance *see* financial sector
interest rates 41–2, 253
and credit policy 144–8
control and deregulation of 126–33
interest payments 41, 253
Integrated Rural Development Programme 134, 140–1
International Monetary Fund 1

Jain, L. C. 203
Janata Government 1
Jawahar Rozgar Yojana 223, 232, 235–42

labour law *see* corporate governance
lakh xiii